The Story in History

THE STORY IN HISTORY

Writing Your Way into
the American Experience

by

MARGOT FORTUNATO GALT

TEACHERS & WRITERS COLLABORATIVE

NEW YORK

The Story in History

Funding for this publication has been provided, in part, by the National Endowment for the Arts and the New York State Council on the Arts. Teachers & Writers also receives funding from the following foundations and corporations: American Stock Exchange, The Bingham Trust, Booth Ferris Foundation, Louis Calder Foundation, Chemical Bank, Consolidated Edison, Aaron Diamond Foundation, Morgan Stanley Foundation, New York Telephone, New York Times Company Foundation, Henry Nias Foundation, Rotary Foundation of New York, Helena Rubinstein Foundation, and the Scherman Foundation.

Teachers & Writers Collaborative
5 Union Square West
New York, N.Y. 10003–3306

Library of Congress Cataloging-in-Publication Data

Galt, Margot Fortunato.
    The story in history: writing your way into the American
experience / by Margot Fortunato Galt.
        p.   cm.
    Includes bibliographical references (p.
    Summary: Discusses various periods or themes in American history, suggests related creative writing exercises, and provides examples.
        ISBN 0-915924-38-2 (cloth : acid-free).—ISBN 0-915924-39-0 (paper : acid-free)
        1. United States—Historiography—Juvenile literature. [1. United States—History. 2. Creative writing.]   I. Title.
    E175.G27   1992
    973'.072—dc20

Cover photos: (front, clockwise from upper right) National Archives photo no. 111-SC-82521; courtesy of Library of Congress; National Archives photo no. 32-148-GW-580; courtesy of War Relocation Authority, National Archives, no. 210-GA-6; (back cover left) National Archives photo no. 129-306-NT-165.139c; (back cover right) National Archives photo no. 42-30-N9006

Design: Chris Edgar

Printed by Philmark Lithographics, New York, N.Y.
First edition

Permissions

Gratitude is due to the authors and publishers who granted permission to use their work. Alberto Rios for his poem "Nani." John Calvin Rezmerski for his poem "Grandmother." Mitsuye Yamada for excerpts from her poem "I Learned to Sew," from *Desert Run: Poems and Stories* (Kitchen Table: Women of Color Press, P.O. Box 908, Latham, N.Y. 12110). Ted Kooser for his poem "Abandoned Farmhouse," reprinted from his *Sure Signs: New and Selected Poems* (University of Pittsburgh Press). Roseann Lloyd for her poem "Lessons from Space." Susan Bergholz Literary Services, New York, for the selection from Sandra Cisneros's *The House on Mango Street.* Copyright © 1984, 1989 by Sandra Cisneros. Published by Vintage Books, a Division of Random House, Inc., New York. Originally published in somewhat different form by Arte Publico Press in 1984 and revised in 1989. City Lights for "The Day Lady Died" by Frank O'Hara, from *Lunch Poems.* Copyright © 1964, 1992 by Frank O'Hara and the Estate of Frank O'Hara. Alfred A. Knopf, Inc. for "The Negro Speaks of Rivers" by Langston Hughes, from *Selected Poems of Langston Hughes.* Copyright © 1959 by Langston Hughes. Reprinted by permission of Alfred A. Knopf, Inc. The Longman Publishing Group for Robert Francis's poem "Like Ghosts of Eagles," from *The Longman Anthology of Contemporary American Poetry,* edited by Stuart Friebert and David Young. Copyright © 1989 by Longman Publishing Group. Random Century Group for the selection from Pablo Neruda's "Birdwatching Ode," from *Selected Poems* by Pablo Neruda, translated by Nathaniel Tarn and published by Jonathan Cape, Ltd. Bill Ransom for his poem "Statement on Our Higher Education," which originally appeared in *Carriers of the Dream Wheel,* edited by Duane Niatum. N. Scott Momaday for his poem "The Delight Song of Tsoai-Talee," which originally appeared in *Carriers of the Dream Wheel,* edited by Duane Niatum. Gwendolyn Brooks for her poem "Kitchenette Building," from *Blacks* by Gwendolyn Brooks, copyright © Gwendolyn Brooks, published by Third World Press, Chicago, 1991. New Directions for "Dog" by Lawrence Ferlinghetti, in *A Coney Island of the Mind.* Copyright © 1958 by Lawrence Ferlinghetti. New Directions for "The Garden Wall" by Denise Levertov, in *O Taste and See.* Copyright © 1964 by Denise Levertov. Dwight Okita for his poem "In Response to Executive Order 9066," first published in *Breaking Silence,* Greenfield Review Press. Copyright © 1992 by Dwight Okita. Houghton Mifflin for the excerpt from *Let Us Now Praise Famous Men* by James Agee and Walker Evans. Copyright 1939 and 1940 by James Agee. Copyright 1941 by James Agee and Walker Evans. Copyright © renewed 1969 by Mia Fritsch Agee and Walker Evans. Reprinted by permission of Houghton Mifflin Company. All rights reserved. Milkweed Editions for Phoebe Hanson's poem "Long Underwear," originally published in *Sacred Hearts.* Copyright © 1985 by Phoebe Hanson. Persea Books, Inc. for Paul Blackburn's poem "The Sign," reprinted from *The Collected Poems of Paul Blackburn,* copyright © 1985 by Joan Blackburn. University of Pittsburgh Press for Patricia Hampl's poem "St. Paul: Walking," reprinted from *Woman before an Aquarium* by Patricia Hampl. Copyright © 1978 by Patricia Hampl. John Minczeski for his poem "My Name." Holy Cow! Press for Joe Paddock's poem "The End of Their Leap," in *Boar's Dance* (forthcoming 1993). Louisiana State University Press for Kelly Cherry's poem "Lt. Col. Valentina Vladimirovna Tereshkova, first woman to orbit the earth, June 16-June 19, 1963," from *Relativity: A Point of View,* copyright © 1977 by Kelly Cherry, published by Louisiana State University Press.

The illustration sources are as follows: Behaim's map, De la Cosa's map, and the western section of the Oregon Trail are from the New York Public Library Map Division. The detail of Descelierts's map of Florida is from the Britism Museum. The photographs of Savage Station (p. 152) and the First Minnesota Squad—After Fair Oaks (p. 161) are from the collections of the Minnesota Historical Society and are reproduced by permission.

Contents

Table of Figures

Acknowledgments

This book has grown out of many encounters with other teachers and writers. Many Minnesota teachers especially deserve thanks. They opened their classrooms to me, shared in my struggle to make a lesson plan work, and offered me their expertise: Pat Hogan and Carol Sheffer from Bloomington Jefferson High School; David Bengston from Long Prairie High School; Al Kvaal, Lorraine O'Connor, Jan Carter, and Bill Whelan from Harding High School, St. Paul; Jill Cacy, Jovita Hernandez, Mary Knezovich, and Gwen Williams from Cherokee Heights Elementary, St. Paul; Annalee Odessky, Greenwood Elementary School, Hopkins; Chris Correa, Mounds High School; Pat Riley, St. Cloud Junior High; Marge Fox, Ramsey Junior High School, St. Paul; Patty Anderson, RTR High School, Tyler; Randy Nelson, Granite Falls High School; Catherine Barner, Battle Lake Schools; Katherine Taack, Oltmann Junior High School, St. Paul Park; Tim Rosenfield, Breck School, Golden Valley; Arlene Ross and Toni Mattson, J.W. Smith Elementary School, Bemidji; Jean McNutt and Wes Sideen, Hazel Park Junior High School, St. Paul. I owe a particular debt of gratitude to Susan Marie Swanson, poet and colleague, who adapted the Sioux "winter count" for classroom use. My colleagues in the Master of Education program at Hamline University were generous with their interest and suggestions. Many others not directly involved in helping me teach about the American experience have encouraged me along the way.

Of the many writers whose expertise, criticism, and encouragement have contributed to my own literary development, my first mentor, Patricia Hampl, and poets Deborah Keenan, Norita Dittberner-Jax, and Mary Schwarz provided help with this book. Thanks also to those writers who allowed me to quote from their work. Visual artist Joyce Lyon, a friend who shares my interest in family history, has extended my sympathy for the link between American experience and the European Holocaust. The librarians at the St. Paul Public Library, including my husband and first-line editor Fran Galt, have given me unfailingly prompt and friendly research service and advice.

This book would also never have come about without the administrative magic of the Minnesota arts agency COMPAS, especially that of Daniel Gabriel and Randolph Jennings, directors of the Writers-and-Artists-in-the-Schools program in Minnesota, community programmer Margret Swanson, and executive director Molly LaBerge. They are models of dedication to the cause of arts in education. Their counterparts at Teachers & Writers Collaborative—especially Nancy Larson Shapiro, executive director, who saw the potential in my approach, and editors Ron Padgett and Chris Edgar—have helped me realize my dream to write a book about the teaching of imaginative writing and history. Thanks also to T&W's proofreader, Jessica Sager.

Portions of this book were written during a stay at the Ragdale Foundation. No other retreat for writers and artists could be more homey and bird-filled. My thanks to director Mike Wilkerson for several satisfying visits.

Finally, my gratitude to my father, Leonard Henry Fortunato, 1909–1990, who, though we often differed in our politics, taught me the thrill of creative teaching and a love of history that eventually I could not deny.

Introduction

As an itinerant teacher of imaginative writing, I often use a subject close to my heart: personal and public history. Entering a classroom as a stranger, I introduce myself not by my hobbies or opinions, but by the history of my names. When I write "Margot Rosalie Fortunato Kriel Galt" on the board, the students gasp.

I explain each name's origin and meaning, the difficulties it's given me, and the way I feel about it now. Soon, students offer their own names for discussion. We talk about the ethnic backgrounds of the names and the reasons students have been given their names. Finally, we exchange stories of immigration and settlement as clues to each student's personal and family history.

With adult writing classes, I introduce myself the same way, emphasizing the way my different names seem to collect periods of history around them. Often writers in these classes have, at some point, changed the way they feel about their names. A nickname may have become too embarrassing or constrictive for an adult: "Sissy" becomes "Christine." Or an adult may have decided to reclaim a family name that was anglicized when a grandfather was admitted to the United States: "Michael" may return to "Mikolowski."

After the students and I discuss our names, I read poems I've written about historical figures, old photographs, or my grandfathers. Evoking my German grandfather's house in North Dakota, I describe memory's marvelous power to combine sharp details and strong emotion. "Memory is the writer's first editor," I say. "It shows us what details to put in." Then I may outline an exercise about grandparents (which you'll find in the first chapter). Students of all ages who draw on their memories of grandparents invariably produce writing that is focused with complex, unmistakable feeling. Starting with memories of personal history helps them avoid generalized writing. I urge them to use specific details in writing about places and people close to their hearts.

I begin my residencies teaching from the past because I grew up steeped in history. My father was a history professor in a small South Carolina college. At the dinner table, he lectured about the French and Indian Wars; he had us seeing Indians behind the drapes. On the road north to visit his Italian-American relatives, we paused to read every historical sign between Charleston and Pittsburgh. The signs seemed to bring history to life before his eyes, but they peeved me—what did I care if General Lee had camped in yonder field? After a hot day in the car, I wanted to dive into the shimmering turquoise of a motel pool. But the time we visited Monticello, I felt the thrill of imagining the past. The present receded behind soft green hills, and I tried to visualize the man who had invented a bed that divided two rooms and could be entered from either, who had played the violin like my father, and who had built a graceful dome in the woods.

When I entered graduate school, I wanted a nourishing mixture of history, visual arts, and anthropology added to my study of literature. I took a Ph.D. in American Studies, and was lucky enough to be able to write, for my thesis, a novel about civil rights and the Gullah oystermen in South Carolina. It's no wonder that, when I became a teacher of creative writing, I insisted that imagination make room for history.

But there are other reasons to work with history and writing. I've found that although writers—newcomers and veterans—enjoy looking back, they don't do it enough. Our up-to-the-minute age doesn't encourage tuning into personal or group memory. Occasionally, well-made TV dramatizations bring historical heroes to life: in the mid-1980s, George Washington was portrayed on network TV as a surveyor, Indian fighter, and New World Don Juan. In 1990 the PBS series, *The Civil War*, made history buffs out of many. But generally our national and personal identities are encouraged to look forward rather than back. Trendy clothes, athletic fitness, and jobs define us; taking a fancy vacation, looking young, and flashing a charge card—advertisements equate these with the good life. I think we're missing out. When we ignore the past, we operate with flimsy, disposable identities. We fail to learn patterns in our families that might help us to understand and accept ourselves. As we forget places, aromas, and moments of high excitement, our individual identities blur. We become "an owner of a white sportscar," rather than "a man who cried when his mother served the pet goat for supper," or "a woman whose first kiss was high in a willow above Lake Elsie."

If we don't delve into our personal histories, the more remote ones become reduced to inert facts, completely unrelated to us. When grandfather hasn't talked about how his paint business boomed after the GIs returned from Okinawa and Sicily, we're less likely to understand, after a contemporary war, a rage for kids' camouflage clothes. When grandmother no longer passes down the delicate rice bowls sent to the Midwest by a California aunt, a modern novel about Chinese-Americans will be less likely to capture our attention. As more of us live in cities and landscapes shaped to look like commercial strips that could be anywhere, we may have trouble understanding the Puritans' shock at landing in a new world so physically different from their old Europe. When our concept of time extends no further back than to yesterday's news bites, we may fail to consider how a public event may linger to wreck or enhance our well-being.

For better and worse, I am an exception to this forward-looking trend, and I've made it my mission to haul whomever I can with me into the past. I had a good teacher: my father showed me how to live with the past. He talked almost nonstop about his childhood. He bemoaned its disappearance and continually resurrected it. He made Pescopagano, his ancestral town near Naples, with its goats and festivals, as attractive to my imagination as the Lone Ranger and his great horse Silver.

Sometimes, though, the past was a burden. I tired of hearing how I resembled Grandma Rose, whose fingers flew up and down the piano keys. I chafed at spelling "Fortunato" for my Carolina classmates, who had "normal" names like Royall and Taylor. But though I might have wished for an identity more common to Charleston, my father made sure I learned exactly how I differed from my friends. Their families boasted 300 years in the Low Country; I was only one generation removed from a grandfather who fled a Neapolitan seminary and his family's insistence that he become a priest.

The past was also very much alive to my Carolina friends. In the 1950s, the South as a whole—and Charleston especially—remained in love with its traditions, its lost war, and its old architecture. Most of my friends wouldn't have dreamed of moving away from their heritage of names, land, and family silver. The rewards for staying were clear—elaborate family support systems, tolerance for any sin except departure, and devotion to civic beauty.

Unfortunately, this allegiance to tradition often had a negative side, too, which spilled over even into our family. As the conservative politics of the 1950s took hold in South Carolina, my father, who knew few blacks firsthand and had not even grown up with any, began to spout violent diatribes against "Negroes" and "colored people." I had no sympathy for the international plot he envisioned.

Yet I learned some unforgettable lessons about history from our arguments. I learned that, sooner or later, past events will affect us in the present. They will shape both our personal and public lives. Like it or not, they will require attention. That was the first lesson, one that continues to inform my writing and teaching. The same for the second one: history is surprisingly a lot like its cousins fiction and poetry.

Granted, history contains real events and people, dates and places, even physical evidence. History is built out of what we call facts. Fiction and poetry are invented out of what we loosely call human nature and the sound and sense of words. Yet, like fiction and poetry, history changes in perspective, content, tone, texture, detail, and language—depending on who is telling it. It changes over time, as events in the present make us review the past for different or previously overlooked facts. Thus, history textbooks in the 1980s contain frequent references to women and minorities, additions prompted by feminism and the civil rights movement. History also changes in subtle or obvious ways as writers interpret it from different perspectives: a modern Native American sees the arrival of Europeans as a disaster for Indian ways, not the "discovery and conquest of a new world," as so many previous historians have phrased it. Such divergent perspectives are similar to what happens in fiction when, say, sisters recall the day the dog had puppies: their versions are all different.

Sources for the study of history have also expanded tremendously in the last thirty years. As the world economy becomes more and more global, as local environmental problems spell trouble for countries far away, as communications networks bring us immediate news from remote regions, it is no longer enough to study our own heritage. Learning about the history of settlement in the Brazilian rain forest, for example, sets the stage for guiding our personal and public responses to the rain forest's destruction. Transporting American historical paradigms to Brazil won't work, either. It's not enough to compare the settlement of the rain forest to the westward expansion of the United States. We need to appreciate the Brazilian story from the point of view of its unique people, environment, and history.

But that means admitting history told by people quite different from ourselves. Such histories can sound marvelous, unbelievable, and quite a lot like fiction. In these cases, the boundary between history and imaginative writing becomes blurred. That is partly why the use of imaginative writing in history is now so important: it helps us get inside the points of view of others, no matter how different they may be from us. In the shrinking world, such an ability may prove not only useful, but crucial.

The connections between telling history and telling a story can thus be used to enhance the writing of each. When interpreted with the techniques of creative writing, history takes on the vibrancy of lived experience. Students can imagine themselves into the past, wearing the clothing and assuming the destiny of heroes or common folk. Undistinguished players—children, servants, hobos, forgotten knitters and quilters—make a difference in the larger world when we see them not only as representatives of group experiences, but also as individuals.

A similar set of benefits enriches creative writing. As students enter their own pasts, they develop their powers of visualization. They learn to see themselves in their minds' eyes. Memory presents unexpected details—the claw-foot bathtub in grandfather's house, the smell of midnight-blue petunias by his front porch. This practice of using memory's strong imagery can also be helpful in writing about the more distant past or describing things and people in the present. Details that reach all the senses and capture the meaning and power of a place function equally well in writing about the past or the present.

Writers can also begin to stretch beyond their narrow age range and explore what it feels like to be older or younger. When they do, the scope of human life opens more generously. Writers struggling to enter the experience of an historical people vastly different from themselves may appreciate how complex we all are, interacting with nature and technology, with beliefs and laws, differently gifted and full of surprises. As a result, not only will students write better fiction and poetry, they will be better students of the human condition and perhaps better citizens of our country and the world.

*   *   *

This book is addressed to teachers from upper elementary to adult level, as well as writers. The exercises are tailored for classroom use, but solitary workers can alter them for individual use. Some exercises are harder or easier than others, but for each I offer suggestions for adjusting them.

The practice of writing poems and stories about American history has attracted many of our best contemporaries, and their work has inspired some of the exercises in this book. I quote their work and the work of students. These latter examples mean a lot to other young writers, and I encourage teachers to use them in the classroom.

Before we begin, let me describe the attitudes toward teaching history and writing that underlie these exercises. The empty page is a scary blank, especially to students whose teachers demand perfect spelling and punctuation in the first draft. Forget standard notebook paper, and leave polishing the language to the end of the process. Instead, use big sheets of paper when brainstorming and drafting, because the large, unlined surface encourages association of ideas and divergence from linear thinking. As a synthesis of the disciplines of history and English, these writing exercises need as much help as they can get in abolishing tight, disciplinary boundaries. Big sheets of paper signal to students that this writing is different from the history term paper or the English book report. This writing needs more room.

Many of these exercises call for some historical research. I encourage students to pair up or triple up for this. Their combined research notes belong to each person in the group; then, if they want, students can also write together. Sometimes the exercise comes with historical background: I tell students what I have found out about a particular subject. Since the primary aim of these exercises is not to promote original historical research, but to recreate the past with full-bodied imagination, I see no problem with the teacher's providing information when it's needed.

*   *   *

In this book, the personal history exercises come first. Students usually gain by studying their own memories and family histories before those of the more distant past. Throughout, the book contains exercises about the recent past, in which the public and private realms overlap. In future years, when students remember the mid-1980s, the TV image of the Challenger explosion will have illuminated each person's memories of private details associated with the disaster. They will remember the new boy in class, the tacos for lunch, and the snow falling outside the windows just before the spaceship disintegrated.

Such exercises help make us aware that public events become personal milestones, that our individual lives can be drastically altered by government programs, that we share common experiences with others of our generation. This emphasis on history-in-the-making comes from a belief that historical acts can be both individual and collective, performed not only by heroes and heroines, but also by the little people. When we write about ourselves with an historical consciousness, we practice newer branches of historical inquiry, focused on family life, demographic records, the poor or disenfranchised, and economic and environmental change. Students who write stories about neighborhood politics use some of the same approaches as a historian writing about a seventeenth-century New England town.

Thus, this book tries to stretch traditional notions of teaching history to include newer, contemporary methods. It also relies somewhat on "process" writing: brainstorming, drafting, revising, and editing. Each step suggests particular strategies; each leads naturally to the next. So in brainstorming, the big sheet of paper mentioned before creates a wide field for drawing and labeling, word mapping, taking notes, and freewriting. Next, drafting attempts a more shapely, organized piece. Revision expands or contracts the draft, adds vivid language, checks for coherence and suitable tone, etc. Editing includes polishing the spelling, punctuation, capitalization, and paragraphing.

Teachers should model this process. The extent of this modeling will vary, of course, with the age and writing experience of the students. But, in general, if students see the teacher actually generating a poem or story on the board, they are more likely to get started themselves. In this book, everyone, including the teacher, is involved in writing.

The teacher can also help students by presenting examples of finished pieces. Sometimes an exercise blends several elements, drawn from different examples; sometimes it begins with one element and then shows how to proceed independent of the model. All writers borrow in these ways, and to expect students to create everything from scratch seems not just contrary to writerly practice, but self-defeating as a teaching method. Many great writers so transform what they borrow that the average reader can't see the connection; inspiration and the writing process will transport many students into new territory, too.

Each chapter in this book contains several major exercises. In some chapters, I add shorter exercises and variations, along with model works. No chapter is meant to be exhaustive, but rather to generate ideas and to show some teaching strategies that have worked well with my students. The first appendix offers tips for creating your own exercises; the second discusses the kinds of sources available from the National Archives and from state and local historical societies and museums; and the third suggests ways to imagine yourself into a photograph or historical place.

Each chapter begins with a short introduction to set the theme for its exercises. Usually, the most fully developed exercise comes first in the chapter, with shorter ones and variations following. Each fully developed exercise is organized as a series of steps toward the completed writing. These steps include models on which the exercise is based and, usually, examples of student writing developed from the exercise. At the beginning of each exercise I indicate the age range for which it is applicable.

My intention has been to describe each exercise flexibly enough that variations on the outline will easily suggest themselves to you. Making a writing suggestion your own inevitably means filtering it through your own history and practice. The writing that results may be quite different from that presented here, which is as it should be. Feel free to follow these exercises until instinct or inspiration or chance takes you and your students in a different direction: your own.

Chapter 1
THE FAMILY IN HISTORY

Close Ties: Poems about Grandparents and Parents

After doing some word mapping, oral history, or journal writing, students write free-verse poems about a relative particularly important to them. (For upper elementary to adult.)

Step One: Conversation about Grandparents

A short discussion about age is an excellent introduction to this exercise. I tell my students that I knew what *old* meant when I noticed the difference between my young body and my parents' older ones, like Annie Dillard's childhood game of pulling up the loose skin from her mother's hand and finding that it stayed put in little peaks and ridges like whipped cream (see her memoir, *An American Childhood*[1]). I was fascinated by my German grandfather's bald head, whose sprinkling of white hair around the back looked like a naughty sugar smile.

From these contrasts—smooth skin versus wrinkles, thick young hair versus old bald head—comes an understanding that older means closer to death. Sometimes you form special bonds with relatives who, you sense, will die soon. When I talk to the class about the illness and death of grandparents, I emphasize that our grandparents teach us about the times before. They are our first connection to the lost days. As our grandparents talk about "flappers" and "tin lizzies" and bed warmers and World War II, they may hint at what makes them different from us, even though they wear the family grin or explode with the family temper.

Separate yet linked to us, their pasts are also our own. Students may wonder what it means that grandmother still speaks Spanish or grandfather once made it home through a blizzard by "giving the horses their heads." Someday, will you regret losing grandmother's language? Someday, will you too have the grit to come home blindly through a storm?

Students' own family histories eventually lead them to explore larger differences in the way people of earlier times interacted with society and nature. Examining our grandparents' (and parents') lives can show us how our families have been affected by massive public events and how society has changed, too.

Grandparents' experiences will vary greatly. Those who arrived during a wave of immigration may have suffered discrimination from more established newcomers, but others may have been helped immensely by church or civic groups. Some worked hard on railroads and in factories, and passed down a pride in physical work well done. Some wanted their children to be professionals and managed to save for their college education. Nowadays, grandparents sound old: they use dated phrases and refer to bygone values, perhaps those of Boston intellectuals, Southern blacks, prosperous small-town merchants, or Latino migrant workers.

Though I don't say this to most students, I believe that writing about older relatives not only helps them understand a less homogenous past, but also gives them a wider range of choices for thinking and acting in the present.

Step Two: Visualizing a Place with a Grandparent

This step uses memory and nothing more. It extends the brainstorming part of the writing process. As the students prepare to close their eyes and begin visualizing, I tell them that those who don't know—or don't have—grandparents may use a parent or another older relative as their subject instead.

"Put your heads down on the desk," I tell the class. "Close your eyes. Now imagine that you are with your grandparent in a particular place. Maybe you are indoors in your grandfather's house. Or maybe outdoors, in a rowboat on a lake, or in a smelly garage, or out in the back garden, bending down to help your grandmother plant squash." Then I tell them that when I think of the summer visits to my grandfather's house in North Dakota, I can smell the midnight-blue petunias that grew on his front porch and the Vicks VapoRub that rose from his bed when I slid in to take a nap. Smells are particularly helpful in recovering memory. A neurologist once told me that smells help us remember because the brain cells that identify smells are located close to those that house memory.

Every once in a while a student will say, "I can't write because I don't remember anything." I know how terrible that feels. Everyone else is energetically scribbling while a solid wall closes down in that one student's mind. The problem is common. Do not despair, because though memories fade, they can be brought back. The more we think, talk and write about the past, the more likely we are to remember. One approach is to ask forgetful students specific questions and write down their responses. If all else fails, have them write about forgetting: "Why *don't* you remember your grandfather?" Sometimes the answer is as good a subject as a memory.

Step Three: Word Mapping on Newsprint

After I tell the students to open their eyes, I have them fold a big sheet of newsprint—plain paper of the quality used for newspapers—in half and open it up again. Then I have them choose one half the sheet for mapping. "Put your grandparent's name (or nickname) in the middle of that half." Then I ask them to draw "roads" or lines, curved or straight, extending out from the name. I tell them to write, at the end of each road, a small detail that refers to one of the five senses. "Use the details of the place where you remember being with your grandparent. Maybe you are out in a boat with Grandpa. Imagine the slosh of the waves, the algae smell, the plop of the baited hook, the wiggle of worms in the carton."

Then I ask them to flesh out the descriptions of their grandparents. What are the features of their faces, hands, or body that make them look like nobody else? What do they usually wear? What are some pet expressions? What do you do together? How do they tease you? Think of their usual activities, or perhaps a piece of their jewelry you like. What does your grandfather collect? What does your grandmother serve for dinner?"

It's best if the details in the word map are as small and specific as possible; for example, "the smell of fish heads in the garbage" rather than "a bad rotten smell," or "the whoosh of traffic two blocks away" rather than "street noises."

Here's an example of how I do my word map on the board:

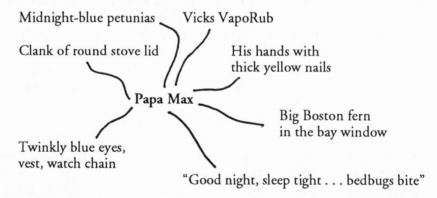

Midnight-blue petunias   Vicks VapoRub

Clank of round stove lid   His hands with
                                   thick yellow nails

Papa Max

                          Big Boston fern
                          in the bay window

Twinkly blue eyes,
vest, watch chain

          "Good night, sleep tight . . . bedbugs bite"

My memories of my grandfather begin with his bald head and move down to the collarless shirt he wore under a frayed black vest. His sleeves, too long for him, were gathered up by elastic bands above his elbows, and a watch chain swung below the vest. At lunch or dinner in the sunny dining room, he tucked a big white napkin under his chin.

I learned about napkin rings there. At each place sat a different ring, some silver, some bone. Later, in the kitchen, Papa Max gave the canary her bath. He poured warm water into a green plastic bath that slid over the door of her cage. Inside she splashed her wings in the water while he spoke German to her. I watched him and tried to imagine what he was saying.

Sometimes as my sister and I climbed the stairway to bed, Papa Max would stand in the hall below and call up to us: "Good night, sleep tight, don't let the bedbugs bite." He smiled and it was funny, but later, after I slid between the cool sheets in the dark bedroom, I trembled, waiting for the bedbugs to march around the end of the mattress and bite my toes.

The story about the bedbugs suggests adding conversation to the maps. "Add your grandparents' favorite teases, the question grandmother asks every time you visit and the words you answer back," I tell the class.

Word maps get students started writing even before they know it. The map's circular array of words lends all the details an equal importance, allowing them a freewheeling interaction that can be both inspiring and true to the dynamics of memory. Soon the maps have begun to describe the feel of a forgotten world.

Step Four: Looking at Model Poems

Next comes the job of shaping these initial memories into small dramas. Lots of poems circle back through repetitions and refrains, but most also proceed toward some kind of conclusion, the way paragraphs or essays do—chronologically from beginning to end, from smaller to larger, from sensation to emotion, from superficial to profound.

The poems I use as models with this exercise vary according to the ages of the students and the amount of time we have to work together. Sometimes, with elementary school classes, I begin with a poem of my own that uses the type of details I've mentioned in brainstorming and mapping:

Sweetie Pie

Papa Max stands by the sink, belly round
under black vest. Even breathing
sets his watch chain swinging.
A yellow bird flutters
from bath to air.

"Sweetie Pie," he chirps,
"Giesst du deine Blume?"

Red his fingers with their
twining care, red the polish
of his apple head.

He has warmed water
for her plastic bath. In
she dips wings and sprays
his hand, vest, trousers.

"Watering your flowers?" he teases.
I know because
bloom
is the same in both
our talk.

A red German saint in dull white
kitchen with his blond
Vöglein, the bird of love.

"Sweetie Pie," he says. "Komm, setz
dich auf meinen Finger, eat
from my hand."

With older students (age twelve and up) I also often use this poem by
the Latino poet Alberto Rios:

Nani

Sitting at her table, she serves
the sopa de arroz to me
instinctively, and I watch her,
the absolute mamá, and eat words
I might have had to say more
out of embarrassment. To speak
now-foreign words I used to speak,
too, dribble down her mouth as she serves
me albóndigas. No more
than a third are easy to me.
By the stove she does something with words
and looks at me only with her
back. I am full. I tell her
I taste the mint, and watch her speak
smiles at the stove. All my words

make her smile. Nani never serves
herself, she only watches me
with her skin, her hair. I ask for more.

I watch the mamá warming more
tortillas for me. I watch her
fingers in the flame for me.
Near her mouth, I see a wrinkle speak
of a man whose body serves
the ants like she serves me, then more words
about this and that, flowing more
easily from these other mouths. Each serves
as a tremendous string around her,
holding her together. They speak
Nani was this and that to me
and I wonder just how much of me
will die with her, what were the words
I could have been, was. Her insides speak
through a hundred wrinkles, now, more
than she can bear, steel around her,
shouting, then, What is this thing she serves?

She asks me if I want more.
I own no words to stop her.
Even before I speak, she serves.[2]

Rios's poem captures the way the boy and his grandmother (*nani*) communicate without speaking, through gestures and the simple act of cooking. As she serves him *sopa de arroz* (rice soup) and *albóndigas* (meatballs), he cannot reply because he has forgotten the Spanish he used to know. Yet her wrinkles speak of events in her life, and because he sympathizes with her and cannot say the words to stop her, he eats more and wonders "how much of me/will die with her."

Both poems use the changes in language from grandparent to grandchild to show the differences between those generations. In my poem, I imagined that I understood my grandfather's German: I admired Papa Max and wanted so hard to understand him that in a way I did. Rios, on the other hand, affirms an affinity to his Nani though he no longer speaks Spanish with her.

Both poems suggest a truth about how poets write history: the small details of one event (a lunch or a bird's bath) make it possible for much of the larger story (cultural assimilation and generational differences) to shine through. When Rios writes, "Nani never serves/herself" and "I watch her/ fingers in the flame for me," he implies her life of extreme self-sacrifice and family service, more common to her generation than to his.

Some writers who respond to these two models write about how cultural identities have marked their grandparents. In the following untitled poem, Helen Gerhardson, a third grade teacher in Bemidji, Minnesota, portrays her Ojibway grandmother as exemplifying a way of life of which the rest of us are often ignorant:

> I wanted to tell that Social Security man
> that every wrinkle in grandma's face
> tells a story.
> The story of how
> she raised four kids alone.
> The story of chopping
> and hauling wood,
> pumping water,
> mending the roof,
> and hitchhiking to Fargo
> for a graduation dress.
>
> I wanted to tell him about
> her planting a garden
> and when it wasn't productive,
> how grandma walked five miles
> on a moonlit night
> to carry a deer home—
> praying she would not be caught.
>
> Asking for Social Security at 88
> took all her pride.
> But that Social Security man told her
> "You never worked!"

The author's strong defense of her grandmother affirms the value of the hard work she did. The grandmother's work also suggests a larger theme: how Native Americans often find it very difficult to fit into the dominant social system.

Another poem I often use as a model with students of all ages is by John Calvin Rezmerski. He speaks openly about his grandmother's illness and death, using details that are sharp and compelling:

Grandmother

In her house I learned to listen to seashells.
The house full of the smells of raisin bread,

chicken soup, blackberry wine,
lavender sachet, laundry bluing, and coal smoke.
The smell of work.

Bronchial pneumonia is a dying old person's
best friend, according to the doctor.
106 degrees for three days,
but cold hands.
She seems to remember everyone all right,
but who knows what she knows,
who knows what she forgets?
"What do you think of an 80-year-old woman
having a baby?" she asks.
"I'm beautiful," she says.

It's finally her day off.

Her homemade rag rugs
lie on the gray linoleum,
the blank TV faces potted plants.
Her wedding portrait rests in the closet,
young and narrow-waisted, holding
blue carnations.

She comes forth like a flower.
And withers.
Blue carnations in her casket,
rosary in her hands:

her last wishes:

"I want my children to take
what they gave me.
I won't need it anymore.
Maybe I missed something
so forgive me."

She has stopped working.
She got sick picking up apples
on the hill behind the house
so they wouldn't rot.
The house is full of medicine
she will not need.
An electric clock buzzes.
The refrigerator hums.
I learned to listen to seashells here.

Her last confinement.
With the skill of a woman
who has done it a dozen times,
she bears down steadily,
gives birth to the spirit
she has carried full term.

Coming in from both coasts,
the family closes around her
like a flower closing for the night.
After the burial Friday morning
we open up,
enjoying each other's company
we have not had for so long,
and settle her estate in an hour or so,
and keep what we had given her,
and sing, and look
through old photographs.
And some who have been feuding
for years
sit down to dinner together.
And I listen to seashells in the attic.
She has not stopped working.
It seems as though we are
gathered around to see her new child.[3]

Rezmerski's details refer richly to the senses. They recreate the atmosphere of the grandmother's house, and offer clues to the old woman's character. She was hard-working, a saver—also one who collected seashells. Rezmerski develops some of these details into evocative motifs that suggest what the grandmother has given the family. He repeats the motif of the first line, "I learned to listen to seashells here," and suggests that she has attuned his attention to mysteries, such as the blue carnations with their unnatural color that mark her wedding and funeral. The birth motif expresses both the gift of life and the way she approaches her death: "she bears down steadily,/gives birth to the spirit."

Creating refrains and expanding motifs or comparisons will unify a poem and, more importantly, introduce meaning without hitting the reader over the head with it. I encourage students to begin and end their poems with echoing lines and to notice how something associated with a grandparent, like the blue carnations, can assume a larger meaning—for instance, the flowers standing for the mystery in the old woman's life.

In most classes I read at least one grandparent poem by a student writer. Hearing what their peers have done inspires students. The following poem by seventh grader Jim Jones develops simple motifs of fishing to create an ending that joins the grandfather's impending death with the thrill of catching a fish:

Grandpaw Leek

Remembering calling him Grandpaw Lake.
When we would fish, gosh
if he caught a fish he would say
"It's not the one." He would just talk
about the walleye, the so-called 25 pounder.
I would think when he would die,
his veins so brittle
with the gentle breeze. And when the sun
was just rising at 6
the golden lake and the green algae
looking so green. Then when gazing out, his pole went down
he said, "Oh God, I've got it."[4]

Another of my favorite student poems (by eleventh grader Tami Carr) uses two strategies adapted from Rezmerski—a refrain and details that expand into a motif.

"Pop": A Cry through the Pines

"POP" is what I called to him
As he tightened the cold, steel vice.

Scents of pine drift into the rafters.
He drank Ancient Age without ice.
The smells wavered freely through air.

He held onto his "little old gramma."
They ran through the kitchen like kids,
Two boxcars, separated not long ago.

He'd rise up early to extend a battered hand.
A comfort for the winter fowl, with some seed and corn.

Bluejays and snowbirds flocked around his cloddy galoshes.
I'd watch from inside the glass.
He would come in to me and ask,
"What do you see, my little chick-a-dee?"
I would laugh with delight as he placed me on his knee.
He stood solid and chugged along till 79;
then the train cracked a "pop" deep within the engine.
A cry through the pines.

The grandfather's affection for the birds extends to his granddaughter, his "little chick-a-dee." The enigmatic "cry through the pines" perhaps refers to her grief as well as the call of a bird.

Brett Opdahl was a twelfth grader, studying auto mechanics, when he wrote "Grandpa's Junk." With many complicated feelings, his poem humorously reminds us not to gussy up our memories. Poems aren't greeting cards, and our connections to older relatives are edged with dislikes, boredom, and occasional fear, as well as sympathy.

Grandpa's Junk

House smells old, musty
Small house, old sheds in back—lots of junk
I see my Grandpa laugh—no teeth
I hear Grandpa play his instruments—he plays everything.
The cellar door open—Grandma is getting canned goods.
I don't like her macaroni and cheese.
Grandpa puts on his harmonica and blows a train
Accordion expands and exhales a fierce sound
Grandpa laughs with joy
He pounds the bass drum.
I want to play—Grandpa laughs as I try.
We walk back to the old sheds—lots of junk
Old cars, black truck—I hate the truck, won't go in it.
Grandpa sets me in it, I scream, he grabs me
Holds me 'til the tears stop.
Walking on further, holding hands, another shed
Explore and find new junk—Grandpa's junk.[5]

Step Five: Drafting the Poem

After reading and discussing several of these model poems, I point out again to students the techniques that they might use in their poems: using repeating lines to link different parts of memory; moving quickly from description to feeling to action; including both the unpleasant and the happy; and focusing on snippets of conversation and small, vivid details.

When the students begin to draft their poems on the adjacent half of the big paper, they can easily refer back to their word maps. I urge them to use most of what's on the map and put in any new ideas. After a few minutes of drafting my own work on the board, I walk from desk to desk, read aloud beginnings that seem particularly strong, and take dictation from students who are stumped. Usually students can produce good drafts in around fifteen minutes.

Though the student poems presented here have been slightly revised, they were essentially completed in one class period. Fundamentally, the poems succeed because the small details from memory evoke the much larger whole of the grandparents' lives and the way their grandchildren understand them.

The poems reveal a remarkable range of understanding. Perhaps the students wrote more knowingly than they realized. Presenting us with sensory images, already imbued with significance, memory rings truer than clichés handed to us from outside our personal experience. Writing such poems is an important antidote to the tendency in our culture to homogenize everyone. With clear rich memories, we become more ourselves, appreciating our idiosyncracies and more sure of a history that gives us an identity.

EXERCISE TWO
Poems of Family History

Personal memory is also a valuable guide to unearthing family history and shaping it in relation to more public events. In this second exercise, which includes a number of possible variations, students use conversations with neighbors or family members to write poems suggesting historical movements these older people were a part of. (For upper elementary to adult.)

Step One: Conducting Oral Histories (or Life Reviews) with Family Members

As people age, they may look back and see moments when their lives changed. Perhaps they see their lives as split into two parts; as my mother says, "B.B." (before babies). Sometimes these shifts correspond to larger social and cultural ones ("before the War"). Shifting the focus from the individual to the group (and back again) is one of the historian's primary functions.

When the information about specific people from the past is sparse, the historian must piece together an individual life or a group profile from records of births, marriages, and deaths; lists of household furnishings; passenger lists; or decrees from monarchs that imply crop failure or plagues. The historian's work then becomes a detective game of inference from remote clues.

With members of our families, we can practice the historian's job of exploring larger historical events by beginning with a private life and watching for ways it represents the fate of many. A whole class can go about this systematically, with each student interviewing a parent or grandparent about an important period of change in American life. Or the students can invite an older neighbor to class, maybe a teacher recently retired from the school or a worker in the region's speciality. Sample topics might be the Great Depression of the 1930s, World War II, the civil rights movement of the 1960s, or modern feminism. A helpful guide to conducting a systematic oral history is Cynthia Stokes Brown's *Like It Was: A Complete Guide to Writing Oral History*.[6]

Preparing students for a group interview takes a class period of discussion. Students of almost any age benefit from filling in a timeline on the board, one depicting, for instance, the town's history. It is surprising how few students (even adults) make connections between an individual's life and the large events in our country's history—World War I, the 1918 flu epidemic, the "roaring" twenties, the 1929 Stock Market Crash, the Dust Bowl and Great Depression of the 1930s, the attack on Pearl Harbor, the end of World War II, the boom years after the war, the House Un-American Affairs Committee Hearings (or the "McCarthy Hearings,"), the initial push for school desegregation in the mid-1950s, President Kennedy's assassination, and so on. Talking to a class about these large events and commenting on their effects on local life can give students some ideas for questions they can ask the visitor.

Another kind of interview is a "life review." A life review does not focus only on one area of a person's life—such as politics or travel—but begins with childhood and ranges over the standard divisions in life: childhood, teen years, schooling, jobs, and parenthood. Some key questions to guide the conversation might be: How do you understand your parents now? Have your feelings toward them changed over the years? If you could change one thing you did or said to them, what would it be? What did they teach you? What were some difficulties you had as a child or young adult? If you could give yourself something now that you wanted then, what would it be? Twenty (or thirty or fifty) years ago, what did you like or hate about food, religion, clothing, houses, games? Could you describe a moment when you "woke up" and saw something differently than you had before? Could you describe someone who left you? What was your reputation in the family, school, neighborhood? What nicknames did you have?

The best life interviews uncover vivid details and anecdotes that the younger generation may never have heard before. Once I was talking with my father, a serious professor. Suddenly, grinning like a conspirator, he started describing being ordered from the table by his father, a stern Presbyterian minister. Upstairs, closed in their rooms, he and his three brothers connived to waken Nonna, their grandmother.

I was all ears. He was talking about a shadowy figure I had noticed in old family photographs. "Who's Nonna?" I asked.

Nonna was the Italian grandmother who came in her eighties from the mountain town of Pescopagano to live with my father's family in Pittsburgh. She never learned English or understood how the household worked. Dinner she took in her room. But she wasn't above sneaking down the back stairs to collect a picnic for her grandsons when they were banished from the table. "She swore us to secrecy and silence," my father relates, "and as we fished bread and cheese from her apron, she would warn us that the evil eye would get us if we told Papa. We teased her mercilessly."

My father's three brothers also teased him. They called him Egg Face. He repeats this each time we talk. I didn't understand the expression. Was it simply that he didn't wipe his mouth? My uncle Frank, the wildest of the four, told me once in a private moment, "As a boy, your father was almost prissy, with his violin and soft cheeks." As an adult, my father became obsessively fastidious, washing his hands, inspecting forks, sponging his trousers. Did being called Egg Face start this?

In another conversation, my father recalled going to the mission church in Liberty Heights where his father was the minister. (His father had converted from the Catholic church soon after immigrating to the United States.) My father says, "To get to the church, we had to take three streetcars. Then we arrived at the bottom of a long hill. It was a hard climb. On either side of the street were houses of Italian-American Catholics. These *paesani* (countrymen) pelted us with rotten eggs and tomatoes, yelling, "Dirty Protestant, heretic, *specie di porcaccio*—disgusting pig." From this story, I understood that my grandfather's religious conversion was bought at a price: he and his family were scorned by their compatriots.

Not every family has problems with their community, but you can count on almost every family's having some vivid dramas. It may take several conversations to loosen their tongues. After all, most relatives aren't used to being sat down and asked to spill out their memories. As with writing, so with speaking: the more you talk about the past, the more there is to say, except when someone deliberately seeks to avoid talking about a person or event. He may be ashamed or uncertain about your reason for probing, or may want to minimize an accomplishment. The best approach is, as Hamlet says, to let "indirection find direction out." For instance, I'm sure that, had I pressed my father to explain his nickname "Egg Face," he would have chuckled and passed over my question. He didn't really know the answer, but I, putting pieces of his story together, see a possible answer, and this insight is my reward for letting him proceed with the account in his own way.

Step Two: Brainstorming and Drafting the Poem

One day, brainstorming on the chalkboard with a class, as I often do, I started with my Italian grandfather from Pittsburgh, Giovanni Battista (John the Baptist) Fortunato. On my word map I put the tidbits of his life and work that I knew from conversations with my father.

When it came time to draft my poem, it was the aptness of his name (The Baptist) for his profession that set me going:

> Named for the evangelist, the voice
> crying in the wilderness
> of America, John the Baptist
> Fortunato boomed for years
> from his pulpit, "a great orator"
> his son, my father
> will repeat, "a great orator."

That's as far as I got, but I knew I was onto something. I hurriedly copied these lines onto notebook paper and took it home to finish. As I worked on it, the poem evolved from my grandfather toward his son (my father), becoming framed by their two names:

> Who led his family, wife and four
> boys, up the slanting
> streets of Pittsburgh into Wop
> Town Sunday after Sunday.
> From the streetcar stop
> they climbed past the raw
> houses of Catholics. "Betrayer,"
> "Heretic," "Dirty Protestant"—
> voices pelted; eggs, tomatoes
> splatted the sidewalk
> and the trousers of the son,
> Leonard my father, who wanted
> to be clean, who could not
> wash his hands enough
> before eating but earned
> the name "Egg Face" from his brothers
> because he had learned
> not to feel the crusted dirty yolk.

The conversion to Protestantism, which made my grandfather true to his middle name, had repercussions for his son. In the razzing each Sunday, the boy collected enough shame to keep him scrubbing for a lifetime. "Egg Face" carries connotations of Easter and Christ's crucifixion, but in writing the poem, I concentrated on recent history. The poem became my family's version of the pains of assimilation, common to many immigrants.

When using this poem as an example, I encourage students to remember key phrases from people they have interviewed, phrases that recall memorable moments of those people's lives, like the typing teacher who mentioned "finger watchers," and remembered being evicted from her college dorm by the "Air Corps Cadets who marched in formation down the halls," training for World War II. I encourage students to write from the point of view of the person they interviewed, or, if they wish, someone else mentioned in the interview.

"Begin your poem with some identification of the person it's about," I say. "Use the first person in your writing if you want, but include details from the past to cue the reader that this poem is not about you." Simple details—such as ration books from World War II, old tools, or ways of growing and preserving food—these immediately set the poem in the past and separate the characters in it from the author.

Poet Joe Paddock bases many of his poems on oral history. In "The End of Their Leap," he uses the experience of interviewing an old man, and watches a story from the past light up his memory:

A glint rising through
the darkness of his pupils,
eighty-five now, he remembers
timberwolves leaping high
at the distant margin
of new field and virgin timber,
him trudging through snow
toward a bone white school,
and the sunrise fired through
the dark fur along the arc
of their backs.

They hung high, those wolves,
at the end of their leap, to see
clearly what he was. A tied bundle
of books in his clutching hand,
the better predator, he pushed on
to District 11, arriving to drill
numbers, rapid fire, through the cold
bright day, the image of living
wolves receding, hanging
in deep black regions
of the mind, far back.[7]

Step Three: Reading Student Examples

The following pieces are by eleventh grade students who conducted
oral histories in two ways. Their class brought in a former teacher, who
reminisced about her days in the college dorm where Air Corps Cadets
were billeted and about how she met her husband. The students in this
class also attended a community "Reminiscence Night" in which three
commercial fishermen described their work in the days before hydraulic
winches, pulleys, and reels. The "pond net" they described was set near
the shoreline in the huge Lake of the Woods between Canada and
Minnesota, to catch "rough" fish (as opposed to "eating" fish) for use in
medicines and animal feed.

The Commercial Fisherman

Dawn. What a cold day
out on the lake.
Can feel the snow on
the weather, the man
a commercial fisherman
working with pond nets,
pulling them up by hand
with lots of fish in them,
selling berbot livers
for four cents a pound
to a pharmacy
to make a substitute
cod liver oil.
Four cents a pound takes
a lot of work
pulling for day
after day
for enough pay.

—*Luke Fish*

*　*　*

When Mrs. Landby Met Her Husband

Mrs. Landby walked into a dance and across the dance floor to the
punch bowl. She waited not too long before a gentleman in a suit came
up and asked her to dance. She told him she didn't know how to dance.
He walked away. Then about ten minutes later the same gentleman came
back and asked her to dance. She thought it was the same gentleman,
and again she told him she didn't know how to dance, and he left.

But not long after, he returned and again asked her to dance. This time she was going to show him she didn't know how to dance. Later she found out that the man who is now her husband had only asked her twice to dance, and his brother, who was wearing the same suit, asked the third time.

—Troy Otto

*   *   *

The Cadet

Sweaty, hot, sticky uniforms, 1942,
St. Cloud. Air Corps cadets
walk down the halls in formation,
miserable, scared of war, scared of
what would happen to them. Klump, klump,
klump down the hall.

—John Bannert

Alternate: Another Model for Writing—The Trip to or from America

A fearsome arrival in a strange land is told simply and powerfully in Mitsuye Yamada's long poem, "I Learned to Sew." Here the grandmother recounts how, when she was seventeen, her family in Japan sent her picture to a man in Hawaii, and when his answer was a marriage proposal, put her on the boat. When the suitor saw her, he rejected her because she was "too ugly for him," and left her stranded. Here is an excerpt from the middle of the poem:[8]

I sat at Immigration for a long time
people came and people went
I stayed
I could not see the sky
I could not see the sun
outside the window
I saw a seaweed forest
the crickets made scraping sounds
the geckos went tuk tuk tuk
sometimes a gecko would come into my room
but I was not afraid to talk to it
it came and it went as it pleased

I was thinking about Urashima Taro
you know the story?

Urashima disappeared into the sea
lived in the undersea world
married a beautiful princess
returned to his village
a very old man
I was thinking
I will leave this place
only when I am an old lady.

Pretty soon the Immigration man came to me
We found your cousin
In two weeks a cousin I met once
in Japan came for me
I stayed with him and his wife until
my cousin found a job for me
I worked doing housework
I did this for one year.

My cousin found a husband for me
he was a merchant
we had a small store
and sold dry goods
my husband died after three sons
your father, my oldest son, was six years old
I could not keep the store
I could not read
I could not write
the only thing I knew how to do was sew.

I took the cloth from our store
sewed pants and undergarments
put the garments on a wooden cart
ombu the baby on my back
we went from plantation to plantation
sold my garments to the workers
I was their only store
sewed more garments at night
I did this for five years.

Her son then finds his mother another husband who agrees to educate
her children. The husband is threatened with losing his job if he does not
put the boys to work on the plantation, but he does not betray his
promise. In the end, the grandmother speaks again:

After that we had many hard times
I am nothing

know nothing
I only know how to sew
I now sew for my children and grandchildren
I turn to the sun every day of my life
pray to Amaterasu Omikami
for the health and
education of my children
for me that is enough.

My child
Write this
There   take your pen
There   write it
Say that I am not going back
I am staying here

Fashioned, I imagine, almost directly from a spoken oral history, this narrative is powerful enough to be told unembellished. Note the powerful image of the "sea change" that occurs in the grandmother's life. She cannot go back to Japan because of the change in her that the journey has begun.

Mitsuye Yamada's poem is a good model for imagining oneself back to the culture (or country) of one's grandparents. By "culture" I mean a way of life, including tools, agriculture, cooking, transportation, family life, festivals, arts and crafts, clothing, housing, and so on. This leap into the past is difficult, but Mitsuye Yamada's poem suggests one way to make it easier: simply to have the grandparent be the speaker in the poem. Students could then also write about how the old ways may be continuing in their own or their parents' lives.

Alternate: Another Model for Writing—The Composite Hero/Heroine

John Minczeski's poem "My Name" tells the story of an anonymous person, newly arrived, stripped of European identity, trying to enter the U.S. without a passport. Like this character, many immigrants lost their names when officials on Ellis Island anglicized or grossly misspelled them.

My Name

for Victor Contoski

My name arrived from Poland in 1910 stowed away
in the engine room of a Swiss freighter. The cook
took pity on it and every day brought sausages, berries
and milk. My name for two weeks was deafened by the sound
of pistons and the turning of twin screws.

My name, without a passport or an extra change of clothes,
without a toothbrush or a brown shopping bag,
swam to Staten Island, barely missed being eaten by sharks.
My name didn't know English. It was taken in
by potato farmers and learned to drive trucks
and drink beer. My name tripped
over a cabbage and was cut in half by a harrow.
Thus I was born. I have given it years of pain.
My name has forgotten how to cry.[9]

The details probably come from bits of family history and a general knowledge of immigrants. Some details are fanciful—berries on a freighter, a freighter from Switzerland. Yet for all its humor, the poem brings to mind photographs of immigrants waiting for the officials at Ellis Island, with a glazed look of estrangement on their faces and their worldly goods bundled in a blanket or shawl.

"My name" in Minczeski's poem suggests not only the complicated identity that the immigrant has begun to lose during the passage, but also how an individual is reduced by being made to feel like a number or just another person on a long list, cut off from his past, his memory, and ultimately his ability to feel. Though not all immigrants' stories are so bleak as this one, the experience of radical change is common to them all.

Minczeski's poem offers another model for combining facts with imagination: rather than emphasizing the unique details of an individual's history, it conjures up a composite story. It's true that "my name," the poem's protagonist, experiences the shipboard passage on an intimate, sensuous level (it eats specific foods, is bothered by particular noises, lacks certain things), but, although it responds like a sensitive human being, it has somehow lost its individuality en route—no family status, no social class, no profession, possibly not even any age or gender.

Using Minczeski's technique in "My Name," students can write compelling adventure poems or stories from many historical perspectives: Japanese interned during World War II, a colonial settler's first decade in New England, a millhand's life in the South, a Creek Indian's trek along the Trail of Tears, a black slave's daily life, a prospector's search for gold. Research about the places, food, transportation, and human interactions common to each of these situations can provide the details that help create an emotional response in the reader.

Variation: Group Poem with Composite Character

Another variation is to learn about historical incidents from a group of older people—family members or friends—and, in a *composite* oral history, construct a collaborative story from the historical details you've learned. Students can interview older relatives or possibly even strangers, and then, bringing the interviews back to class, write a group profile. Or a class can work on shaping their stories with the old people themselves. Participating in a successful collaboration can give the older people the thrill of seeing their memories become part of a composite tale. It's fun to collaborate on content and help with the collective search for vivid language. Working together on developing the material, coming up with good images, ordering the whole, and bringing it to a conclusion can teach students a lot about how to shape a dramatic narrative. It also shows how both history and writing are fed from a dynamic, communal source.

EXERCISE THREE

Collecting Clues from Historical Sites and Objects

Prose or poetic vignettes of family life in various times and locales. (For upper elementary to adult.)

Step One: Discovering the Artistic Appeal of Historical Sites and Objects

For years, when I passed old barns, weathered mansions, or boarded-up tenements, I wanted to stop and study them. I didn't. Fear of trespassing, of being found out, or of falling through the floor always held me back. But whenever I could visit a museum or historic landmark, I did. What was I looking for beyond a melodramatic shiver?

I didn't know until I found Ted Kooser's poem:

Abandoned Farmhouse

He was a big man, says the size of his shoes
on a pile of broken dishes by the house;
a tall man too, says the length of the bed
in an upstairs room; and a good, God-fearing man,
says the Bible with a broken back
on the floor below the window, dusty with sun;
but not a man for farming, say the fields
cluttered with boulders and the leaky barn.

A woman lived with him, says the bedroom wall
papered with lilacs and the kitchen shelves
covered with oilcloth, and they had a child,

says the sandbox made from a tractor tire.
Money was scarce, say the jars of plum preserves
and canned tomatoes sealed in the cellar-hole,
and the winters cold, say the rags in the window frames.
It was lonely here, says the narrow gravel road.

Something went wrong, says the empty house
in the weed-choked yard. Stones in the fields
say he was not a farmer; the still-sealed jars
in the cellar say she left in a nervous haste.
And the child? Its toys are strewn in the yard
like branches after a storm—a rubber cow,
a rusty tractor with a broken plow,
a doll in overalls. Something went wrong, they say.[10]

When I read this poem for the first time, I understood what drew me
to old, ramshackle houses. The sagging roof lines and tattered wallpaper
were clues to the stories of people who had left, and the insatiable
historian in me wanted, among other things, to test how saddling a horse
to ride to town would have made the texture and events of life different
from driving a car. I wanted to explore a lot of those differences, from
washing the dishes to washing the dead.

When I was a girl in South Carolina, historical romance novels and
films satisfied me by dressing up courtship in quaint trappings. Flirtation
in carriages, behind fans, and on moonlit verandas never got as sticky as
holding hands at the drive-in. History's distance, its veil of gentility and
sentiment, was more what I was after. I wanted to step into the southern
belle's shoes, to blush and pine with her.

True historians dismiss such palpitating excesses. But this first
attraction to the romanticized past does teach something. When imagination cloaks us in the past—whether it involves frontier life, the number
of beaux Scarlett O'Hara captured, or legendary baseball players—we try
on for ourselves the way the past might have felt. We breathe life into
history's clues. We imagine how old artifacts shaped everyday life.

Step Two: Asking Questions about Historical Sites and Objects

For a moment, have students put romance aside and simply look at
things, perhaps a hundred-year-old trunk or the furniture of an early
New England farmhouse. Ted Kooser's poem is a good model in the way
it suggests a process for learning how household items and farm practices
affect the lives of the people who have used them, and how imagination
can drape a fabric of sensations, desires, feelings, and ideas over a skeleton
of objects.

You might choose another scenario entirely; maybe you can visit a museum with rooms from different regions and periods, such as the miniature rooms in the Chicago Art Institute or the board-by-board relocations of colonial and Victorian rooms in the Minneapolis Art Institute. Perhaps you can visit colonial Williamsburg, or a recreated summer Indian encampment. If you can't arrange a field trip, try using postcards; for instance, of Louisa May Alcott's home. Photographs of Old Sturbridge Village, Massachusetts, also show details of old furnished rooms. Students might also write about old items from their own families—Bibles, handkerchiefs, dolls, jewelry.

I chose a New England colonial house as a subject because I've read Puritan diaries and Yankee autobiographies and because I want to put my imagination to work on artifacts that are far removed from dishwasher and microwave. Technological change has occurred so rapidly in the last hundred years that to find truly different modes of cooking and heating and washing it's necessary to go back only to the generations of the 1880s or 1920s. Washboard, wood stove, and ice box—these implements aren't all that much advanced over the implements of the colonists.

Lacking a period room to visit, you might use books about early New England, such as *Home and Child Life in Colonial Days,* edited by Shirley Glubok from an 1898 two-volume work by Alice Morse Earle (Macmillan, 1969); *Colonial Living* by Edwin Tunis (World, 1957); *Early Americans* by Carl Bridenbaugh (Oxford, 1981); *The Puritan Family* by Edmund Morgan (Harper and Row, 1944, 1966); and *Colonial America* by Louis Wright (Putnam's, 1965). Students in classrooms, especially if they're trying to finish the writing in a few days, will probably have time to consult only one or two books.

Here is a list of details that intrigued me as I read through these books:

New England thatched roofs had chimneys made of logs that caught fire readily. Fire buckets kept by door. Whole town was a fire brigade.

First windows oiled paper, small. Then came small panes of heavy, wavy glass.

First, tall palisade, until the Indians retreated. Then double rail fence to keep in cattle. As timber disappeared, stone walls.

Light from knots of fat-pitch pine burned in the chimney. Candles were expensive. Tallow for candles came from bear grease, deer suet, or moose fat. Some dipped candles by hand; others used candle forms.

Tinder box with flint, steel and some kind of material to catch the spark. If house fire went out, a child ran to neighbors to bring back coals on a shovel or piece of bark.

Kitchen had huge fireplace with seats inside the chimney. At the back of the fireplace hung a bar made first of green wood. From this "back bar" hung the pots and kettles. Often the back bar burned through and dinner fell in the fire. Later the bar was made of iron.

Pots and kettles and skillets up on legs. Some pots were huge, iron weighing 40 pounds. Many utensils on long handles to keep the cook away from the fire.

Roasts hung on spits from the ceiling next to the fire. Often a turnspit dog, a terrier with short legs and a good disposition, was trained to climb a wheel that turned the roast.

Bread, pies, beans were baked in ovens built into the chimney or later in ovens set before it. A long-handled utensil called a "peel" slid the bread into the oven and removed it.

Houses were frigid except for the kitchen. Beds were hung with curtains and supplied with deep feather mattresses. Bedwarmers were essential to take off the chill. Sometimes they scorched the bedding. Water froze in washbowls.

Tables made of boards set on sawhorses. Few families had china. They ate from trenchers, wooden troughs shared by several. No forks, only spoons and knives. They used their fingers. Cups shared.

Corn was ground into meal for porridge or corn bread or pudding. Mixed with beans for succotash. Corn was shucked in the winter, sometimes at a town party. A red ear meant good luck. Children played games with corn kernels—checkers, fox and geese. Families burned the cobs. Deer, pigeons, fish all salted to preserve the meat. Children often stood during the meal; others sat on long benches called "forms." A rule for manners: "Take salt only with a clean knife."

Forests quickly cut down to clear fields, wood burned to make pitch or charcoal. Deer driven into the middle of the forest by burning the forest. Or a circle of men and boys would press animals and birds before them into the middle and shoot them. This was called a "drift of the forest."

Excesses of nature sometimes led settlers to tell tall tales: a watermelon vine that grew so fast it yanked the melons along the ground.

The streams and rivers and ocean full of fish. A horse might step on one as it crossed a brook. Boys signed onto fishing vessels.

Many children died in first year of life. Names recorded in family Bible. Names came from moral ideas or the Bible: Comfort, Deliverance, Prudence, Charity, Mary, Margaret, Sara, Samuel, Isaac, Jacob, Forbearance, Increase.

Families were large, 10–12 children. Children helped with house and field work.

As I leafed through the books mentioned above, I began to note more than just the material objects of a typical New England family of the period; I also was beginning to describe their customs and practices. This is the next step: from physical clues, to create a fuller picture, including guesses as to behavior, attitudes, and feelings.

Step Three: Interpreting Life from Everyday Objects

As I studied the objects used by the Puritans, I began to interpret how the New England environment—especially its harshness and its abundance—may have shaped the settlers' attitudes. For help, I turned to a poem from the period, Anne Bradstreet's "Here Follows Some Verses upon the Burning of Our House, July 10th, 1666. Copied out on a Loose Paper."

> In silent night when rest I took
> For sorrow near I did not look
> I wakened was with thund'ring noise
> And piteous shrieks of dreadful voice.
> That fearful sound of "Fire!" and "Fire!"
> Let no man know is my desire.
> I, starting up, the light did spy,
> And to my God my heart did cry
> To strengthen me in my distress
> And not to leave me succorless.
> Then, coming out, beheld a space
> The flame consume my dwelling place.
> And when I could no longer look,
> I blest His name that gave and took,
> That laid my goods now in the dust.
> Yea, so it was, and so 'twas just.
> It was His own, it was not mine,
> Far be it that I should repine;
> He might of all justly bereft
> But yet sufficient for us left.
> When by the ruins oft I passed
> My sorrowing eyes aside did cast,

And here and there the places spy
Where oft I sat and long did lie:
Here stood that trunk, and there that chest,
There lay that store I counted best.
My pleasant things in ashes lie,
And them behold no more shall I.
Under thy roof no guest shall sit,
Nor at thy table eat a bit.
No pleasant tale shall e'er be told,
Nor things recounted done of old.
No candle e'er shall shine in thee,
Nor bridegroom's voice e'er heard shall be.
In silence ever shall thou lie,
Adieu, Adieu, all's vanity.
Then straight I 'gin my heart to chide,
And did thy wealth on earth abide?
Didst fix thy hope on mold'ring dust?
The arm of flesh didst make thy trust?
Raise up thy thoughts above the sky
That dunghill mists away may fly.
Thou hast an house on high erect,
Framed by that mighty Architect,
With glory richly furnished,
Stands permanent though this be fled.
It's purchased and paid for too
By Him who hath enough to do.
A price so vast as is unknown
Yet by His gift is made thine own;
There's wealth enough, I need no more,
Farewell, my pelf, farewell my store.
The world no longer let me love,
My hope and treasure lies above.[11]

Bradstreet's religious cast of mind was strong among the first and second generation Puritan settlers, but began to wear thin for their grandchildren. Although I kept this information in mind, I didn't want to write from the Puritans' point of view. Instead, I simply wanted to begin with their material life and see where the objects led me.

Step Four: Preparing to Write

Ease yourself back by degrees, first by remembering your grandmother's stories of growing up. Close your eyes and picture a room in one of her stories, noting everything in detail. Then open your eyes and look at the room you're in. This going back and forth from imagination to "reality" is good practice for what follows.

The next step is to close your eyes and imagine the sensations, actions, and events suggested by the objects in question. In the case of the Puritan household, I imagined sitting down on a bench and looking at a trench on the table in front of me and a huge fireplace off to the side where black kettles hung from an iron bracket. Then I quickly jotted down some of these scenes. This imaginative recreation of the past is an important step because it calls up the interaction between people and things that can then suggest how they affect each other.

Step Five: Organizing and Drafting the Poem

Before writing my poem, I looked back at Kooser's. In it, the details build up, lending a sense of drama to the piece. Poems don't have to have a "big finish," as Kooser's does, but they should move in some direction. Just before writing, I reminded myself about good ways to organize a poem, such as using contrasts; for example, arranging pleasant details first, then unpleasant ones, or describing the top of a trunk, then the bottom.

I began another way, using Kooser's technique of letting the things speak. Here is part of my first draft:

The Puritans

They were severe, say the unpainted houses,
And worked hard to grow food, say the fences of rocks.
Their families expanded, it was hard to keep warm,
says the one open hearth.

Corn was a deliverer, say the kernels and cobs.
They ate it and burned it, and fed hogs on the stalks.
Fire was precious, say the spunks dipped in sulfur.
And light hard to feed, remarks grease from a bear.

They prayed in the dark, say the snuffer and candle.
They drank from one cup, says the big wooden punch bowl.
The babies died young, reads the list in the Bible....

This first draft adopts Kooser's method of letting meaning arise from clues. Reading it over, I felt challenged to make the poem more my own, to play with the language until I found my own way to evoke a story from physical objects. Here is the second version:

The Puritans

We know them by their unpainted houses
    dirt floors, small windows.
Rock fences kept their fields to themselves,
    their hands in the dirt.

Fire was precious but warmed
    just one side of them.
Many scorched sheets with
    long-handled warmers,

charred wooden hearth rods
    tumbled dinner to ashes.
Log chimneys torched houses, whole towns
    fought the fire.

They prayed in the dark and saved
    the deer candles.
For food they were grateful to Indians
    and traders.

Sugar loaves tempted them, corn
    was a deliverance.
They drank from one punch bowl
    passed at the table.

Many babies died young.
    More were soon born
among vast, lonely forests
    with too much of everything.
Fifty-two pigeons, hundred duck, two deer
    down with one shot.
Severe at their tasks, they cut down
    the woodland.

A drift of the forest pressed deer
    to the kill.
Prize to a rider who pulled a head
    from a goose.

Looking over this second draft, I like how it balances the Puritans' hardships with their destruction of the forests of New England. Three centuries after them, I have written from a perspective of environmental crisis. I reacted with distress to what probably was the Puritans' unconcerned delight in the bounty of nature.

This brings up a very important point about interpreting history. Interpretations of the past come and go, but the historian's first responsibility is to try to understand the intellectual context of the past. Rather than interpreting the Puritans in the religious context they might have chosen, I have used a modern attitude to assess them. The Puritans were no more cruel or destructive than their contemporaries; renaissance English folk of other religious persuasions also enjoyed games such as cockfights and bullbaiting that to most of us seem cruel. To the colonists the wilderness looked abundant and vast. The idea that they might deplete it probably never entered their minds. Unlike the Native Americans, the Puritans as a group did not have a high regard for the natural world. Their eyes were on survival, heaven, and, soon enough, a prosperous life.

Variation: Writing about Family Heirlooms

Pat Riley, an eighth grade teacher in St. Cloud, Minnesota, decided that she did not want to do research on the Puritans. She wanted to write about a "relic" from the more recent past, a trunk, whose history she already knew. Before writing, she imagined herself sitting beside the old trunk up in the attic, left behind by her family. She began her poem in the third person to indicate that the trunk belonged to family members before her, then she switched to the first person for her own memories of it. She wrote a list of details and random memories first, then two drafts of the poem. This is some of her second draft:

The Trunk

It was left behind.
It was too big, too heavy.
There was no room for it in the house in town . . .

It had been there before them.
It had served three generations of Whalens and Flaigs.
The rumors of how it came to be were vague.

Some thought it came from Willow Lake Township.
Others suggested Prairie du Chien or Ontario, or even the old country.

As the walls grew around it, it became family.
And it was left behind.

Its sad, seaport-grey exterior extolled the practicality of early Redwood
    County homesteaders.

Its utilitarian look matched those folks who had made do
Those who had survived in spite of drought, hail, and grasshoppers.

It was stocky, the walls six inches thick.
It was sturdy.
In its attic home, it bore the hottest hot of summer and the coldest
    cold of winter, and the lonely isolation.

Nor was it the romanticized cedar chests of the media.
It was just the old grey trunk.
And it was left behind . . .

I could only inhale the pleasant sweet smell of generations past.
And it was left behind . . .

It was magic—it became our golden egg.
From its bottomless depths it produced a wealth of treasures,
Some with stories told, some with stories felt.
Great-great-grandmother's lace wedding dress.
Her bedspread.
Grandma Hanson's crocheted spread and tatted pillowcases and
    Grandpa's galvanized milk pail
Pictures for family reunions.
Baby clothes for those lost babies . . .
An original 1920s flapper dress, a legacy from a grandmother known
    only through stories . . .
Prom dresses of the 60s and the dress for the farmgirl in the dance line
    . . . the extra blanket needed for just in case, hinting of the cold,
    snow-filled and storm-bound Minnesota winters of decades past.
But on that sad November day, its magic ceased.

It was empty.
The last harvest was over.
It was time to move on, to move on without the trunk,
And it was left behind.

Now it stands alone in the empty attic in the empty farm house in
    Charlestown Township
Waiting. Its heritage lost to those who might explore and to the next
    generation.

Eighth graders doing research on their families respond enthusiasti-
cally to writing about family mementoes. One day I asked them each to
bring in an object to write about—a mother's doll, a family tree, an old
Bible, or jewelry. Most of them did, and I had those who forgot draw

such an object before writing. For brainstorming, the whole class answered the following questions: What is it? How old is it and how do you know it's old? Who gave it to you? What has this item endured? What memories does it evoke in you?

When the class was ready to write, I encouraged them to begin by noticing where their eyes first went when they looked at the object, and to describe that detail. Then I asked them to weave together information and description with memories. Here are a couple of their poems:

Family

The length of the tree shows how hard he worked.
He went from town to town tracing them.
When he was done, he had plenty, which
is told by the dates. 1455 he got back to.
So many stories to tell.
From the depths of ages, out comes
the truth. Kenneth was his name.
He did plenty. Brought out all the names.
The first was William who took land
from the Lord of Soudry.
My mom's dad found out everything.
So far back King Henry the
Seventh was there.

—Adam Paulson

*   *   *

Poem

Cracked at the corners
the oak box that
held so many secrets is now
worn from the long trip from England
with the initials of his
loved one inlaid in the black
hardwood. The man worked
for hours a century ago.
The metal letters were parted
by a mother-of-pearl heart
that showed the immense love he felt
for his teenage girlfriend.

—Jenny Gustafson

EXERCISE FOUR
A Lesson in Names

Writing short prose pieces or poems about the origin and history of our names. (For upper elementary to adult.)

Step One: Discussing the Origins of Names

Anyone who has taught for a while knows that first names come in and out of fashion. One generation will name its girls "Ashley" and "Amber," or "Jennifer" and "Jessica." Another will call its boys "Charles" and "Craig" or "Sean" and "Stewart." Along with such whimsical tides of fashion are deeper ethnic and regional currents that affect all of us. To many of us, names such as Larson and Olsen sound simply Scandinavian, but those among us of Scandinavian ancestry can distinguish the Danish names by the "sen" spelling of the last syllable. The same holds true for new immigrants from Southeast Asia, whose names sound similar and derive from a common culture, but a culture that has linguistic differences.

In Spanish-speaking countries, many people use two last names, combining their parents' last names, the father's positioned first, the mother's positioned second. So, the son of Lorenzo Lopez and Maria García may become Felipe Lopez García. If the mother dies and the father remarries, half brothers will have different names: "Lopez García" and "Lopez Cardona." Married American women nowadays often keep their maiden names or use them as middle names.

Among many Native American peoples, a tribal elder names the children. This elder waits for a vision or dream to present an image that suggests a name. These names are distinct from the Anglo-American practice of giving a first name and a family name. Today, many Native American people have two sets of names—one that they use in the tribe and one that they use elsewhere.

Step Two: Using Native American Naming Events to Suggest Other Common Naming Practices

After the general discussion about names, I read the class selections from an anthology of Native American writing, *Shaking the Pumpkin*, edited by Jerome Rothenberg.[12] In the section called "A Book of Events," Rothenberg has gathered different rituals and activities—some quite old—that loosely resemble modern theater, particularly the performance pieces called "happenings." The "Naming Events" from the Papago are especially inspiring in helping the class to recognize how they themselves are also named, over and over, in their lives. Here are excerpts from those events:

1) A shaman has a dream and gives a child a name inspired by the dream. Among such names are Circling Light, Rushing Light Beams, Wind Rainbow, Feather Leaves Flowers Trembling, Chief-of-Jackrabbits, Short Wings.

2) A person receives a name describing something odd about him or her, always derogatory; for instance, Grasshopper-Ate-His-Arrow, Gambler, Blisters, Fish-Smell-Mouth, Bed Wetter, Rat Ear, Yellow Legs.

3) A group of namers gathers around a dead enemy and shouts abusive names at the corpse. These names are then given to the shouters. They include: Long Bones, Full-of-Dirt, Back-of-a-Wildcat, Yellow Face.

4) A person buys a name or trades names with another person. For example, Devil-Old-Man exchanges names with Contrary, but has to give him something in addition because of the desirability of the name.

"My Name," a short chapter from Sandra Cisneros's *The House on Mango Street,* introduces students to another tradition of naming, the Mexican-American:

> In English my name means hope. In Spanish it means too many letters. It means sadness, it means waiting. It is like the number nine. A muddy color. It is the Mexican records my father plays on Sunday mornings when he is shaving, songs like sobbing.
>
> It was my great-grandmother's name and now it is mine. She was a horse woman too, born like me in the Chinese year of the horse—which is supposed to be bad luck if you're born female—but I think this is a Chinese lie because the Chinese, like the Mexicans, don't like their women strong.
>
> My great-grandmother. I would've liked to have known her, a wild horse of a woman, so wild she wouldn't marry. Until my great-grandfather threw a sack over her head and carried her off. Just like that, as if she were a fancy chandelier. That's the way he did it.
>
> And the story goes she never forgave him. She looked out the window her whole life, the way so many women sit their sadness on an elbow. I wonder if she made the best with what she got or was she sorry because she couldn't be all the things she wanted to be. Esperanza. I have inherited her name, but I don't want to inherit her place by the window.
>
> At school they say my name funny as if the syllables were made out of tin and hurt the roof of your mouth. But in Spanish my name is made out of a softer something, like silver, not quite as thick as sister's name—Magdalena—which is uglier than mine. Magdalena who at least can come home and become Nenny. But I am always Esperanza.
>
> I would like to baptize myself under a new name, a name more like

the real me, the one nobody sees. Esperanza as Lisandra or Maritza or Zeze the X. Yes. Something like Zeze the X will do.[13]

After enjoying the creativity, humor, and fantasy of these writings about names, the class and I discuss our own names: first, middle, and last. I write my five names on the board and tell them that my middle name, Rosalie, comes from my little Italian grandmother whose "fingers flew up and down the keys," according to my father. I have them guess what my family name "Fortunato" means in Italian ("fortunate"). That name came to the United States in 1900 with my grandfather.

Lareina Rule's *Name Your Baby*[14] contains the origins and translations for many first names currently used in this country, as do most dictionaries. Students love to learn what their names mean. Also, learning about the ethnic backgrounds of names and their meanings helps students appreciate the similarities between naming practices in different cultures.

Step Three: Brainstorming through Mapping

Using outsize newsprint, folded in half, have your students put their names in the middle of one half of the paper. This is the start of a word map about their names. Next, have them add information about the origins of their names: who named them, where their names come from (what countries and languages), and what they mean. Next, ask them to add nicknames, past and present, and how they acquired them. Finally, have them write about their initials; for example, Mario might write, "M is a hammock between two trees, or a mountain." Judy might write, "J is a bow tie."

Then, after reminding the students about the Papago Naming Events, have them recall parts of their dreams ("I dream that a tiger is chasing me," or "In my dream I walk down stairs into a dark basement over and over"). Recurring dreams are often easier to remember and sometimes more frightening. Have the students make up dream names for themselves and add them to the map. Dream names might be "He-Who-Rides-a-Bike," or "Tiger-Chases-After."

Next, have the students move to family naming practices. I ask them to remember what their parents or siblings call them when angry: "sloppy" or "lazy," or an intentionally garbled nickname. "What do they tell you to do next?" I ask. Students then add these names and commands to the word maps. Finally, the students write what their enemies might call them. Sometimes embarrassing nicknames come from enemies, and students won't even write them down.

Step Four: Drafting the Poem or Prose Piece about Names

While it's good to let students choose their own forms to write in, many need some direction. Two good ones are the short essay and the name acrostic, examples of which are below. Depending on your students, you might want to reverse steps four and five.

If students have trouble beginning, I put a starter on the board, such as "If you see a [fill in description of yourself], then you'll know it's [your name]." I encourage students to describe themselves fancifully. Often I let them practice on me first: "If you see a hair-twirling, loud-voiced, eye-glassed lady with wild stockings, you'll know she's Margot Fortunato Galt."

Variation: The Finger and Hand Addition

Sometimes I add another approach. I have students draw around one of their hands and then make comparisons. "This is your hand, but what else does it look like?" Students answer: "A palm tree, a parking lot with lots of bays, a head of wild hair." Then students write about what their hands look like, where the dirt is, what scars are where and how they got there, rings, shapes of nails, fingernail moons, tricks the hand can do. Finally, students write about what their hands do to help them, how their hands get them in trouble, and what their hands give away, in gestures and in gifts.

Step Five: Reading Student Work

Here are two short pieces written by fourth grade students:

> If you see a blond-haired, green-eyed, gentle, tall, slow-moving girl, you'll know that's Crystal Marie Williams. If you hear Crystal the Pistol, Crystal Marie Williams, Crissy, or "Disaster Area," you'll know it's me. My name is Crystal Marie Williams. My mom named me that. Neither one of us knows what it means but she says I am as sweet as sugar.
>
> If you see a big hand with light fingernail polish, a peach-colored, long finger-nailed hand doing homework, you'll know it's Crystal Williams's hand. If you see a hand that looks like a tree, a spider, five carrots, a swamp monster, you'll know it is my hand. My five people help me write this poem.

*   *   *

> If you see a yo-yo spinning, twisting around, yo-yo rolling in the wind, in the summer breeze, you will know it is Y.E.D. in a helping way. My name Esperanza means Hope. Diaz means days. My godfather gave me

Esperanza. My dad gave me Diaz. My names, Esperanza and Diaz, are Mexican. Yo-yo stands for the first letter in my name. My enemies call me Olanda. Yolanda came from my godfather. The D in my name is like a baby upside down. Y upside down is like a fork.

If you see a hand with a B-flat clarinet in it, with a short nail, hand with a parking place drive in it that helps make beautiful ice-capade pictures, you will know it's Yolanda Esperanza Diaz.

A sixth grade student wrote this acrostic poem:

J – a hook to catch a huge whale.
My name changes my brother's
stinky diapers.
A – a finger with a bandage on.
My name got lost in the store
and went to sleep in the
Cheerios box.
C – a half of a belly button. My
name said his chores were done
but they were not.
Q – a cat in an accident with a truck.
My name wishes he had four
of each brother and sister.
U – a jump rope getting ready
to be used. My name helps elderly
people across the street.
E – a sideways M. My name likes
to play hide-and-seek with
the orphanage kids.
L – a cane to help elderly people
walk. My name says it will be
sunny and it is.
Y – a broken umbrella. My name
spanks kids and makes them
cry really hard.
N – a sideways S. My name gets in big
trouble, and I take the place
of someone else. I hide.

Some second grade students also wrote about their names. Here are two of their prose poems:

My real name is Katherine Beth Childs. My grandma calls me Missy. My brother calls me DeDe because he cannot call me Katie. We call my sister Jenny Penny. We call my brother Cubby. My grandma calls me "deep-diving fish" because I am a good swimmer. At school they call me Katie. Oh, my dad calls me Blueberry. Because I like blue.

* * *

My Nickname

My real name is Casey Robert Pavel. But my mom and dad call me Chuck, Caboose, Mister, Wimp, Dude, Rob, Robert, Shrimp, Case, Pave. Aseekay and Dude are my nicknames. Aseekay is pig-latin for Casey. I don't like Shrimp and Wimp because they're bad names.

In the final example, a senior high student in Spanish class mixes English and Spanish in writing about her name:

Nombre

Me llamo Deanna Michelle Payne. Deanna means "bright as day" in Latín. Mis parientes named me Deanna after la cantante, Deanna Durban. Since I am católica, I had to have a saint's name somewhere in my name. So they named me Michelle, which is derived from the saint, Michael. Payne es de Inglaterra.

Mis apodos buenos son Dee, Mickey, Chief, y Susana. Mis apodos malos son Diane, Anna, Deanne, Dust, y Deanna the banana who lives in Indiana. I think the *d* en mi primer nombre reminds me of a lagrima. The *m* en mi segundo nombre reminds me of camello, the *p* in my tercer nombre reminds me of a whale standing on its head. When I am bad, mi madre yells "Deanna Michelle Payne."

En mis sueños, estoy en Florida con muchos chicos guapos. My nombre will be on ESPN para kickboxing. Yo quiero ser La Champion del Mundo. Para divertirse, mi nombre would be in *Cosmopolitan* as a model. Mi nombre ayuda a los niños porque I will be a social worker.

Each beginning letter of my name means something to me. The *d* reminds me that daisies are delicate. The *m* reminds me that memories are forever. The *p* stands for pain is temporary.

Like Pat Riley's poem about the trunk that her family left behind, poems about our names and the families that bestowed them bring us closer to understanding our connection to the past. Names, family rituals, and heirlooms are all handed down to us by older relatives. In describing family rituals such as the opening of Christmas gifts—reading the silly notes, posing for goofy photos, eating tangerines from the toes of the stockings, and wadding up the giftwrap and throwing it to the dog—we gradually discover our personal history and begin to understand it.

Chapter 2
HEROES AND HEROINES: PRIVATE MOMENTS AND PUBLIC LIFE

Public Hero, Private Person

(For upper elementary to adult.)

After students have written about things close to home, it's good for them to try the other end of the spectrum: the lives of famous people. In this exercise, students imagine a prominent American hero or heroine in the midst of a private moment. The exercise aims to show students that heroes are more than one-dimensional. Historical figures are more than a profile on a dollar bill, a man in a coonskin cap, or a teacher in a space suit. Seeing a hero in a personal situation, students come to understand how that individual has influenced world events and affected the lives of many.

The student poems that result from this exercise are usually dramatic monologues, most often showing the hero or heroine speaking or writing to someone. Doing prior research allows students to draw on historical facts—medical practices, styles of furniture, cultural assumptions, social conventions, political events, and religious attitudes—to create a fuller picture of the hero's or heroine's surroundings.

Step One: Background Research

To begin the exercise, students take notes about the hero or heroine they've chosen to write about. Resources can include textbooks, encyclopedias, biographies, letters, contemporary accounts, diaries, or even historical fiction.

The entire class might want to write about the same person. For example, if a junior high history class is studying the Revolutionary War, they could pool their background information when writing about George Washington. If, however, they all choose someone different, they'll have to do more research, which may be what you want—it will give each of them experience collecting information.

In either case, starting with the encyclopedia or a reference book such as *American Biography* will help students acquire general information that they can fill in from other sources. With younger or less experienced students, the teacher can help by gathering source materials and bringing them into the classroom.

Let's imagine that the entire class has decided to write about George Washington. After a homework assignment to look up information about him, the class can come together and create a big communal "research sheet." When I collect information about a historical figure, I write down not only the general facts (e.g., that Washington was General Braddock's aide during the French and Indian Wars), but also any interesting small details that help to flesh out the figure's experience (Washington's diary tells us that at one point he had to use a piece of bark as a plate). Encourage your students to achieve a similar mixture of information, reminding them that they should try to imagine the everyday lives of their subjects, not just the skeletal facts of accomplishments.

Here are the facts and impressions I assembled from a standard junior high American history text, the long biographical entry about Washington in the *Encyclopaedia Britannica*, and some original sources, such as Washington's letters and diaries:

George Washington

Born Feb. 22, 1732. Childhood on wilderness farms. The Mason Weems biography of 1806 created the story of GW cutting down the cherry tree and not telling a lie. GW studied math, gauging, mensuration (measurement or surveying), trigonometry. He also copied out rules for behavior.

His father died when GW was 11. GW's first job (at 16) was as a surveyor in the Shenandoah Valley. Diary notes "sleeping under one threadbare blanket with double its weight of vermin such as Lice and Fleas," and an encounter with Indians carrying a scalp. He described Pennsylvania-German immigrants as being "as ignorant a set of people as the Indians, they never speak English but when spoken to they speak all Dutch." Washington had to eat a serving of roast wild turkey on a "Large Chip," had no dishes.

His older brother Lawrence died. GW, at age 20, became the head of Mount Vernon. He considered farming "the most delectable" of pursuits. "No establishment is more pleasantly situated," he wrote to an English friend about Mount Vernon. He wanted to be known first as a farmer.

He excelled in all outdoor sports, from wrestling to colt breaking. A friend described him: "straight as an Indian, measuring 6'2" in his stockings . . .

muscular, broad-shouldered, 175 lbs., long arms and legs, penetrating blue eyes, heavy brows, nose large and straight, mouth large and firmly closed. His movements and gestures are graceful, his walk majestic, and he is a splendid horseman."

At age 21, GW went to warn the French away from building forts on the Ohio river. Indians shot at him from 15 paces. He fell in the Allegheny River, almost froze in wet clothing. Wrote, "I have heard the bullets whistle and believe me there is something charming in the sound." In 1755 he became General Braddock's aide in the French and Indian War. He warned Braddock that the redcoats should hide behind trees. Braddock wouldn't listen. GW fought shoulder to shoulder with Braddock, had two horses shot from under him and bullets pierce his clothing. He became so ill that he had to use a pillow instead of a saddle. Braddock was shot and killed; GW took the army back to VA.

As lord of Mt. Vernon, GW made the estate self-sufficient. He said of Mt. Vernon: "Middling land under a man's own eyes is more profitable than rich land at a distance." GW kept many slaves, but would not sell them. Carefully clothed and fed them, hired a doctor for them. "I am principled against this kind of traffic in the species," he said. He played cards, liked theater, afternoon tea, concerts, cockfights, balls.

As trouble with British began, he said in May 1775, "I will raise one thousand men, subsist them at my own expense and march myself at their head for the relief of Boston." GW a radical in the Continental Congress but did not think of independence.

Voted (May 1775) by 2nd Cont. Congress to head army: GW darted modestly into an adjoining room, whereas loser John Hancock flushed with jealous mortification. Hearing of Bunker Hill, GW said, "The country is safe." In Boston, he drew his sword under an elm and wheeled his horse and took command of the troops as men paraded by. Refused payment, took care of his own expenses, and declared himself unfit for the job.

Naturally bold and dashing, he repeatedly followed advice for evasion and delay, which lost battles. Stern disciplinarian, energetic, rallied men. Army alternately dwindled and increased as soldiers who left came back. Ill-fed, ill-clothed, ill-paid, his army was prostrated by sickness and ripe for mutiny.

Crossed the Delaware, Xmas eve, 1776, in rowboats while the Hessian soldiers fighting for the British partied. GW's dawn attack a surprise. He captured 1,000 Hessians. Cornwallis, the British general, said of GW that he would wait to "bag the old fox." That night the wind shifted, roads froze hard, and GW stole away leaving campfires burning. Went around Cornwallis, killed 500 at Princeton. This heartened the Americans after disastrous defeats in N.Y.

Valley Forge: continental army twice beaten at Brandywine and Germantown, ill-housed and fed, thousands of GW's soldiers "barefoot and otherwise naked." Exhausted, half-starved.

Victory at Yorktown credited to GW, the finest single display of his generalship. War ended.

GW stayed with Congress to make sure the army was paid. One Col. Nicola offered GW a plan to use the army to make himself king. GW refused.

Dec. 4, 1783, GW took leave of closest officers at Fraunces Tavern. His personal expenses for the war were £24,700, presented a bill to Congress in his own careful handwriting.

Back at Mt. Vernon, he laid out new grounds, sunken walls or ha-has, planted mahogany, palmetto, and pepper trees. As a national figure he "entertained" a lot.

At the Constitutional Convention, he was president and broke his silence only once for a minor matter. He supported the Constitution in Virginia, said, "It or disunion."

The electors unanimously elected GW first president of the U.S. Years later, when war between England and France was declared, he worked to keep the U.S. neutral.

As President, he returned no visits and shook hands with no one, but bowed instead. For receptions he wore a velvet suit with gold buckles and yellow gloves, powdered hair, cocked hat with ostrich plume, and a sword in white scabbard. Accused by anti-Federalists of being a king, but his distant behavior was the result of his natural shyness.

In retirement, he was exposed to cold and snow while riding. Exhaustion led to quinsy or laryngitis. His doctors bled him, drew five pints of blood in twenty-four hours, then applied "blisters" of dried beetles to his throat. He pleaded for no further cures. He said, "I die hard, but I am not afraid to go . . . I feel myself going. I thank you for your attentions, but I pray you to take no more trouble about me. Let me go off quietly. I cannot last long."

Step Two: Freewriting Imaginative Scenes about the Hero or Heroine

Next, students do some directed freewriting about their hero or heroine, imagining the character in a particular time and place during a moment of high excitement or danger, or a simple one of quiet and calm.

In either case, it's important that students describe where the hero is—for example, in a tent at Valley Forge, winter 1778. Then they freewrite from the point of view of the hero, who is thinking or speaking about an event, past or present. (If there is enough time, they can write about two different moments, each in a different place.) These pieces of writing should tell the reader something about the hero, some of his quirks and dislikes, fears and memories. Remind students that the hero can move backward and forward in his mind, thinking about a past victory or worrying about the future.

One good organizing technique is contrast. I often have students look over their research sheets and circle moments when their hero's luck is either very high or very low, and look for a contrasting situation; for example, if the hero is in a happy situation, have him remember some of the trials leading up to it. If the heroine is in trouble, let her fantasize about how she'll get out of it. Students can have their hero or heroine speak to people, think out loud or silently, move around and do things, or daydream, but the goal is to show the person experiencing some of the events that the history books describe, while at the same time revealing private moments that show the person's inner life.

Here is a freewriting example from eleventh grade history student Mark Sauntry:

> GW floating down the river. He screams for help as the swift current carries him along. As his clothes get soaked with the frigid water, he attempts to yell louder but cannot, for he has yelled his voice hoarse. He realizes that he is about to die and starts thinking of his life. The wonderful farm with his father—it was so hard on him when his father died. The smell of fresh cut trees, the taste of cherry pie. His school days, all the math classes, that surveying job . . . with all those bugs and that disgusting turkey on the oak bark. The bugs could be seen crawling on it! Brrrr, the water is cold. He wonders if anyone will see him, remembering watching the slaves jump when he called for them after he became the head of Mt. Vernon. Then he sees a farmer at the side of the river. "Help," he manages to croak out. The farmer jumps into the water with a line and saves them both. He pulls Washington back to shore and wraps a blanket around him. "Thanks," says George as he shivers.

In the following piece of my own freewriting, Washington surveys his troops at Valley Forge and sees his wife in the distance, a grey figure writing a letter home for a scurvy-ridden soldier.

> The army dissolves into winter mist, and the next day I find grey corpses in the snow or shadows in the place of deserters who've gone home to the warmth of kin. By a tent my wife sits with a half-clad, starving New Englander. She writes his bad news of cold and hunger home to his rock-clogged hills. I must send my own message to the quiet woods of Virginia, to my trees, mahogany, palm, and pepper seedlings that wait in the quiet of winter rain for the sun to warm them to growth.
>
> Each man's estate, be it rock-filled or fertile like my Mount Vernon, "the best situated" of life's prospects, we must defend here. I know the resolve of the British. Our kinsmen in word and blood, the redcoats died with their General Braddock in the Indian wilderness, their blood-red coats stupidly open to the arrows. Yet here they could prevail, here they

could conquer us. I must mold this starving, ragtag army into a fighting force. Call on my memories of freezing swims in swollen rivers, nights spent shivering, the venison served on a bark chip, Indians with a neighbor's scalp hung up for trophy. If we are to survive with the rights and privileges of free men, we must work ourselves into instruments of war. I, the shy yet strong, will conquer their division, their weak desire for home. I will forge an army in the snow.

In this scene, Washington talks of various soldiers and empathizes with them. Such other characters, who are rarely mentioned as individuals in the history books, help give drama to the scenes we imagine. They also can suggest ways to mold the poem, as described in the next step.

Step Three: Shaping a Dramatic Monologue

In this step, students select one of their pieces of freewriting and begin to shape it into a poem in which the hero is speaking. His words may be addressed to a stranger or a significant person in the hero's life. Or the poem may relate a conversation the hero is having with a family member, friend, or visitor. In a monologue, the conversation is one-sided, but, as you write it, it is important to keep the other person in mind. Remind students that what their hero says will partly depend on who that other person is.

In my poem "Florence Nightingale Receives a Visitor," Nightingale (the founder of modern nursing) addresses a young man whose father she nursed in the Crimean War. Now a much older woman, she has spent years collapsed on her couch:

> Don't ask me if I remember
> your father. I cut the blood-soaked
> cloth from his legs. After the Battle
> of Inkerman, men lay in their own filth.
> I ordered scrubbing brushes and beds.
>
> The minarets of Mihrimah Cami mosque
> rise outside the second-floor window.
> I coil ropes of linen. At night
> a nurse falls in her own stupor,
> skirts stain a punctured chest.
> She is removed to England.
>
> > For thirty years I've lain here,
> > letters and viceroys pass the straits.
> > Your father lived with a lost leg.

Under the dome of the Hagia Sophia
a cat stalks, its eyes wide
like the wake eyes of wounded
in pain. Divine wisdom
brought me here, out of whale-boned
convention, to treat an army.
Each crusted face and open wound,
I bathe and wrap.
Distant and sharp, a bell rings,
pebble slaps the surface.
I fall through clear water to rest,
my head to the East.

> Don't think I cannot see you.
> Like your father, you want me
> to fall in your eyes. Young man,
> I am already drowned. I snubbed
> Lord Herbert before he died.[1]

The arrangement of the poem separates Nightingale's words to the younger man (indented) from passages of free association. The alternation of monologue and stream of consciousness suggests the multiple levels on which humans function simultaneously: as she speaks about her nursing during the war, she remembers images of mosques and a hospital, the corsets and church of her English youth, the filthy hospitals she cleaned in the Crimea, and finally her snubbing a dying friend.

Once the students have decided on the setting of their poem, they can then use passages from their freewriting and factual details from their research to help flesh out the poem. The setting will suggest details for the hero to notice. It helps to include the hero's feelings about present and past, tying them to immediate events in the setting and to memories of past events. Thus, Washington's despair at his soldiers' bloody feet and hungry stomachs could come through as he also remembers difficult times in his youth, soldiering for the British.

Reviewing my piece of freewriting about Washington, I saw that it suggested a letter poem that he writes from Valley Forge.

In my freewriting, I had GW simply musing about his troops at Valley Forge. But then I decided that the piece would be more dramatic if instead he were to write to someone, possibly someone in his family. Because I could not decide if this would work unless I knew more about his actual correspondents and his epistolary style, I looked at a collection of his letters, *Affectionately Yours, George Washington*, edited by Thomas Fleming.[2] There I found that in the winter of 1778, he wrote regularly to his brothers Samuel and John, and to friends in high political places.

Since Washington's style was fairly dry and formal with all these correspondents, I was not inspired to use them in my poem. Instead, I tried to imagine a letter he might have written to someone he'd never met, someone to whom he owed thanks or had to tell bad news. In my own experience I am sometimes more open and revealing with strangers than I am with family.

With this in mind I decided to have GW write a thank-you letter to the mother of a soldier at Valley Forge. Knowing that Washington's own mother had pestered him when he was a young soldier, I read a few of his letters to her from 1755. For instance, his mother had asked him to find her a Pennsylvania Dutch overseer and some butter while he was working as General Braddock's aide. His somewhat tart responses to her suggested some details that I added to this imaginary letter, written years later from Valley Forge.

The title of the poem came to me immediately. Of course, this doesn't always happen, so it's good to remind students that they can make up a title after their poems are finished.

Here is my poem about Washington:

George Washington Returns Thanks from Valley Forge

Madame, with the good sense I read in your son's stalwart bearing, you
have sent us socks.

Throughout this winter of despair, my army
dissolves into winter mist, cold fires left

by barefoot, naked wraiths who run
for home. Your son remains, his sentry post

trod with blood.

My tent is the hive for plots
and forgeries, spread north and south. I wonder

if you've encountered them on your
rock-clogged road from Boston. Providence and

drill alone can mold this starving, ragtag
army into force enough against the British.

Memories urge us on: as Braddock's aide, I was lucky
to survive a swim in a frozen river,

bullets sounded charming until two horses
were shot from under me and General Braddock died.

Still I laughed at how the ranks of blazing
foolish redcoats caught the Indians' arrows.

We colonists hid behind the trees. Now
you embarrass no son with calls to camp

for butter as once my honored mother did.
Fight for just right and privilege, you urge,

for common good from piney South
to rocky North. I agree. Madame,

my feet and I declare our gratitude.
We salute you. And I save my hopes

of future retirement to nurture
trees of palm and pepper. Now I

remain here, strongly bent to arms and
union, here to forge an army in the snow.

Discovering Washington's dislike of his mother's meddling gave me
an interesting memory to include in my poem as a contrast to the mother
he writes to, who has been only a help. As we lift details from the historical
record or begin to create details out of what might have happened, we can
keep asking ourselves, what would this person have worried about,
remembered, thrilled to, hated?

Alternate: Descriptive Poem

Another approach to writing about a hero is to describe him in the
third person, but with intimate details, as if you are standing nearby,
watching. In Walt Whitman's long poem, "The Sleepers," the author
created close-up portraits of Washington, first suffering the loss of his
troops, and then saying goodbye to them at the end of the war:

Now of the older war-days, the defeat at Brooklyn,
Washington stands inside the lines, he stands on the intrench'd hills
    amid a crowd of officers,
His face is cold and damp, he cannot repress the weeping drops,
He lifts the glass perpetually to his eyes, the color is blanch'd from his
    cheeks,

He sees the slaughter of the southern braves confided to him by their
    parents.

The same at last and at last when peace is declared,
He stands in the room of the old tavern, the well-belov'd soldiers all
    pass through,
The officers speechless and slow draw near in their turns,
The chief encircles their necks with his arm and kisses them on the
    cheek,
He kisses lightly the wet cheeks one after another, he shakes hands and
    bids good-by to the army.[3]

Both Whitman's poem and mine describe public moments with
private reactions: Washington and Nightingale show us what it may have
felt like to live with the risks of political and social power on a grand scale.
How their lives have been affected by their positions becomes, thus, part
of the emotion they show and what they speak about. They help us
experience history from the inside.

Step Four: Reading Student Examples

Actually, you can present examples to students at any point you feel
appropriate. The following piece about Washington is by Mark Sauntry,
a student in an eleventh grade history class. (His freewriting is quoted
earlier.)

A Letter from George Washington to His Old but No Longer Friend William

William, you sad creature,
you left me, your country, in

the time of need. You left
us just as you left me when

I fell in the river. You were
not there then, and you are not

here now to help me. What
has happened to you since we

fought together with Braddock?
You fought side by side with

me as I did with our worthy
leader, but now you run and

cower in your warm house
as we at Valley Forge freeze

and starve. You are no better
than any of the others that

have left us. I shall even
call you it—you deserter.

This memory shall live in
your family, scarring

your name forever. You
used to be such a great

warrior, but now you
hide from such an unformidable

enemy as cold and hunger.
You leave the defense of your

country to the "boys" that
you said would "never last a

minute in a real battle like
the ones in the French and Indian

Wars!" Well, my friend, they
have outlasted you, it appears.

You helped me to find another
horse after both mine were

shot from under me, and I
was to give you powerful control

at Mt. Vernon while I was
at Congress, but that I can

not do to such a vile creature
as William, a traitor to his people.

In freewriting, Mark placed Washington in his younger years as an
aide to General Braddock, but in the poem placed him in his later role

as General at Valley Forge, remembering the earlier battle and spill in the river. By the way, the cowardly William is entirely Mark's invention.

In Becky Sohn's poem below, George remembers paddling his way with his men across the Delaware. He is smart enough to know to put rags on the oars so he won't wake the British. Every move anyone makes has to be silent. The British, celebrating on Christmas Eve, are not aware of George's sneak attack. He feels nervous nonetheless, because there is a chance that the British troops are decoying him:

> People may ask why I did it on Christmas
> Eve. Why use violent actions on the Eve
>
> before Christ's birth, why . . . I did it because it
> was necessary. Don't think that I don't care about
>
> this celebration of Christ, rather think
> about this as being the time for
>
> the birth of a new country. A time to celebrate, a
> time of peace . . . My thoughts were mixed when we crossed the river.
>
> I was scared and cold. What if the British troops woke up,
> the consequences would be terrible. Every single
>
> move anyone made had to be silent. We moved
> slowly across the icy water. Slow and silent, nothing more.
>
> Our presence was unknown, we didn't wake a
> soul, not even a bird. Only the God above knew
>
> about us, about our attack, about how we felt inside.

Here is a dramatic monologue by junior high student Kari Hamlin:

George Washington's Long Death

As I walk down the long halls, I think of when I was first in school, playing with other children as the teacher watched with joy.

When I go back to my room, I sit on the bed thinking I have lived sixty-seven years and I want to see tomorrow. I know everybody dies someday, but I don't want to die now. I have three more bleedings to go. I hope I can survive. As I lay in my bed after my fifth bleeding, and after they applied "blisters" of dried beetles on my throat, I no further felt like living. When they did my bleeding it felt like taking a sharp knife and slitting my wrists.

I remember the time when I was on death road. I was crossing the Delaware, Christmas Eve, 1776. We were in rowboats while Hessian soldiers fighting for the British partied. As I rowed away, the fires were burning high into the night. Then there was the time when I was fighting shoulder to shoulder with Braddock. I had two horses shot from beneath me as bullets pierced my clothes.

As I woke up and looked at the sunlight on the leeches, I felt queasy all over. I think I am going to die soon.

Following are research notes, freewriting, and a poem by Letitia Delaney, a junior high student in a humanities class.

Frederick Douglass

Shortly after fleeing from his life as a slave, twenty-three-year-old Frederick Douglass joined the American Anti-Slavery Society as a traveling speaker. Captain Thomas Auld became Douglass's master shortly after the slave turned fifteen years. According to Douglass, his master found religious sanction for his cruelty. Douglass first learned how to read under the guidance of Sophia Auld. However, these lessons were soon stopped by her husband who feared that education would make Douglass unfit to be a slave. Douglass often found slaveowners to be hypocritical in their actions. They would profess to be God-abiding, yet their treatment of their slaves was certainly less than angelic. Douglass said his life as a slave was hard. "We were worked in all weathers. It was never too hot or too cold. It could never rain, blow, hail, or snow too hard for us to work in the field."

Douglass first sensed what it must be like to live as a free man when he was hired out as a worker at a shipyard in Baltimore, Maryland. Along with fighting for emancipation of slaves, Douglass joined in the battle for women to receive the right to vote. Douglass wrote an autobiography called *Narrative of the Life of Frederick Douglass, an American Slave.* Addressing an English audience during his visit to London in 1846, Douglass spoke against a war between England and the U.S., even though he said a war between them would eventuate in the "emancipation of three million of my brethren who are now held in most cruel bonds."

* * *

Douglass sailed to England on the British steamship *Cambria.* He was forced to stay in the steerage which made him feel angry. It reminded him of slavery when the slaves were forced to work in all weathers. It was never too hot or too cold, it never rained or hailed too hard for them to work. So here he was in the goop of the steerage where it was sloppy and cold, wet and damp, never too unfit to put a tired, worn-out slave in for who knows how many sailing days and nights.

*   *   *

A Letter from the Steerage

To My Dearest Anna,

Here I am sailing
to England on the British
steamship *Cambria.*

I was forced to stay
in the steerage, which
makes me angry.

It reminds me of
slavery when we
were forced to work

in all weathers. As
you recall, it was never
too hot or too cold,

it never rained or hailed
too hard for us to work.

So, here I am in the goop
of the steerage where it's
sloppy and cold, wet and damp.

But don't worry, honey, I'll
keep my feet dry and warm.

I often ask why they say the
steerage is never too unfit to put
a tired worn-out slave in,

for who knows how many
sailing days and nights?

I may be a free black
man, but I ain't
nobody's dog.

I often have to remember
to keep my head held

high and remember what
I am fighting for.

Emancipation of slaves
is the most important
thing.

I am also in the battle
for women to have
the right to vote.

Boy, I am glad I learned to
read and write, I don't
know what I'd do to keep
in touch with you.

I love you, and hug the
children for me. I'll be
home soon.

Yours truly,
Frederick Douglass

Fifth grade students wrote poems based on the characters in Elizabeth Yates's *Amos Fortune, Free Man*. Amos was an African chieftain's son captured and sold into slavery. Amos's African name, Atmun, and his sister's name, Athmun, appear in Lara Gerhardson's piece:

Letter from the Ship

Dear Ath-mun,

The people here have great birds that
sail on water. Food is scarce and I am
afraid you won't notice
ME! The water is often
fought over and
spilled.
The people wear STRANGE
hides. I wonder what
these animals look like.
They must be horrid.
The people punish
us with bracelets that are
skin-tight and are stronger than

the strongest beast, yet they fall
apart when a stick goes into them.
I fear I will never see you again.
Thinking of you,
At-mun

Lara drew on settings and characters from *Amos Fortune, Free Man*, but her poem shows her own sensitivity to the personal effect of the middle passage on the new slave: the Africans were chained below deck and not allowed to move for the long weeks of the trip. In her short piece, Lara recreates Atmun's experience and his struggles to make sense of a culture so different from his own.

EXERCISE TWO
Modern Ballads

In this exercise, students write ballads using the words of heroes or heroines. (For upper elementary to adult.)

The ballad is a venerable form, narrating the exploits of real or imaginary people. The ballad usually has a stanza or line that recurs (perhaps with variations) as the story progresses. Alternating with these refrains are verses that advance the action, describing the setting, the characters, and their adventures. Often ballads are set to music and sung. An interesting, but little-known American ballad is Stephen Foster's "I'm Nothing But a Plain Old Soldier." It is written from the point of view of a veteran of the Revolutionary War, who later, during the Civil War, thinks back and urges the divided country to remember its early union and glory under George Washington.

Modern ballads from the point of view of modern heroes or heroines work especially well if the character happened to have spoken some remarkable words in a speech or interview, words we can use. Martin Luther King, Jr., is a good subject for this exercise partly because his "I have a dream" speech is full of visionary and poetic phrases that resound in the context of a ballad's refrain. The verses of student ballads about Dr. King could come from students' own experiences of discrimination or from research, or both. The ballads may touch on general themes such as racism, sexism, or agism, or they may focus on the civil rights movement and King's fight against segregation. The January holiday commemorating King provides the perfect occasion for this exercise.

Students can write about an anti-slavery hero from the more distant past or other civil rights figures from the 1960s and 70s, such as Stokely

Carmichael; the group of students who started the sit-ins in Greenville, North Carolina; Fannie Lou Hamer; Rosa Parks; or Malcolm X. Student ballads can also treat heroines from the women's suffrage movement or their counterparts in modern feminism. Many other heroes or heroines from past and present suggest themselves as subjects for a ballad.

Whatever the subject, writing ballads helps students to identify words, ideals, and actions that continue to challenge us. This exercise shows students two important qualities of history: the way obscure people can become known through events; and the way the leaders themselves remain powerful long after they are dead.

Step One: Listening to or Reading a Ballad

Begin by listening to a ballad. Stephen Foster's "I'm Nothing but a Plain Old Soldier" is an unusual one because it has a distinct speaker telling his own story, whereas most ballads tell a story through a distant narrator. Foster's ballad also shows the way a popular song (like rock songs and rap these days) can take a political stand. (A recording of this ballad is included in *Songs by Stephen Foster*, available on the Nonesuch label, H-71268.)

I'm Nothing but a Plain Old Soldier

I'm nothing but a plain old soldier,
An old revolutionary soldier.
But I've handled a gun
Where noble deeds were done
For the name of my commander was George Washington.

(*Verse*) My home and my country to me were dear.
And I fought for both when the foe came near.
But now I will meet with a slight or a sneer.
For I'm nothing but a plain old soldier.

(*Refrain:* I'm nothing but a plain old soldier *etc.* . .)

The friends I loved the best have departed.
The days of my early joys have gone.
And the voices once dear
And familiar to my ear
Have faded from the scenes of the earth one by one.
The tomb and the battle have laid them low,
And they roam no more where the bright streams flow,
I'm longing to join them and soon must go.
For I'm nothing but a plain old soldier.

(*Refrain*)

Again the battle song is resounding.
And who'll bring the trouble to an end?
The Union will pout
And secession ever shout,
But none can tell us now which will yield or bend.
You've had many Generals from over the land,
You've tried one by one and you're still at a stand,
But when I took the field we had one in command,
Yet I'm nothing but a plain old soldier.

(*Refrain*)

Notice that the verses give little vignettes of the soldier's life on the battlefield, while the refrain, repeated between each verse, describes him. This is a typical ballad structure, with verses and refrain alternating, but it has nine lines in some verses instead of the usual four. Foster gives himself more room to describe the soldier's experience and to heighten the latter's admiration for Washington.

It's okay to bend some of the rules of the form and write verses of varying lengths, not just four lines. You may also want to forgo meter and rhyme, because they often lead to awkward syntax and clichéd phrasing. At the same time, though, it's good to try to retain the larger shape of the ballad, verses followed by refrain, with the verses telling different things and the refrain repeating the same words.

Step Two: Brainstorming Ideas for a Ballad about Martin Luther King, Jr.

The way I begin this step is to discuss with students their own experiences of discrimination and prejudice. Perhaps the class contains people of different ethnic and racial backgrounds. These days Latinos, Native Americans, Asian-Americans and African-Americans may experience sharper prejudice than ethnic minorities, but virtually everyone has had some experience of discrimination. Being excluded or called names seems to be part of growing up. For instance, I tell students how kids in my junior high labeled me Roman Nose because I am Italian. By talking about the way prejudice has affected us, we can then integrate the negative effects of racial discrimination with the positive vision that King provided.

Next, the students can make a word map for their own lives, collaboratively on the board or individually. For individual maps, I recommend using large sheets of newsprint. Have the students fold them in half and open them again. One half of the paper is for the mapping and the other half for writing the ballad.

Here is the word map I made about the racism I experienced growing up in the 1950s:

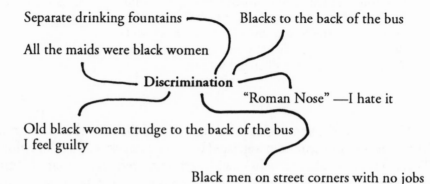

Step Three: Reading Martin Luther King, Jr.'s "I Have a Dream" Speech and Selecting Phrases from It

Pass out copies of King's speech and read it aloud to the class. Have students underline phrases that move them or seem particularly strong.

Next, make a list of these phrases on the board. For example:

- When all God's children will sing together
- Let freedom ring
- I have a dream that . . . black boys and girls will join hands with white boys and girls and walk together as sisters and brothers.
- With this faith to stand up for freedom together.
- Free at last, free at last, thank God Almighty, we're free at last.

Have your students make another list of phrases that describe their freedom to value all people. For example:

- When no one need march or sit-in, when we all sit down as one, at the same table
- When racial domination is gone, and all can read and write to understand together
- When we hear all voices, and listen even if we don't understand
- When we value all skins, as we care for the earth, trees, water, air.

Step Four: Composing the Ballads

With their lists and word maps, the students are ready to build their ballads. It may help to write one first as a collaboration on the board. Each student can then write one individually.

The first step is to write the refrain. You can use King's vibrant, hopeful, and powerful lines—of which there are many—or your own lines.

Next come the verses, to go between the refrains. Labeling the refrain "A" and the verses "B," I then write the following scheme on the board:

A
B
A
B
A
B
A

etc., as long as you want.

Beginning and ending with the refrain gives the ballad a satisfying sense of unity and closure.

Step Five: Reading Student Models

Here are some ballads by ninth grade civics students. The refrain in the first poem was inspired by the teacher's description of a black childhood friend her parents disapproved of.

Ballad

I was her white shadow.
We were like Siamese twins.
You don't forget your first friend.
How delicate we are as human beings.

We were just little kids playing bounce ball
4th or 5th grade, age is lost.
We didn't know it was wrong, we had all
seen it on television, prejudice.
We were just too little to know
that we were the hands with the knife cutting
Anthony because he was black and
littler than us. We didn't have to
tease him.

I was her white shadow.
We were like Siamese twins.
You don't forget your first friend.
How delicate we are as human beings.

Although we were lost
I can still see us thinking
we're big grown-ups, how
sorry I am.

How delicate we are as human beings.

    —Tim Willite

*   *   *

Poem

Blacks at the back of the bus.

I saw a little black boy
who was being made fun of.

Blacks at the back of the bus.

A person who doesn't do well
in tests was given harsh treatment
by everyone.

Blacks at the back of the bus.

A person of a different nationality
was stepped on.

Blacks at the back of the bus.

A new student in lunch couldn't
find a place to sit down.

Blacks at the back of the bus.

A person wouldn't lend a pencil
to an Asian even if his father
was president of a pencil company.

Blacks at the back of the bus.

    —Rick Estrellada

*   *   *

I Do Not Know

I've always wondered
what it would be like
to be that black man
in the mid-age of life.

Would I feel happy
and glad?
Or tormented
and sad?

I do not know . . .
I do not know . . .

I've always wondered
what it would be like
to be that black man
in the mid-age of life.

Alive
and well, or tired
as hell.

I do not know . . .
I do not know . . .

When the days grow short,
and he is old and gray,
how does he feel
at the end of the day?

Glad to be alive,
still?
Or wish he were dead
by now?

I do not know . . .
I do not know . . .

How the kids ridiculed him
as he walked down the street,
throwing stones and rocks
all aimed at his feet.

I felt sorry for that man,
kind of glad that he's now dead,
so he can go up to heaven
where no man has to dread.

I do not know . . .
I do not know . . .

　　—*Eric Breneman*

Step Six: Individual Ballads

The ballad refrains do not have to be long. Look at Rick Estrellada's: only one line. Let students know that they can choose a line or group of lines that make a strong point, adding their own words when they want, and that it's best to write the refrain first.

Then they can think of the other verses either as various examples of prejudice or as a step-by-step description of a single example of discrimination. Tim's poem relates his own and his friends' harsh treatment of a younger black boy. Tim alternates description, action, and feelings, giving a strong weave to the poem and helping the reader understand the shift in time that takes place in the poem.

Tell students that it's okay to use short lines and to eliminate the clutter of connecting words like *and* or *then*, and that when poems make leaps in time and place it usually improves them.

EXERCISE THREE
The Glare of the Historical Moment

(For upper elementary to adult.)

Sometimes an event in the public world hits us like a lightning bolt. It illuminates private lives so fiercely that we remember, in precise and vivid detail, where we were, what we heard, what we were doing, what we immediately thought. Writing prose or poetry about such experiences can help us to understand how the public event—the assassination of President Kennedy, the explosion of the Challenger spacecraft, or even the death of a great entertainer—has become a milestone in our individual lives just as it has in the life of a community or the entire country.

Like the first exercise in this chapter, this one encourages students to recognize the significance of public figures in personal lives. Sometimes the results are surprising. Perhaps students will discover that, for many people, President Kennedy was less important than his wife Jackie, that she was the symbol of what the country's girls wanted to be when they grew up. Or that Christa McAuliffe, the teacher who was killed in the Challenger disaster, has already come to symbolize the brave and adventurous teachers in our lives. Students may also learn that they absorb ideals, knowledge, and behavior from public figures that seem to be quite remote. Becoming conscious of one hero's power may make us more attentive to how other public figures affect us.

Step One: Discussion of Different Kinds of Memories

To begin this exercise, discuss with students the way we remember events. Some events in daily life repeat and repeat until they blur into a continuous series and become "the way my father came home every evening and dumped his briefcase on the floor, as he called out the baseball scores." This moment of the past has a timeless quality that embeds the events deeply in memory. Other events stay with us because they happen only once and with such force that they illuminate the daily happenings around them. This exercise focuses on this latter kind of event.

After helping students become aware of these differences, I then focus the discussion on one "big" event. I choose an example, depending on the students and how I'm feeling that day. I ask students to remember the moment just before the public news broke, and then how the news instantly made daily life seem mundane and insignificant. Such moments are fixed in personal history as "the day John Lennon was shot," for example. The point is to have students recall not only the event itself, *but minute details of where they were, what they were doing, and how they heard the news.* The event recalled could be a personal or family event, but for purposes of this exercise, let's use one from the public world, as poet Frank O'Hara did in his poem (below) about the death of singer Billie Holiday, known as "Lady." Tell students not to worry about O'Hara's allusions to people and places. Even though his references may escape younger (and some older) students, his poem is a good model to follow in writing about the glare of the historical moment:

The Day Lady Died

It is 12:20 in New York a Friday
three days after Bastille day, yes
it is 1959 and I go get a shoeshine
because I will get off the 4:19 in Easthampton
at 7:15 and then go straight to dinner
and I don't know the people who will feed me

I walk up the muggy street beginning to sun
and have a hamburger and a malted and buy
an ugly NEW WORLD WRITING to see what the poets
in Ghana are doing these days
 I go on to the bank
and Miss Stillwagon (first name Linda I once heard)
doesn't even look up my balance for once in her life
and in the GOLDEN GRIFFIN I get a little Verlaine
for Patsy with drawings by Bonnard although I do
think of Hesiod, trans. Richmond Lattimore or
Brendan Behan's new play or *Le Balcon* or *Les Nègres*
of Genet, but I don't, I stick with Verlaine
after practically going to sleep with quandariness

and for Mike I just stroll into the PARK LANE
Liquor Store and ask for a bottle of Strega and
then I go back where I came from to 6th Avenue
and the tobacconist in the Ziegfeld Theatre and
casually ask for a carton of Gauloises and a carton
of Picayunes, and a NEW YORK POST with her face on it

and I am sweating a lot by now and thinking of
leaning on the john door in the 5 SPOT
while she whispered a song along the keyboard
to Mal Waldron and everyone and I stopped breathing[4]

O'Hara's poem gives an accurate rendition of the process we often
follow in absorbing sudden drastic events: the trivia of the errands and
thoughts of his lunch hour become etched into the poet's memory after
he learns of Holiday's death.

Step Two: Choosing and Discussing an Event for Writing

Of course, students have to decide what event will be their subject.
The assassination of an important public figure or the death of a beloved
singer or athlete are natural choices. You might encourage students to
choose a fairly recent one, such as the Challenger disaster. Christa
McAuliffe signified to a lot of young people the best of what a teacher can
be. Everyone in class can tell where they were when they heard about the
explosion, how their families or schools responded to it, and the tiny
details of time of day, the surroundings, dress, food, errands, conversations, rooms, etc. from the moments just before, during, and after the
disaster. Such group discussion helps loosen up each individual's memories.

Step Three: Freewriting Details about the Event

For some students, it's extremely helpful to get the details they remember on paper before they begin their poems. Ask them to describe where they heard the news, what they were doing and thinking just prior to hearing it, what they heard about the disaster and what they saw, and what the aftermath was in their thoughts, feelings, and behavior. Advise students to write quickly and not to worry about spelling and punctuation.

As an example, here is a piece I wrote about the day I witnessed the Challenger disaster. As I wrote, I was surprised by little memories and by what the event meant to me.

I was visiting a school for a week's residency in creative writing. It was a cold January 28th with lots of snow in the fields as I drove to the rural school. Mid-morning, I was resting in the teachers' lounge. In this old-fashioned school, the lounge was on the second floor, a big sunny room with the same narrow maple floorboards as the rest of the building. As I read through students' papers, I munched on doughnuts and drank weak coffee. Teachers' lounges are the best place in the world for munchies.

Some regular teachers had turned on the TV to watch the Challenger take off. My attention was drawn to it as the countdown began. I rose from the table and stood with the clump of teachers, my eyes focused on the TV screen. I thought that these teachers cared more about this space flight because one of their own, a woman teacher from New England, was on the flight. That week the local newspaper had printed a story about how her family was missing her, her husband had taken over her household duties, and her two young kids called her and wrote to her as she prepared for the flight.

The spacecraft rose in a cloud of smoke and steam. It was exciting. My heart raced as the gleaming bullet rose straight up. Then I was distracted; someone called me from the table and I left the screen. A second later a gasp came from the teachers around the TV and everyone in the room raced back to the set. Pieces of metal were spraying through the air. The bodies were disintegrating, too, I thought. I was struck dumb with the horror of the loss and with the shock of watching it happen. Somehow our watching made the disaster worse, and I thought then and later how TV turns us into passive bystanders of events, and that although we can't do anything, we watch each horrible moment, fixated on the unfolding of violence.

Later I did think about her. I thought how horrible for her family to be watching her blown to bits. I mourned for her children, who would carry with them these images and probably be frightened by them for years. I wondered if they would be able to imagine her whole, would the idea of her going to heaven be possible for them. I found myself more dissatisfied than ever with TV as a means of receiving information. The immediacy it created that morning actually told me very little about the reason for the explosion; in fact, the experience was more about TV than about space flight. I'll remember for a long time the sickening feeling I had as I empathized with the teacher's children who had seen their mother's death so vividly, yet so distant.

Step Four: Evaluating the Freewriting

Most people who jot down quick memories of a national disaster will discover some surprises, which can form the basis of a good discussion. In my case, I did not expect to remember feeling concern for Christa McAuliffe's children or getting angry at the TV. I was surprised at how I associated myself with her, and thought nothing of the men who also died in the explosion. Fathers, husbands—they too left families behind. But my immediate recollection was of Christa's family, perhaps because the newspaper had focused my attention on them, perhaps because I too was the mother of a young daughter. Students have other reactions, but all of them have a historical dimension that reveals something about a generation.

Step Five: Shaping a Poem or Prose Piece from the Freewriting

Reread Frank O'Hara's poem to the class. Though it appears casually written, O'Hara crafted it to convey a jaunty noon-walker's pace and the breathless schedule of a busy New Yorker. Point out how the poem seems to be one big rushing sentence that comes to an abrupt stop, just as Billie Holiday's life did.

With the O'Hara poem in mind, have students look over their freewritings and circle the small details that surrounded the historical moment: actions, observations, thoughts. Like O'Hara, students can treat their thoughts and actions like headlines, and then, for contrast, introduce sly humor—"Miss Stillwagon (first name Linda I once heard)/ doesn't even look up my balance for once in her life"—or descriptions of the natural world—"muggy street beginning to sun." An accumulation of quick details can build to the moment when we discover the news.

Next, have students arrange these details in chronological order, mixing action, description, and thoughts. One of the best things about O'Hara's poem is how he's in no hurry to get to the "important" part of the poem. He lets the mood of the writing shift, as if by itself.

As a variation, the class could create a group poem composed of the little details of many lives, contrasting the different ways students learned of a single event, and perhaps concluding with a collage of students' individual memories of it.

Variation: Consulting Another Model

The following poem by Roseann Lloyd offers another approach. She does not even mention the Challenger disaster by name:

Lessons from Space

Astronaut is a foreigner in a silver suit
walking on the moon but *Teacher*
is our familiar—only one step
away from *Mother*, the first step out the door.
Teacher, we say, and we can see her hands again
covered with the chalky dust
of our own first grade. We can hear
her voice, insistent, explaining
why and *how to* as we print
with our fat, red pencils—
lower-case *s*'s
fill all the spaces between the sky-blue
dotted lines.

Now we are paying attention
to the front of the room where Ginny Lindstrom
is holding up an orange, representing earth,
and Walter Locke is holding up a lemon,
representing moon. Stephanie Jones gets to hold
the flashlight, representing light.
Teacher, we say, *we don't get it.*
Just try, she always answers, *everything*
will be O.K. if you will only try.

Now she is mixing bright blue tempera
which we will apply—*not too thickly*—to our maps
around our wobbly pears
of continents, whose names we must also
memorize. *You must learn*
all about the universe. Teacher is moving
about the room, her sleeve is smudged and dusty
like everything else in here, even the solitary
plant that shoots its flat spikes up
in front of the blackboard, which is
also swirling dusty white, like the Milky Way.

After lunch, we put our heads on our desks.
Teacher is reading. She explains the hard parts,
how it is possible in the story

for Harriet Tubman to be underground
and following the stars at the same time.
This is as inconceivable as death or the idea of space
having no end.

We turn away from knowledge
and admire our snowflakes, falling across
the glass. We folded white paper and cut them out
yesterday. Teacher says every snowflake
is unique, which means, unlike any other. Teacher
says each of us is a unique individual, special
unto ourselves. It is snowing now, for real.
We can't see the stars at the end of the sky.

If Teacher goes away, who will teach us *how to*
and *why*? How to cut out free-hand
hearts. How to find the drinking
gourd on a starless night.
What is burning in those smudge pots
in the orange groves? What happens to machines
when it's freezing cold? Why does the T.V.
say *blow-up, melt-down, O-rings*
out-of-round? Why
are they looking for freedom up there
in the swirling clouds, the sky-
blue sky?[5]

Lloyd suggests the historical significance of McAuliffe's death by placing it in a setting distinct from the event, telling it from the point of view of a student during an astronomy lesson. You might point out to your students how flexible Lloyd's poem is. It moves back and forth between reverie and "real life," from wonder to fact, allowing us to see the many ways history affects the lives of children. By searching for a heroine's significance through her impact on other people, we may learn about ourselves as well, and where we fit into the scheme of things.

Chapter 3
DISCOVERY AND TRADE

The traveler first sees with eyes from home, so it's not surprising that the Europeans who first crossed the Atlantic tried to shape the Americas in their own image. In the past some historians carried this impulse to the point of assuming that the New World was waiting in the dark to be "discovered." Such historians imply that after 1492 the Americas took shape essentially from the tools and ideas brought by Europeans and Africans.

Nowadays we know that the influence went both ways. Europeans and Africans brought their place names, tools, scientific categories, roads, town plans, songs, and languages, but the Europeans also took home enough gold and silver to change the basis of European currency. American foodstuffs changed eating practices worldwide, and, in the case of the potato, started a European population explosion.

The natives taught the newcomers about rivers and plants, showed them tribal versions of democratic political systems, and gave them their first look at what we now call "guerilla" warfare. The colonists would have starved if they hadn't learned from the Indians how to eat off the land.

The exchanges weren't always beneficial: the Old World visitors brought smallpox and alcohol; the New World natives probably gave them syphilis in return. European conquerers tried to change the clothing, religion, and politics of the American tribes.

Many Europeans felt that the American tribes had to be converted to Christianity to make them human. But many Indians were understandably not eager to convert to European religions. For every sympathetic missionary who treated the natives kindly and—like the Spaniard Bartolomeo de las Casas—tried to protect them, there were many other Europeans who enslaved them and tortured them when they did not produce gold, silver, or other products.

To many Europeans, the New World was simply a source of pelts and plumes. The abundant resources of the unexplored continents seemed endless, compared to the depleted soils, forests, and wildlife of Europe. Little wonder, then, that a dichotomy developed in the way Europeans and European-born settlers often thought about their new home: America was huge, untamed, raw, and uncivilized, whereas Europe was refined, sophisticated, and educated.

Though to European trappers and woodsmen the American "frontiers" seemed (and were) lawless and brutal, they gradually became tamed. In many areas of North America, bringing white women to a frontier was considered the necessary first step to importing culture and refinement. The white women brought European education, arts, and furnishings. But the immigrants couldn't impose European ways on the newly discovered continents without being changed themselves. As the diaries of women traveling the Oregon trail or raising families in sod huts in the Dakotas show, the American frontier drastically changed the immigrants' domestic life.

The immense distances of the Americas, the extreme weather, and the gigantic size of many plants and animals—from forests to geese— surprised new thoughts out of the settlers. Lonesome cowboys and lonesome wives sang ballads of loss set in the scope of the whole continent. Hunting, fishing, farming—every interaction with the natural world could overwhelm the newcomers with abundance or disaster. Out of these encounters grew a humor that fooled around with scale— tall tales played with the tenderfoot, who might scoff at the story until he met his first bear. African br'er rabbit spoofed br'er fox in the American briar patch and survived, much as the slave threw a thicket of double meanings around his white masters. It took some Old World eyes a while to see what was what in the New World.

This chapter and the one that follows present writing exercises designed to shake up our traditional textbook notions of discovery and domain. We'll look both ways to see what the new land taught the newcomers, and what the European travelers brought from home. Students will write about maps, place names, and native American foods and plants.

All these exercises are designed to broaden students' views of the encounter between Old World and New. I also hope that, in the process, students may come to realize that historical perspectives are still expanding, and that the ways we treat our land, resources, and each other can still be informed by lessons from the past.

EXERCISE ONE
Maps of the World

Short prose essays that explore the way our early childlike sense of geography changes to more mature versions of the world. (For upper elementary to adult.)

Step One: Discussing Place Names

I take one class period to talk about Columbus's first voyage and to discuss how places in the Americas got their names.

The way early European settlers named places, peoples, cities, mountains, rivers, and oceans tells us a lot about how they viewed themselves and what their aspirations were. It's common knowledge that Columbus made a mistake about where he landed: he named the people who greeted him "Indians" because he thought he had arrived at the East Indies. Like many educated people of his day, Columbus was willing to sail into unknown waters because he was convinced that the earth was round and that he would eventually reach land. Many before him thought the earth was flat and rested on the backs of animals—elephants or turtles, because they live long enough to hold up an old, tired world. Sailors believing this were afraid to venture too far from land because they feared they would fall off the edge of the world.

Columbus had the best European maps of the day, like the one sent him in 1481 by Paolo Toscanelli, an astronomer of Florence, that located Japan and India about where Columbus eventually found the Americas (see fig. 1 for Behaim's 1492 map, similar to Toscanelli's). Yet few before Columbus had sailed into the *Mare Tenebrosum* (Dark Sea), as the Romans called the Atlantic. He was one of the first Europeans who dared to cross it, and he described the new experience by constantly comparing it to old ones. "The weather was like that of April in Andalusia," he wrote. "The sea was as calm as a river." Several times the sailors mistook cloud formations for land, and were baffled by the numbers of land birds that crossed their path.[1]

After a voyage longer than any of the crew expected, Columbus had a near mutiny on his hands. He had falsified the distances reported to his men, but after a month even they realized they had traveled more than the 2,400 miles the voyage to Japan was supposed to take. At his crew's demand, Columbus adjusted his course to follow flocks of birds to the west-southwest. Three signs of land appeared floating in the water: a branch with leaves and berries, a board, and a handcarved wooden staff.

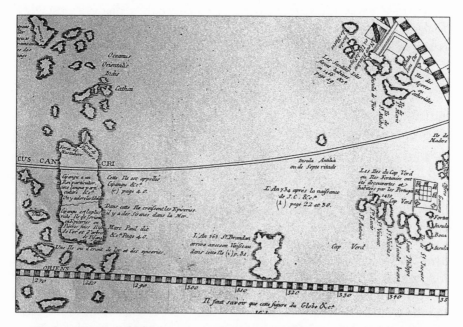

Fig. 1: Detail of Behaim's map (1492): the Canary Islands (lower right), Cipangu (Japan, large island on the left), the legendary island of St. Brendan (center, bottom), and in between, an empty space (the future Americas).

When land was sighted in the early morning hours of October 12, 1492, his three ships drifted with sails down until daylight, when Columbus was rowed ashore in a small boat, carrying the Spanish royal standard. There, instead of meeting richly clothed and urbane Japanese or Chinese, he found a crowd of naked men and women. He named the island San Salvador, or Holy Savior. The native tribe, the Arawak Indians, called the place Guanahani or Iguana Island. The Arawaks were timid. They called the Spaniards men from heaven, and their enemies (who sometimes ate them) the Caribs, or Canibs. Two words have come down to us from the Arawaks: *Caribbean* and *cannibal.*

When Columbus reached Haiti, his next stop, it reminded him so much of Spain that he named it Hispaniola. The Islands of the Bahamas he designated Ferdinandina, Ysabela, and Juana after the Spanish royal family. Columbus not only continued to believe he had reached the Far East, he continued to adapt names out of his European heritage.

Gradually, as other explorers nosed around the outline and interior of Columbus's "new world," they drew its shape differently and disproved him. But they too made mistakes about what they discovered: Amerigo Vespucci, an Italian banker, astronomer, and explorer, sailed with a

Portuguese expedition down the coast of Brazil to discover, on New Year's Day, what looked like a river. The crew named the spot Rio de Janeiro (River of January). It turned out to be a bay, not a river at all.

After Vespucci's letters were published, people began to associate him with the "discovery" of the New World. His first name, Amerigo, the Italian form of a German name meaning "rich in wheat," stuck to the entire hemisphere—not a bad name for lands so fertile, but historically as much of an accident as Columbus's naming of the Indians. But "Indians" stuck too, as did other names imported from Europe or fashioned out of misconceptions about the Americas. (For 1992, the 500th anniversary of Columbus's landing, many new books have been published about Columbus, the early European interaction with the native people, and the effect of American culture on the world[2].)

Many European settlers brought visions of home with them. So, many towns, cities, and states in the Americas have "new" in front of them—New York, New London, New Hampshire, New Harmony, New Orleans, New Rochelle, New Richmond. The settlers of these places perhaps hoped to transplant a bit of home to this New World that was not always hospitable to them.

At the same time, Europeans appropriated some of the names given by the tribes—Mississippi, Alabama, Tennessee, Okefenokee, Cheraw, Cherokee, Shawnee, Sisseton, Mankato, Seattle. With meanings drawn from nature or a tribal people's vision of themselves, the native names ring differently in European-American ears.

Step Two: Making a Drawing or Word Map of Our Early Worlds

Ask your students to imagine the way a little child thinks of the world; for example, what is a four-year-old's notion of the size, shape, and location of China? In certain ways, early explorers' and map-makers' conceptions of the earth's geography seem quite childlike. As we venture out, exploring first a room, then a house and neighborhood, we gradually learn about the larger world, while still holding on to the idea that everything radiates from the center of our home. We identify foreign places by the haphazard and scanty information we've been given. We imagine foreign places in ways that eventually we learn are inaccurate.

Early maps of the world had traits similar to those of our childhood mental maps: pictures of animals and people studded them, the familiar home country was at the center of the paper, and at the edges, unfamiliar lands were represented by mist or blobs. Mapmakers who believed the world to be flat placed a heaven above and a hell below, with animals supporting the land. Sometimes mythical creatures swam in the oceans, sometimes a portrait of an explorer hung inside unexplored territory.

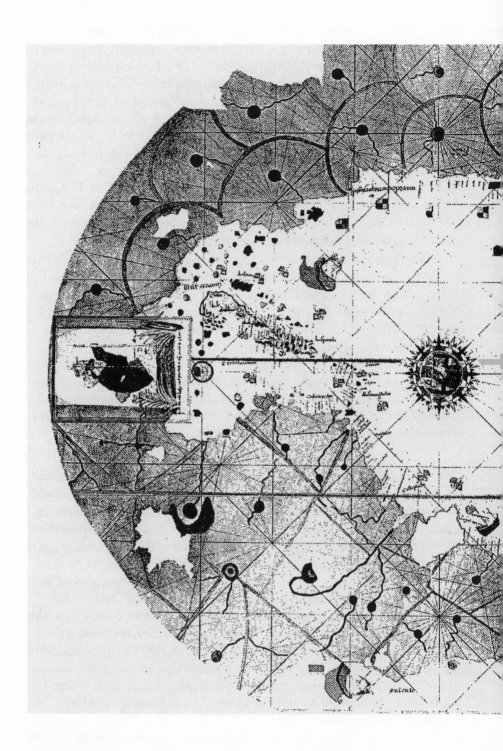

Fig. 2: Juan de la Cosa's map (1500), the first attempt to depict the entire New World (at left).

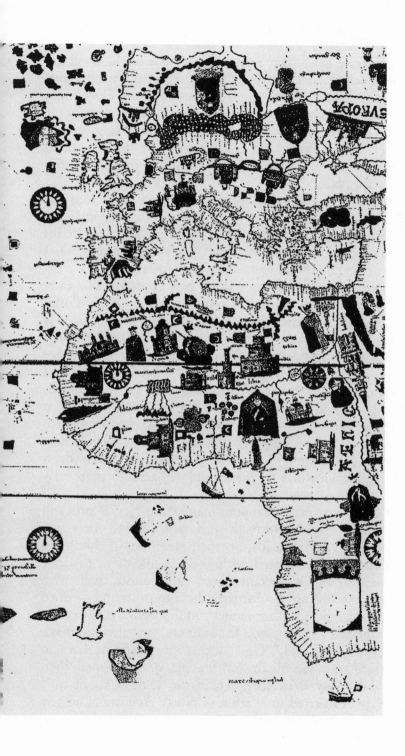

Distortions of distance, location, and size were common when mapmakers tried to conceive of faraway places.

Students can create their own early maps of the world by either drawing one and labeling it or by writing a word map. First, I tell students to close their eyes and imagine themselves back at age seven. They might begin by imagining themselves sitting at a school desk or resting at home in bed. I ask them to think of the world radiating out from that spot: they are at the center. In the first circle around them are neighborhood landmarks, then places near home, then those a little further away, and so on to very distant places.

Songs, games, and traditional folklore about places—such as the common childhood fantasy of digging to China—may also be included in the map. The songs my parents sang about the Blue Ridge Mountains of Virginia, about Gettysburg, and about the University of Minnesota— all figured in my own childhood fantasies of these places.

Early European maps give us clues about how to design our early maps. For example, take the first attempt to show the entire New World, drawn on oxhide in 1500 by the pilot-navigator of the Niña, Juan de la Cosa (fig. 2). He places a picture of St. Christopher carrying the Christ child over the coast of Mexico, yet unexplored. La Cosa drew the bulge of Brazil further east than it has since proven to be. On Africa and Europe, saints and castles stud the land. Little ships ply the water off the coasts. Another interesting early map (1550), of the unexplored interior of Florida, is by the French cartographer Desceliers. It shows unicorns and pygmies hunting long-necked birds that are a cross between herons and flamingos (fig. 3). You might want to encourage students to draw hybrid and outlandish creatures on the unexplored areas of their early maps, too.[3]

Showing students these early European maps of the New World will help them get started. While word maps work well, I like to encourage kids to draw, because I find that it spurs their memories of childhood places and the incidents associated with them. I ask them to draw landmarks, coastlines, and important states, and identify them with pictures and labels, according to what they thought in second or third grade. These labels can include place names and short phrases to explain how they are connected to each place; for example, "I visited the Black Hills with my mom and dad." Or "Mexico, my grandma lives in Mexico." If in third grade we saw the Earth as pie- or egg-shaped, then we should draw it that way. What foreign lands did we think about, how did we imagine them situated in relation to North America? Did any events happen there, any discoveries or earthquakes or wars or coronations? I tell my students to try to be as true as possible to the way they

Fig. 3: A detail of Desceliers's map (1550), showing a unicorn, pygmies, and a flamingo-like bird.

imagined the world then; for example, to keep the "mistakes"—one state larger than life, distances stretched or squished—just as the early explorers did.

To make word maps, I have students put in the middle of their papers the title: "Map of the World, Age Seven," then arrange around it answers to questions such as:

1. Where is the center of the world?

2. What object does my state look like? What geographical features do I place in it?

3. What are my landmarks, for the neighborhood, for the U.S., for the world? What do I associate with them, from family experiences, songs, stories, or books about exploring or foreign places?

4. What shape is the world? How are the oceans and land arranged? What does *terra incognita* (unknown land) look like on my map? What lives in the unknown land?

5. What pictures do I place at various points on my map?

6. How have I learned about the world so far—what books, stories, other maps, movies, etc. have given me ideas about it?

7. How will my map of the world change and what will bring that about?

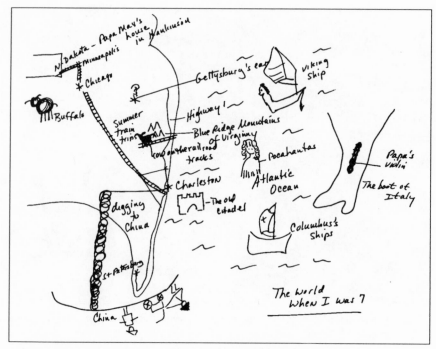

Fig. 4: Example of a map of the world remembered as if at age seven.

Here are examples of a graphic map and a word map from my childhood:

Big Atlantic Ocean, unknown Pacific Ocean

S. Carolina, a triangle on the ocean, Charleston the seaport, a palmetto tree and sand dunes

China directly under us on the other side of the paper. In China people walk upside down.

Italy, a boot, is where Grandpa came from Papa got his violin here.

Gettysburg, Pa. where Papa went to school

Map of the World at Age Seven

Driving north to the Blue Ridge Mountains, a cow on the tracks
Monticello with columns and a bed separating a room, Jefferson's home

A train track angling north, change trains in Cincinnati (the Chessy cat trains) and Chicago

University of Minnesota where mother went to college, near North Dakota with threshing machines, sloughs, cow pies

Step Three: Prose Based on the Maps

Here is a prose description of my childhood version of the world.

Map of the World

Until fifth grade, I was convinced that the Old Citadel where we lived lay at the center of the universe. I carried a map of the world in my head, the flat kind with slit ovals for oceans. The picture books I read about explorers—Leif Erickson and Columbus—said that they had landed at points north and south of my dot on the Atlantic, but my world radiated from Charleston, South Carolina. I saw their tiny vessels struggle up and down huge waves, and I craned my neck to see where they came ashore. I expected them to notice my harbor and wave to me from the wall of trees that greeted them.

When I thought of the United States, after putting the colored states in the puzzle, I traveled north on a slant to North Dakota to visit Papa Max, or straighter on many summer trips to North Carolina mountains or Virginia battlefields where my father stopped to read historical signs.

In the Blue Ridge Mountains of Virginny, a cow stood black and white on a railroad track at the top of the peaks. How did I know that? My mother sang a song that said so. We visited Monticello, the home of President Thomas Jefferson. His bed was built in a wall separating two rooms; he could get in bed from either room.

Sooner or later, however far away we drove, all the roads led back home. Driving into Charleston at night, I held my pounding heart in the front seat; spied the Cooper River Bridge, stilt-tall and open like lace. I knew I was home because black people whirled on street corners, lights glanced off their purses and teeth. And we were going down King Street past the Colonial Store where my mother bought bags of groceries with celery sticking out of the tops. A stoplight caught us.

I recognized Amar's Drugstore—huge colored vials slept in its dirty window. We were almost home. My father turned the wheel, the car edged into a walled parking yard, bumped over cobblestones and came to rest with its nose pointed at the wall below our window. We climbed out. My heart raced. I wanted to see my turtle waiting for us, clawing the side of his bowl. I had to rush in to him. He carried my world on his back.

Later when my father played the violin he had bought in Italy, I placed that country on my map of the world. Italy stuck a boot off the stomach of Europe; I added a triangle for India whose point caught Vasco da Gama as he sailed round Africa for the first time. Another party of ships went west, around the hooked end at the tip of America called Cape Horn.

The ships sailed across the huge Pacific which I knew meant "calm." As they sailed, they pulled the dawn with them to meet another flotilla of ships from the dark. A crash of bright light. They encircled the globe.

Another day had started. My world was round; my map wrapped around an orange. Mrs. Weston switched on the overhead light and everybody in fifth grade science blinked.

Chairs scraped back and Ellen's dark curly head stood out against the white cloth where the planets' shadows had fallen. I had mixed up two voyages: Magellan's first triumphant sail around the world and Mrs. Weston's demonstration of the planets revolving around the sun.

For long after, whenever I heard the word "earth," I saw a medium-sized orange ball on a wire. It took third place after tiny Mercury and bigger Venus. Behind it lagged Mars, Jupiter, Saturn, Uranus, Neptune, and, way out in the darkness of space, tiny Pluto, like the Walt Disney dog with floppy ears in the funny papers.

Vast as the round Earth might be to us when we stand on it, I also saw it from the incredible distance of the dark music room, and knew finally it was only a medium-sized planet, lucky to be not too close to the sun and burned to a crisp, or too far away and frozen solid.

From then on, the explorers with their search for spice and gold clanked as antique as their swords. They had little to tell me anymore. I thought I could learn more from a series of rubber balls revolving dark to light to dark again. When in college I learned about Pythagoras, I added the phrase "the music of the spheres" to my repertoire, and my personal universe was complete. From then on I listened to the music the whole earth made in the darkness of space and did not heed so much the noise of small mortals traipsing like armored ants across its surface.

As always, the goal is to get students to respond individually and imaginatively: maybe walking downtown or along a railroad track takes them out of familiar territory into the *terra incognita* of tall façades, unexpected corners, or strangers resting in a ditch, or a photo album shows them relatives from a foreign country who take their places on the word maps. Maybe a stamp with an exotic blue bird brings them news from a pen pal and lights up an island in blue ocean.

It's good to have students begin their prose pieces by placing themselves in a dramatic moment. Small details of car, sidewalk, buildings, people, and sounds give the reader a vivid experience of the map. Or students can begin by describing their drawings of the world: how is the world shaped? What is center or home base?

Step Five: Reading Student Examples

The following are short essays written by fourth grade students Nalie Ly and Jonathan Kanavati, respectively. Notice that sometimes they write not about their past ideas, but about their present maps of the world.

My map is flat like a big blob. It looks like a chart full of states and countries. My states are far apart from my countries. There is a state that looks like a flashlight on my map. Minnesota is colored blue. Florida is like a giant foot. California is like an old sock.

My home base is Minnesota. The most comfortable place in Minnesota is my bedroom. My bed is soft like a furry rabbit. I like to sleep away in the darkness.

I have traveled to California. I went to visit my grandmother. I was two years old then. It was summer over there. We stayed about two weeks.

I would really like to visit New York, Laos, and Rhode Island, but mostly New York because I heard that it is very fun there and there are a lot of people there.

I've been to Baker's playground. Me and my mom and sisters and brother were there. We played on the swings and on the other things at the playground. We played till it was almost dark. When we got home, I wanted to go again, but my mom said next week. But next week she didn't take us to Baker.

I used to believe that if you dug deep enough, you could be in China. I used to think the sun is always in Florida. I used to think New York is the shape of a flashlight. Now I don't believe in these things anymore. I believe that you have to take an airplane to get to China. I believe that the world turns, not the sun.

*   *   *

In my fourth grade map, the United States looks like it is twenty thousand years ago. Minnesota looks like it's holding Wisconsin by a thread. Texas is a soggy ice cream cone. Inside my map the states are floating. The states on my map are Minnesota, Wisconsin, Chicago, Texas, and Israel. Minnesota is where I live. I go swimming, boating, and sledding all the time. Sometimes I visit Duluth to go swimming. There are lots of reptiles there.

In Wisconsin I visit my aunt. She buys us ice cream cones with about five scoops. I went for a vacation in Chicago. Their zoo is gigantic. Sometimes they let animals loose. In Texas there are parrots for less than twenty dollars. We wanted to buy one, but there were no more. Israel is where my parents were born. There are mountain entrances that you can go to by camel.

I used to think that there is air in space. I used to believe that we are fleas on a ball and the ball is floating in a bowl of water. When we go swimming in a lake or river, we are floating in the bowl. Now I know that there is no air in space and we are in the world. Right now I believe the Earth is going to explode after World War Three.

Here is an essay called "My World up to Third Grade," by Sing Tsai, an eighth grade student:

My house was the center of my world. It was there that I lived out my daily life, where I started off from and where I always came back to. The little white house with its yellow trim along Carroll Street was the place I called home, while all the other streets in Denton, Texas, were a maze that only my parents could figure out.

My house had a big backyard. The two pear trees bloomed with fruit and flowers every spring and summer. They provided good climbing and pears that were more crunchy than you could find at any store! Along the fence way out back, honeysuckle flowers and blackberries grew. That little drop of honey on the end of the pistil from a honeysuckle and the sweet berries my brother and I would later dip in sugar were worth the risk of poison ivy that we knew was present.

In the front yard, on the carpet of coarse green grass, were four trees— two big ones and two little ones. Their leafy branches formed a canopy above the sidewalk leading to the door. It was in this yard that, after the awe of our first snowfall, we built our snowman. (It was such a pitiful sight, but fun nevertheless.)

My schedule was pretty much routine. Every schoolday, my mom drove me to school. Newton Rayzor Elementary was just a big brick building where I had to go every day. In the summer, my dad would bring us to Dr. Wolski's office, where my mom worked, so we could go out to lunch, all four of us. Then, in the evening, my mother would take us to the university so we could pick up Dad to have supper. Once a week, we went to Mrs. Farish's house for piano lessons. On Friday or Saturday evenings we'd often go shopping at the mall, eat out, and, if we were lucky and the weather was warm, be treated to ice cream cones.

Every weekend, I was either at my own house, at Carrie Rishel's house up the street or at Wendy Huang's apartment. With Carrie, I always had a good time and laughed a lot. Wendy and I played together using our imaginations constantly. We have been princesses, detectives, millionaires, Wonder Women, architects, teachers, and all sorts of characters from books. I don't know what I would have done without my friends.

Now and then, my family went out and did special things together. Once a year, the fairgrounds would have a fair with its giant Ferris wheel. In the summer we held picnics by the recreation center and the playground. The playground was by the lake which had snakes in it that all my friends had seen, but I hadn't; I pretended I had. Occasionally we drove to Dallas. On the way we crossed Lake Louisville with its purple waves, and once we arrived in the city we looked at the tall, shiny buildings with mild fascination. When we drove down the long highway, over the red river and past the giant rocks, we ended up at the zoo in Oklahoma. These trips were what I did with my family.

Since third grade, my family has moved three times. The most important and influential move was our move from Texas to Minnesota. I came to know of a society and a lifestyle different than what I was used to. I had moved to an almost all-white environment where many were seemingly ignorant of differences, and people talked differently, too. My friends were no longer there whenever I needed them, and these new, strange people at my bigger and more sophisticated school seemed to be in groups that I was a little apprehensive to be a part of. I met a new, different piano teacher and, of course, lived through my first "white Christmas." This move gave me a broader view of many things, including people. People can be very much alike, yet be totally different. That was very confusing, and it was then that I realized how lucky I had been before, when these thoughts had never even entered my mind.

This exercise works well for adult writers too. Second grade teacher Kent Levine wrote "My Map of the World—Age 7, January 1955" with some of the same appreciation for family travels as younger writers:

My personal map of that personal world back in those very personal Eisenhower-filled days I remember as exciting. My weekly travels only got me as far as Gram and Papa's house, located about one mile away, the grocery store where the invention of TV dinners and sugar-coated cereals kept my interest, the drugstore comic section, Sunday church, and of course second grade.

Second grade was filled with all kinds of maps and places of interest. Mrs. Smith liked me a lot. I sensed that she understood my need to talk about places and things. My most recent trip to the relatives in Iowa was exceptionally interesting to her. Those annual trips served as a springboard for me in knowing a little more about the greater world.

By age seven we had a real car. The first five years of my life were spent in the back seat of dad's business coupe. The business coupe wasn't really a car. It was flesh in color with no back seat. My sister had the elevated position of sitting on the top of an orange crate while I was lowered to Great-Grandpa Parks's ratty old horsehair hassock.

But by age seven we had a real car with a back seat. It was a dark green Buick that brought us the 300-plus miles to Grandpa's farm in southern Iowa. I especially remember the roads being so very narrow but paved. I could never understand why Minnesota had wide black roads, and Iowa had narrow gray.

"License-plate bingo" was the game of travel. Just how many of the forty-eight states could I find before my sister? Everything was always so competitive. How unfair! After all, she *had* three years to practice before I was even born, and five years in the business coupe high on the orange crate.

The license-plate bingo did teach me a lot! Such interesting facts: some states spelled out the county, some the city or town, and all of them had a catchy phrase to remember. I never understood Missouri's SHOW ME (but was so proud of Minnesota's 10,000 LAKES). Did Iowa even have a lake? No, just narrow gray paved roads that interrupted miles and miles of corn.

My world dropped suddenly back in time once we reached the farm. Why couldn't I have lived here? Why couldn't I have lived before the car? How could they let a building fall down from neglect? Didn't they know what a fresh coat of paint could do to make the old barn look new again? I guess not. They were too busy. Oh, to be busy and not just a kid from the city. A kid from the city that everyone knew would get hurt if he really got to experience farm life.

Alone in an upstairs bedroom came the real excitement! Out of a bedroom closet would come THE MAP. The map was special. As far as I knew, it only got used once a year. Once a year when I visited the farm. I would carefully dump the forty-eight wooden pieces on the linoleum floor patterned to look like carpet. Ready? Now the true test. Name them. Name them and carefully place them back in their place of honor. Minnesota . . . 10,000 Lakes. Iowa . . . Hawkeye State. Missouri . . . Show Me.

Someday I would visit all of these places. Someday I would know all of their nicknames. Someday I would own a business coupe and put my little boy high up on the orange crate. I'd help him play license-plate bingo so that he could win! We'd visit more than just Iowa. But if we didn't, I would promise that I'd let him cover every inch of his Great-Grandpa's farm and I wouldn't worry *if* he got hurt.

Variation: Maps Close to Home

Some students want to draw maps of their neighborhoods, not of the larger world. These may include streets and familiar buildings, playgrounds, and bridges. Other students want to draw pictures of places that are special but not often visited—a grandfather's farm, for example, or a foreign city where relatives live.

Variation: Older Writers' Visions of the World

In Kelly Cherry's poem, "Lt. Col. Valentina Vladimirovna Tereshkova, first woman to orbit the earth, June 16–June 19, 1963," the author views the earth from the perspective of space, adding an interesting twist to the themes of this exercise. Also, as a model it encourages students to write a poem rather than a prose version of their maps of the world. Note that this poem might be too difficult for younger students:

It looked like an apple
or a Christmas orange:
I wanted to eat it.
I could taste the juice
trickling down my throat,
my tongue smarted,
my teeth were chilled.
How sweet those mountains seemed,
how cool and tangy, the Daugava!

What scrawl of history
had sent me so far from home? . . .

When I was a girl in school, comrades,
seemingly lazy as a lizard
sprawled on a rock in Tashkent,
I dreamed of conquest.
My hands tugged at my arms,
I caught flies on my tongue.

Now my soul's as hushed as the Steppes on a winter night;
snow drifts in my brain, something
shifts, sinks, subsides inside,

and some undying pulse hoists my body
like a flag, and sends me up,
like Nureyev.
From my samovar I fill my cup with air,
and it overflows.
Who knows who scatters the bright cloud?

Two days and almost twenty-three hours
I looked at light,
scanning its lines like a book.

My conclusions:

At last I saw the way
time turns,
like a key in a lock,

and night becomes day,
and sun burns away the primeval mist,
and day is, and is not.

Listen, earthmen,
comrades of the soil,
I saw the Black Sea shrink to a drop
of dew and disappear;
I could blot out Mother Russia with my thumb in thin air;
the whole world was nearly not there.

It looked like an apple
or a Christmas orange:
I wanted to eat it.
I thought, It is pleasant to the eyes,
good for food,
and eating it would make men and women wise.

I could taste the juice
trickling down my throat,
my tongue smarted,
my teeth were chilled.
How sweet those mountains seemed,
how cool and tangy, the Daugava![4]

In a humorous and jaunty way, the poem reminds us of our immense power, and our immense responsibility, now that we have so thoroughly conquered the earth.

EXERCISE TWO
Naming the New World

Writing poems about names given to places, rivers, mountains, lakes. (For upper elementary to adult.)

In poems about America's rivers, Langston Hughes and Robert Francis explore the theme of the New World and what immigrants have brought to it. Hughes's poem below tells what rivers a twentieth-century black American contains within him, all the rivers his people have known, in the Old World and the New:

The Negro Speaks of Rivers

I've known rivers:
I've known rivers ancient as the world and older than the flow of
human blood in human veins.

My soul has grown deep like the rivers.

I bathed in the Euphrates when dawns were young.
I built my hut near the Congo and it lulled me to sleep.
I looked upon the Nile and raised the pyramids above it.
I heard the singing of the Mississippi when Abe Lincoln went down to
    New Orleans, and I've seen its muddy bosom turn all golden in the
    sunset.
I've known rivers:
Ancient, dusky rivers.

My soul has grown deep like the rivers.[5]

Hughes's rivers represent different episodes in the history of black people. Other races and nationalities can trace back their own movements by identifying them with rivers.

In another poem, Robert Francis reminds us of the many Native American names given to North American rivers:

Like Ghosts of Eagles

The Indians have mostly gone
but not before they named the rivers
the rivers flow on
and the names of the rivers flow with them
 Susquehanna   Shenandoah

The rivers are now polluted plundered
but not the names of the rivers
cool and inviolate as ever
pure as on the morning of creation
 Tennessee   Tombigbee

If the rivers themselves should ever perish
I think the names will somehow somewhere hover
like ghosts of eagles
those mighty whisperers
 Missouri   Mississippi[6]

Variation: Writing River Poems for Different Nationalities (For upper elementary to adult.)

In this exercise, students consider their ancestors' journey to this country; they can trace on a globe the rivers, lakes, and oceans these forebears might have known, and then make a list of them; they might also make a list of songs that mention rivers. The ballad "Shenandoah" is an example to sing or play for a class.

Hughes mentions work that his forebears performed beside the great rivers. Students can imagine meals, dances, or battles that may have brought their own ancestors to the banks of rivers. Encyclopedia entries about rivers associated with particular races or nationalities—the Nile and the Egyptians, for instance—will give students some sense of the history associated with various rivers.

Once students have gathered some information and imagined some events involving their ancestors and bodies of water, they can reread Hughes's poem and notice the way he imagines himself beside each river. Using the first person this way allows Hughes to be both intimate and expansive at the same time. Let your students know that they don't have to describe only what they know literally happened to their particular ancestors; they can speak for their whole nationality or race.

Variation Using Robert Francis's Poem

Have students reread Robert Francis's poem. It focuses on the rivers themselves, and the changes that have occurred to our landscape since the Native American tribes named them. It's interesting to pair Native American names with European ones, to find out what the names mean, and then to write a poem about them, perhaps with a refrain like Francis's. The refrain could contain words from one tradition, or could alternate those from both groups.

A good way to start is to make one list of Native American names, and then a second of European names. Good sources for these names are Henry Gannett's *American Names,* George R. Steward's *American Place-Names,* and Myron J. Quimby's *Scratch Ankle, U. S. A.*[7] After looking up the origins of the names and doing some reading about the U.S. as it was when the colonists and pioneers found it, students can write a poem. Below is a sample list for a comparison poem, with Native American names on the left and European names on the right. Each pair comes from a single state:

Manhattan	New York
Cheraw	Charleston
Miami	St. Augustine
Natchitoches	New Orleans
Yosemite	San Francisco
Dakota	Bismarck
Missouri	St. Louis

Variation: Poems about Places We Have Known

A poem about American place names that links the migration of our own family (or an individual) and places where they paused or stopped. (For upper elementary to adult.)

Step One: Making a List of Places

Using the same sources as in the exercise above, have students make lists of alternating Native American and European names. I give a list of my own as an example. It starts with my grandfather's arrival, then my own adjustment to New York, years later. It then continues with my birth in Pittsburgh, my move at age four to South Carolina, and so on:

New York	Manhattan
Pittsburgh	Allegheny and Monongahela (rivers)
Charleston	Cheraw
New Orleans	Natchitoches
Rolla	Niangua (river)
Saint Paul	Minnesota

Step Two: Looking Up the Meanings of the Names

When students look up the meanings of the names in their lists, they're very likely to find others that are loaded with rich meanings and may demand to be inserted in the list. As I began to compose stanzas around the meanings of the places where I or my family had set foot, I continued to rummage around in the name books and substituted a few gems for some of the duds. The Santee, a South Carolina river originally on my list, was not mentioned in any of the sources I consulted, so I used Cheraw, a lovely tribal name that reminded me of Girl Scout summers at camp nearby.

When I came to the Kansas-Missouri interlude in my life, I found that Rolla, Missouri, has a wonderfully humorous origin. Though I actually only passed through the town a few times, I fudged history a bit and imagined myself nearby, canoeing on the Niangua River in the Ozarks. The list is simply a device to get students started; they can change it as they discover better names and remember episodes from their travels.

Step Three: Drafting a Prose Poem from the List

A prose poem combines the compression and imagery of poetry with the longer lines and looser cadences of prose. The prose poem is a hybrid that dates from the nineteenth century; its practitioners range from Baudelaire to present-day poets such as C. K. Williams.

Using the prose poem allows students to draw information, memory, and metaphor into a fairly loose structure. In my own piece, I tried to begin or end each section with a place name:

> New York the city, half-named from Dutch *Nieuw*, the Amsterdam replaced to honor the Duke of York entrusted with the English colony where my grandfather and hundreds of others passed immigration 1900 to sit wordless on a church step until a *paesano* policeman fed him words for the new land.

> Within it Manhattan, island named "Island" in Algonquin, bought for a handful of beads and the good will of the tribes, where I drove three blocks in three hours the day before Thanksgiving, 1964, and thereafter took the word *car* out of my vernacular to use in Manhattan.

> The city of hills and steel mills where I was born after a midnight ride to spend four years in its environs, first named for French Duquesne, then for English Pitt and the winning general added "burgh"—the Scottish *h* his only sign, Pittsburgh;

> where two rivers meet and flood into tributaries the Beaver rose over our doorstep and set us afloat to the attic to sleep on pallets my sister new born, one river Allegheny, "most beautiful best stream" in Algonquin, the other "high banks falling down," Monongahela.

> We took trains to the big city on the mouth of the Gulf, toured French-lace balconies and spear-sharp steeples. Sisters in twin dresses we dined at the Court of the Three Sisters in the export-import French confection, voodoo-bayou New Orleans.

> And its cousin upstream where, grown, my husband and I forded a river with New York license plates stopped by a herd of mourners heel-cooling in the stream, the body in its box hung out the truck, Indians called themselves pawpaw eaters, we got there and called ourselves lucky, then drank a Coke, Natchitoches.

> The mountain town echoed of blue spring, and late nights after we canoed the hound-hollering Niangua, I picked up spills of radio from far away as Chicago, D.C., I couldn't tell the guide's meaning when he called the green heron "shypoke" the town's namer, homesick, said "Raleigh," the other locals heard it "Rolla."

> Minnesota home now as "cloudy water" river in Siouan where Indian

names fall like coups on a shield: Winona first-born female, Wabasha and Sleepy Eye chiefs, Mendota where one river joins another, Watonwan fish bait, Kanabec snake, Kandeyohi where the buffalo fish come, Wadena little round hill, Waseca fertile field, Anoka both sides of the river. Here I return to family name Fortunato as in Poe, as in St. Paul where I name my postage-stamp yard Cedar-Fenced Green-Eye or Maple-Door or Ground-That-Eats-the-Snow.

Native American names, so prevalent in Minnesota, inspired me to create some names for my backyard that come from Native American naming practices: compound words that connect pieces of the natural world. Naming a residence this way draws attention to those natural features that orient us and make us know we are home.

Fifth grade teacher Jane Reynolds ignored the prose poem idea, but used names of rivers from her life as markers for experiences in her life:

Rivers of My Life

Oh rivers
bringers of life
bearers of abundance
you course through valleys and carve out the plains
so too do you meander through me

a child makes a spelling game
the letters shape the river known as Big Muddy

and what of your urban sister
Chicago?
Why do they dye her green
to celebrate their silly March holiday?
surely they don't mistreat the River Shannon this way

the Fox
your waters flowed through rural Yorkville
where they lapped at the banks of Mim's neighborhood
and at the summers of my childhood
you brought mayflies
and funny insects
creatures I'd never seen before
or since

the Rock River
farther from home
my circle widens

but you are there
for continuity

the Kishwaukee
my first time in a canoe
unprepared
capsized in October
bell-bottom pants weighing me down
pulling me into your icy grip
I am here for the learning place
the college
but the river teaches me a lesson today

Totogatic
Namekagen
St. Croix
these are rivers of now
adulthood
what adventures will we have together?
what memories will be born in their waters?
the river knows
but she
is not telling.

EXERCISE THREE

Modern Odes to the History of Flora or Fauna of the Americas

Long skinny free-verse poems about plants and animals native to the Americas. (For upper elementary to adult.)

Odes date back at least to the time of ancient Greece (the Greek word *oide* means "song"). In ancient Greece, odes were intricately rhymed poems usually sung by a chorus in praise of heroes or deities. Thinking about those performances, I can imagine a chorus in white fluted garments raising laurel branches while their voices proclaimed a victorious leader. It's interesting how history becomes smoothed of its colors: most of the Greek buildings we've known as white were originally brightly colored. Imagining the Greeks in red and orange makes them seem less lofty, more human.

Step One: Finding a Model

One of the best authors of modern odes is Pablo Neruda. When I introduce Neruda's work to students, I ask them to think about his name, then guess his ethnic origin. Mexico, Spain, and Italy are usually high on the list. When I narrow the possibilities to countries in South America, I show students a portion of his "Birdwatching Ode" (below) and say, "His country of origin is the same long skinny shape." Almost immediately a student will say, "Chile."

Neruda wrote a wonderful array of odes. Informal and earthy, his free-verse odes are about elephants, salt, clocks, socks, watermelons, and the "mad, lovesick birds" of jungle and forest. Before I read the poem in class, I again draw students' attention to its long skinny shape, and ask them to consider the effect of all the line breaks on the way I read it. This helps students to understand a little more about modern, free-verse poetry.

Birdwatching Ode (*excerpt*)

Well now
invisible
birds
of jungle and forest,
of pure bowers,
acacia birds
and birds of evergreen,
mad,
lovesick birds,
surprising,
singing,
stuck-up
migrating musicos,
one last
word with you
before
I turn
with soaking shoes,
dry leaf and thorn,
back to my house:
vagabonds
the way I like you,
free,
far from gun and cage,
fugitive
corollas,

I love you
thus,
unattainable,
faithful and sonorous
society of heights,
leaves
on the loose,
stunt-riders
of the air,
petals
of smoke,
free,
happy,
flyers and singers,
airfree and earthbound,
wind navigators,
happy
constructors
of the softest nests,
unwearying
pollen messengers,
matchmakers
to the flower,
uncles of seed,
I love you,
ungrateful ones:
go back
happy to have lived out with you
a moment
in the wind.[8]

Each time Neruda breaks a line, he asks us to pause a bit, thus giving more emphasis to the words at the ends and beginnings of lines. This prompts us to read the poem slowly and attentively, enabling us to focus our attention on Neruda's many allusions and metaphors.

Even though the poem works well with students of all ages, you might want to discuss some of the words and references in it. For instance, I tell my students that a corolla is the covering of a seed. Then I ask them about some of the images in the poem: When do birds look like a seed all folded up before blooming? When do they look like "petals of smoke" (one of my favorite comparisons in the poem)? Perhaps when flying far off in the distance, each bird seems only petal size, the cloud of them moving like smoke. Why are birds "uncles of seed" and not parents? Not all such questions need have right or wrong answers.

Step Two: Choosing a Subject, Researching, and Brainstorming

Many native American plants, animals, or birds make wonderful subjects for an ode. These subjects can be exotic or mundane: a toucan, because we saw one in a zoo; a coatimundi, because once we took one home from a pet store for a week; or the humble peanut, because we like it salted, roasted, steamed, creamed into peanut butter, or spiced in exotic Thai sauces.

Before students do any research, I ask them to take a big sheet of paper and draw the plant or animal in the middle. Then they can play the "looks like" game to generate some visual metaphors. If the subject is the peanut, I tell students, "Forget this is a peanut. What else does it look like?" In this game, the poorer the drawing, the more likely you are to see other things in it. If students are having trouble finding comparisons, I have them concentrate on only one part: for example, the toucan's beak may look like a fat scimitar or a blue and orange nutcracker. I have them write down their comparisons around their drawings. When the students write their odes, the comparisons usually add humor and lead their imaginations to unexpected places.

I then have the students do some research on flora or fauna. Source materials are easy to come by. The encyclopedia is a logical place to start. Jack Weatherford's *Indian Givers* contains some lively discussions of tomato and potato.[9] Science teachers and librarians sometimes know of interesting sources. For my own ode to the peanut (below), I found some curious pamphlets published by the U. S. Department of Agriculture, the American Peanut Research and Education Society, the U. S. Food and Drug Administration, the University of Georgia, *Countryside and Small Stock Journal,* the National Peanut Council, and Peter Pan Peanut Butter Company. Of course, students wouldn't be able to come up with such an assortment in a day or two.

I also leafed through a 1915 book titled *The Peanut Plant: Its Cultivation and Uses,* by B. W. Jones. He writes:

> One cannot pass along the streets of any of our larger cities and towns, without encountering, at every turn, the little peanut stands, where roasted peanuts are sold by the pint. They are kept for sale in numerous shops, they are peddled on the railroad cars, and sold to the loungers at every depot. Roasted peanuts are more common than roasted chestnuts once were, and almost everybody eats them. Even the ladies are fond of them, and frequently have them at their parties.[10]

Mr. Jones's emphasis suggests that, as I've read elsewhere, peanuts were previously considered food for the poor and unsuitable for "the ladies." By 1906, a fellow named Amadeo Obici had progressed from selling peanuts from his fruit stand in Wilkes-Barre to founding the Planters Nut and Chocolate Company. By 1915, the Planters logo depicted a peanut decked out in top hat and tails and walking stick, refined enough to accompany any lady down the street. Because American chestnut trees had suffered a blight, peanuts had moved up to take their place. Peanuts were on their way to being a modern national staple. The lowly peanut, originally exported by the Spaniards from Peru and Mexico, had found its way to Africa, from where it was brought back to the western hemisphere by African slaves. For years it was grown in the South to feed pigs and poor people. Thus the peanut presents a curious case history of how attitudes, commerce, advertising, and technology can affect the status of a food. Today peanuts fly with us to Europe, and return in exotic dishes with Southeast Asian immigrants.

After reading about the peanut for a while, I knew that I had done enough research when I began to run into the same information again. Next I started to arrange the tidbits that intrigued me on three word maps, labeled "Peanuts, History," "Peanuts, Agriculture,"and "Peanuts, Cooking." When I reached the point at which I felt that I knew more than I'd ever expected to know and more than I could imagine fitting in any one poem—about where peanuts are grown, about peanut harvesting and processing, about their uses, and about their history—I stopped.

Step Three: Focusing the Ode

Neruda's "Birdwatching Ode" has a dramatic setting: the poem's narrator walks through the jungle and forest, his shoes soaked, his trousers studded with leaves and burrs. He seems to be addressing the birds in the treetops above him, immediately snatching ideas from their flight. Students can create the same sort of drama by addressing the foods, plants, or animals that are the subjects of their poems. I ask students to describe the setting: maybe the bird is in a cage at the zoo; the coati is chained to a stump outside a thatched, open shop in the Yucatan; or the peanuts, unshelled, are riding in their hands. I also point out that at certain points in their odes it helps to introduce dramatic situations— maybe crack the peanut and eat it or offer the toucan a banana through the bars, or buy the coati and introduce it to the North American raccoon.

Good odes of this type combine both history and imagination. Arranging the historical information chronologically helps the reader follow the story. I tell students to use comparisons and descriptions (and any other poetic techniques) anywhere in the poem, especially among the historical information. As an example for this exercise, here is my "Ode to the Peanut":

Incan legumes
with pretense
to nuts, let me
tell your story
while you
ride
your striped canoe
in the waves
of my hand.
Four named: Virginia,
Valencia,
Runner,
Little Spanish—
I crack you
at baseball games
home run
between
the teeth,
cousin
to black-
eyed pea,
you're no
luck at New Year,
buried with
Incas, snacks
for the other
world
we munch you
high on
Pan Am,
United,
Trans-World.
You returned
with slaves,
Congolese
called you
goober,
pease, pease, pease
eating goober pease
goodness how delicious.
300 miracle recipes
of George Washington
Carver

to turn
the boll weevil
South to gold.
First peanut-
butter patent
to Dr. John Kellogg—
his sanatorium
patients
preferred you
to Breakfast of
Champions.
Picked,
dried,
leaves left
for fodder,
you're
washed,
graded,
A-plus for
protein,
C-minus
for fat,
skin blanched
lest peanut butter
be red-flecked
or you paper
our teeth,
9th richest U.S.
crop, you're
consumed
9 pounds
a year
by each
of us—
candy crunch
sweet brittle
fake pecan
lipstick base
for sticky kisses
you speed
wheels and cures—
penicillin base,
axle grease,
peerless oil
you burn clean.
Skippy

on my shelf
in glass, not
plastic,
you built
a big profit
for Amadeo
Obici, Wilkes-
Barre, PA.
from fruit stand
to salted,
chocolate-
coated Peanut
Man, Planters
1915
in top hat,
white tie
and tails, our
national
hick food
turned
sophisticate.
Thai satay
peanut sauce,
our new immigrant,
oldest native
you came from
China with
the first
Eskimos,
crunch-
aficionado
I prize your
split personality,
sticky smooth
you ruin
my smile
glob in
my mouth,
I eat you up.

Students may discover, as I did in my research on the peanut, that the histories of other native American flora and fauna turn out to contain surprising clues to the web that unites us to diverse peoples and places around the world. The spring after Hurricane Hugo hit Charleston, South Carolina, suburban lawns began to sprout sunflowers and petunias in varieties never before seen on the Atlantic seaboard. Some say the flowers came from Jamaica or Africa on the high winds. Plants and animals reflect physical changes parallel to those of human history. Writing about them helps to wake us up to our impact and dependence on the environment, and to read a fuller version of our history, one that is entwined with toucans and peanuts, tomatoes and pelicans, petunias and raccoons.

Chapter 4
TRACKING YEARS AND
LAND IN NORTH AMERICA

Wilderness. That's what early European travelers to North America said they found: dense forests, wild and dangerous animals, and native peoples who might either scalp your children or offer helpful hints on what to eat. European settlers came to the New World on a mission to subdue this wilderness. But "wilderness" and "virgin land" were concepts the Europeans brought with them; to the tribes who inhabited the forests, prairies, and hills of North America, both ideas were utterly foreign.

The European notion of wilderness as an overgrown place threatening orderly moral life dates back as far as the Greeks. The wilderness had to be "broken" to benefit human life. For the most part, the idea of Europeans living in harmony with wild plants, birds, and wolves, treating them with respect and as equal creations, had to wait until the eighteenth century, when the scientific spirit of the Enlightenment encouraged some attention to the workings of the natural world. Some of the solitary naturalists who trekked the prairies and canoed the rivers of the New World came inspired by new respect for the surprises and intricacy of nature, and by the Enlightenment notion of the Noble Savage.

Apart from these few enlightened naturalists, however, the overwhelming majority of European colonists felt compelled to subdue the virgin wilderness and make it yield its bounty, or else, they felt, the savage land would defeat them. They extended this attitude to the native peoples. The Indians were human counterparts of the wilderness. Since the Europeans had no sense of the land as an ally, they could not appreciate how the Indians lived in balance with the environment.

EXERCISE ONE

Keeping Track of Years and Writing about Cultural Contact

In this two-part exercise, students write "winter counts" (a Sioux tradition), then combine actual "winter counts" with the journals of European naturalists to create verbal collages of life on the Great Plains during the period of early cultural contact. (An extended exercise for junior high to adult. Each part may be done separately.)

Step One: Understanding Early Contact between European and Native Cultures

Just as Native Americans and European immigrants viewed the land quite differently, the various native tribes responded differently to European influence. Some—such as the Cherokee—adopted European styles of farming, converted to Christianity, and chartered towns. However, many Plains tribes, such as the Sioux, resisted changing their nomadic hunting life and, when it became clear that their traditional life would not continue, played out their despair with the visionary Ghost Dance religion.

Some elements of early European contact, such as the fur trade, were common to nearly all native tribes. The fur trade, conducted first by French and English trappers and later by colonists from the eastern United States, drew single European men further and further west into North America where, for ironware, blankets, beads, and liquor, the Indians exchanged beaver pelts and the hides and feathers of other animals. This two-century exchange eventually opened up the continent to European exploration and settlement, and in the process both radically altered the culture of the indigenous peoples and brought the beaver, trumpeter swan, and buffalo close to extinction.

The fur trade epitomizes what was different in the ways of European and Native American peoples. As historian Peter C. Newman describes it, the European fur trade was an "extractive industry carried on by overseas monopolies for the gain of private shareholders . . . to the one-way benefit of the owners."[1] Adventuring free of family, church, and legal restraints, the European men who paddled the canoes, ran the trading posts, and explored and mapped new territory had essentially one aim: to extract as much material wealth from the wilderness as they could and to come back alive.

For most Indians, however, the accumulation of wealth for its own sake had little value. Living off the land, they had to share what they had to stay alive. Their ways of life were closely tied to the local supply of game, to weather and growing patterns. So when beaver and buffalo were depleted in a given area, the Indians living there suffered. The European traders, on the other hand, had no such roots. After a summer season in the woods, they left; when the fur trade was no longer profitable because beavers were hunted out and fashions in Europe changed, the European traders turned to other merchandise. Their lives were dictated by movement, transfer, and profit, not bound to any particular environment.

If the fur traders viewed themselves solely as businessmen, they were also human. They often adopted the ways of their Indian trappers, putting on elaborate ceremonies in the Indian manner to greet their counterparts and exchange goods. Some took Indian women as wives, though they often left them after the trading season.

Both the European merchants and Indian hunters superficially benefited from the fur trade. The Europeans found in the Indians a cheap and knowledgeable labor force. As for the Indians, Peter Newman writes that "the white man's goods transported them instantly from the Stone Age into the Iron Age . . . meals could be cooked in copper pans over fires instead of in birch bark cauldrons containing red-hot rocks, and fish could be caught on strong metal hooks instead of threaded carved beaver teeth or bird bones."[2] Yet as the Indians traded beaver for spoons, ice chisels, hatchets, gloves, pistols, and combs, they also exchanged an independent way of life for possessions that only superficially improved their standard of living. What followed was for most Indians far from an improvement: the European settlers that came on the heels of the fur traders usurped tribal lands, helped decimate the Indians' traditional food supply (for example, the buffalo), and herded the Indians like cattle into reservations often located on undesirable land.

The fur trade also introduced the Indians to the scourges of measles, smallpox, and alcohol, with results that dismayed even some traders. The naturalist and artist John James Audubon recounted how smallpox was passed to the Mandan Indians when one of them stole the blanket of an infected steamboat watchman. The disease quickly spread because the Indians would not follow the advice of the traders to desert their village. Audubon wrote:

> They thought the whites had a preventive medicine. It was explained to them that this was not the case, but all to no purpose; the small-pox had taken such a hold upon the poor Indians, and in such malignant form, that they died oftentimes within the rising and setting of the day's sun. They died by hundreds daily; their bodies were thrown down beneath the high bluff, and soon produced a stench beyond description. Men shot their

wives and children, and afterwards, driving several balls in their guns, would place the muzzle in their mouths, and, touching the trigger with their feet, blow their brains out.[3]

Though not immediately so life-threatening, the effect of alcohol also radically changed the lives of the native tribes, and (rather ironically) provoked the stern judgment of many white travelers. Yet the Europeans continued to ply the native tribes with alcohol, and the Indians in turn learned to test its strength by spitting it in the fire—thus the term *firewater* for water mixed with enough alcohol to flare up. At a critical time in the tribespeople's history, alcohol weakened their family and tribal ties and made them dependent on trading posts.[4]

Artist George Catlin, traveling along the Missouri in the 1830s, also witnessed how the Plains Indians were abused by white traders. "After a few weeks on the frontier, many whites run home to write about the 'glutted and besotted' natives," wrote Catlin, but only "where white people have made beggars of them ... Amongst the wild Indians ... there are no beggars—no drunkards." Catlin argued that "there is no subject [on which] the civilized world . . . [is] more incorrectly informed than upon that of the true manners and customs, and moral condition, rights and abuses of the North American Indians."[5]

The tribespeople knew what was happening to them. Their chiefs were often eloquent in testifying to the loss of a satisfying way of life. Chief Seattle spoke of this in 1854:

> I will not dwell on nor mourn over our untimely decay, nor reproach our paleface brothers with hastening it, as we too may have been somewhat to blame . . . Day and night cannot dwell together. The Red Man has ever fled the approach of the White Man, as the morning mist flees before the morning sun.

This decline of his tribe and their movement by the whites into a reservation saddened Seattle but did not make him mourn. With a foresight that reaches into the present, he concluded:

> But why should I mourn the untimely fate of my people? Tribe follows tribe, and nation follows nation, like the waves of the sea ... When the last Red Man shall have perished, and the memory of my tribe shall have become a myth among the White Men, these shores shall swarm with the invisible dead of my tribe . . . At night when the streets of your cities and villages are silent and you think them deserted, they will throng with the returning hosts that once filled and still love this beautiful land. The White Man shall never be alone.[6]

With so much of tribal life radically changed, we have difficulty understanding what it was like. Few individual records (such as the "Winter Count" discussed below) are available today. In some cases, Europeans destroyed what records there were—such as in Mexico, where the Mayan texts were burned by the Spaniards. Despite the lack of written records, if we are to understand American history better we need to try to experience the lives of the tribes through their eyes; that is, to imagine them as vividly as possible. One way to start is to measure tribal views of the Americas against those of the Europeans.

Step Two: Reading Ben Kindle's "Winter Count"

Many Native American peoples have had a tradition of keeping an oral history of the tribe, handed down for generations. Ben Kindle learned his tribe's "Winter Count" from his grandfather, Afraid-of-Soldier. Winter counts are oral calendars that mark each year with either a vivid, rhythmic phrase, or a pictogram that helps remind the storyteller which stories go with which years. Many Dakota tribes (also called the Sioux) kept "Winter Counts." Ben Kindle's tribe, the Oglala Sioux, had kept this yearly count from 1759 until Ben Kindle told it to anthropologist Martha Beckwith in 1924, the year he died.

Following are some entries from Ben Kindle's "Winter Count." Note that the ideas and images are condensed and often extremely complex. Fortunately, Ben Kindle elaborated on them (below) when he told the "Winter Count" to Beckwith. (I include the original Oglala tag lines for the first two entries.)

1789 *K'agi' o'ta c'uwi'tat'api.* Crows / many / they freeze to death.
Many crows die of the cold. These are not the summer crows but a bigger crow that stays in the winter.

1790 *Miwa'tani num c'ahc'o'ka wic'a'ktepi.* Mandans / two / out on the ice / they are killed.
Two hostile Indians came down to the Sioux camp on the ice and, when the Sioux pursued, they killed them on the ice.

1792 Woman / a / white / they see.
Once three Indians had gone after buffalo and were returning with the meat tied to the saddles. They looked up toward a hill just at sunset and saw a woman in white looking toward the sun. They ran back to camp and before dawn twelve young men went out to investigate and saw the woman in white at sunrise looking toward the sun. They believed this to be a spirit warning them of the approach of an enemy and they moved camp.

1801 They break out / with a rash.
The second epidemic of measles.

1802 White man / a / good / he arrives.
The first white preacher came to the Sioux.

1803 Horseshoes / many / they bring home. (They brought home many shod horses.)
    The Sioux were going to steal horses and for the first time saw horseshoes on them.

1808 Red Shirt / he wears / a / meeting / in an anti-natural manner / he is killed by those arriving. [A clown or anti-natural in the tribe does everything the opposite from the way it is supposed to be done, to entertain, and to confound bad spirits.] An anti-natural does the opposite of what the others on his side are doing, and so confuses the fighters that his own side [unwittingly] kill him.
    The Crow Indians are fighting the Sioux and the clown, wearing no mask but a red shirt, runs toward the Crow and shoots at the Sioux, and the Crow kill him.

1810 Beaver / Little / has his house burn down. (Of itself, i.e., without anyone planning it on purpose.)
    A white man set up a store and collected beaver skins. The Indians called him "Little Beaver." His camp burned.

1821 Star / a / with voice / it went by.
A shooting star flew from east to west with a noise like thunder.

1823 Corn / much / it is bad.
    Much corn spoiled. White men camped and the Indians took their sacks of corn to be ground and it got wet and moldy because they did not know how to keep it.

1825 Water / they die. (They drown.)
    In March the people camped across the Missouri River. One morning before sunrise someone called to wake them because the water was coming. One heard the voice, but no one would listen. The banks did overflow and some of the old men and old women were drowned, while the able-bodied had to swim in the broken ice to reach high land. The horses were tied and could not get away, so they were all drowned.

1830 White buffalo / leg / it is broken.
    They kill many white buffalo. [White buffalo were rare and considered priceless. Some in the tribe gave them a supernatural power.]

1834 Cheyenne / established in his home / a / they kill.

A Cheyenne of good family is killed by another Cheyenne because he is so rich in horses. [The Oglala and Cheyenne fell into and out of friendship with each other, as did the Oglala and many other tribes.]

1835 Buffalo-bull / a / it is fat / they shoot with an arrow.

They kill a fat buffalo bull.

1836 Branched stick / with / they sing over each other.

(The branched stick is a part of a bough with several branches or forks left on, like an elk-horn.) A man about to give the sign of adoption saw some buffalo coming and thought they were soldiers. In his haste he waved a stick instead of the horsetail over the adopted person.[7]

The adoption ceremony was an important ritual in Oglala life: to have the main participant make a mistake during the proceedings would undoubtedly cause notice. Apart from that, the incident suggests a lot about the recent experience of the tribe. The Oglala may have laughed in relief when the soldiers turned out to be buffalo, but the incident came to represent the whole year in their memories, a year when they believed they would be attacked.

Step Three: Interpreting the "Winter Count"

Some winter counts were pictograms of the important events that the tribe chose to record each winter. The pictures were often made on buffalo hide with a brush of bone taken from the knee of a buffalo; the brush had a sharp edge for drawing fine lines and a broad, flat side for spreading paint. To color the drawings, the artist used minerals, powdered and mixed with water or oil. Some of these pictorial winter counts are now displayed in museums.[8]

The pictorial winter counts served to jog the teller's memory, both of tribal and personal events. One picture, for example, shows a white man wearing a tall hat; this represented the coming of Europeans. The next picture shows a little boy with a bird in his hand. The old Dakota man telling the count explained this:

> My mother died when I was a baby, and my grandmother took care of me. When we were going from one camping place to another, I tried to kill birds with my bow and arrow. I took the birds to my grandmother, and when we camped at night, she cooked them for our supper. The picture shows me with a bird I have just killed.[9]

Having someone on hand to explain the "Winter Count" is the best way to understand it, of course, but there are other things a class can do to interpret winter counts on their own. Paying attention to the number of times something is mentioned in the "Winter Count" helps students to gauge how significant it was to the Dakotan tribes. In Ben Kindle's "Winter Count," for instance, the category of events mentioned most often (forty-nine counts) is warfare (or making peace) with neighboring tribes. Next most important (forty counts) is contact with white people. Next were important people killed or dead (twenty-eight counts). Religious and social events, and illness and disaster each got twenty-one counts. Hunting, food, and housing rated nineteen.

When something occurs for the first time in the "Winter Count," it quite possibly marks a change. Ben Kindle's "Winter Count" suggests some of these "firsts," which may have been significant for other tribes as well. The entry recording the first outbreak of measles in 1782 marks one such change. Two years later, the "Winter Count" records "Soldiers / many / they freeze to death." This is the first mention of the Oglala's having found whites in their territory, soldiers who were frozen to death.

More than a century later, in 1912, came a turning point in the tribe's history: "Flag / upward / they raise it." In this entry, Ben Kindle remembered helping to raise the American flag at the U. S. Bureau of Indian Affairs agency building, after the tribe had been brought in to live around the agency. From this entry until the last one, in 1925, all but one of the yearly counts concern either events in Europe, American involvement in World War I, or a government agent's action against the tribe. This shift after 1912 signifies that the tribe had begun to disintegrate as a people with their own history. It was becoming absorbed into the history of the United States.

Step Four: Brainstorming for Personal Winter Counts

Now it's time for students to try naming the years in their lives after the fashion of the Sioux winter counts.

Although English doesn't invert modifiers the way Oglala does—putting the *a* after the noun, for example—writers in English can adopt the compression and vivid focus of the Dakota naming practice. Here are some suggestions for how to begin.[10]

For students who are twelve to fifteen years old, the job of naming every year since they were born may seem daunting. I tell them not to worry about being absolutely thorough—they can skip a year. It may also be difficult to pinpoint the dates of some events. Not to fret. If students have a general notion about how old they were—toddler, pre-school, kindergarten, early elementary, etc.—that's good enough.

What kinds of events lend themselves to vivid naming? It may help some students to begin by making a word map, putting their names and nicknames in the middle of the page and then writing their memories around the periphery. I offer suggestions as they work: include an accident, a favorite song or game, the arrival of a pet or new bicycle, a move, the first days of school, a new brother or sister, a moment when weather intruded, a memorable moment such as a mudpie extravaganza, backyard skit, piano recital, or telephone gag. Recalling what the Dakota included in their winter counts also helps students to identify major moments in an ordinary life: when somebody dies, when pets do something odd, when someone unusual enters the scene.

Most of us don't remember back before we were two or three. For those early years, we have to rely on other people's accounts. My father recalls driving my mother to the hospital forty miles away at midnight so I could be born. Such early stories about us also belong on the word map.

Here is an example of a word map I made up from my own first twelve years:

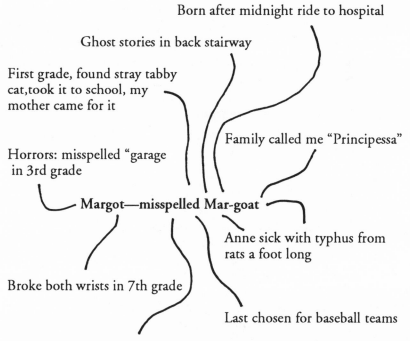

Born after midnight ride to hospital

Ghost stories in back stairway

First grade, found stray tabby cat,took it to school, my mother came for it

Family called me "Principessa"

Horrors: misspelled "garage in 3rd grade

Margot—misspelled Mar-goat

Anne sick with typhus from rats a foot long

Broke both wrists in 7th grade

Last chosen for baseball teams

Piano recital jitters, Miss Miller, my teacher, gave me a locket

Step Five: Drafting the Personal Winter Count

Point out to students that the season in their winter counts does not have to be winter. For the Sioux, winter was the quiet time, probably a time for reflection. The students' counterpart may be summer.

The counts can take various forms. One winter count places the season at the end of each naming phrase:

> 1798–99 Many-women-died-in-childbirth-winter.
> 1799–1800 Don't-Eat-Buffalo-Heart-made-a-commemoration-of-the-dead-winter.
> 1800–1801 The-Good-White-Man-came-winter.

This device may appeal to some students. The repetition of the season at the end of every line gives rhythm and sonority to the count. But perhaps more important here is the notion of making each naming line as condensed as possible, yet still intelligible. Students should try to include vivid details of color, taste, smell, and sensation, as well as humor and variety. Variety and vivid moments are key here: each count should take the reader back to a moment of intense life.

Students should take the ideas from the word maps and transfer them to a chronological list. Some writers like to list the years first at the left side of the paper. Others simply arrange the events chronologically, adding the years in the margins.

Step Six: Reading Student Examples

The first example, by a fifth grade boy, does not include dates; it jumps around from season to season:

What Happened in Seasons

born-early-winter
moved-from-little-white-house-on-an-alley-spring
gave-Dad-black-eye-two-years-old-winter
went-to-California-for-fourth-birthday-winter
Great-Grandpa-died-of-old-age-spring
brother-born-OK-summer
brother-born-had-trouble-getting-out-but-fine-fall
Great-Aunt-died-of-Alzheimer's-summer
bees-lived-in-wall-summer
first-time-skiing-at-Buck-Hill-winter
beat-smart-aleck-Uncle-in-poker-on-a-pair-of-twos-winter.

The next example is a selection from a collage by a sixth grade class. Each student contributed his or her best line to a collaborative poem (which then served as a model for other individual pieces):

Was-born-with-hole-in-heart-fall.
Piece-of-glass-in-my-foot-summer.
Tiny-clay-pitcher-summer.
Made-a-card-for-my-dad-with-a-ripped-piece-of-paper-summer.
Brother-who-draws-spiders-on-walls-born-spring.
Went-out-shoveling-and-caroling-winter.
Lady-in-spooky-house-died-winter.
Left-the-friend-that-I-went-sledding-with-winter.
Ten-bats-came-out-of-the-attic-fall.
Saved-blackbird-spring.

Revision can help make the counts more vivid. The goal is to retain the compression of the models, but make each event sparkle. For example, "Fell-off-bike-summer" would create a better picture in the reader's mind if it were "Fell-off-bike-into-mudpuddle-in-front-of-girlfriend's-house-summer." Some writers have to get the idea down first, then go back and spark it up a bit. The trick is to add just enough detail to make a bright image in the reader's mind and to carry some of the feeling of the event, but not so much detail that the "Winter Count" begins to sound like a story.

The Sioux did tell stories associated with each winter, after they had said the special naming phrase. We can do the same, reading through our winter counts and then going back to add all the gory details.

EXERCISE TWO
Extending a Winter Count into a Collage Poem

Using winter counts (discussed in previous exercise) and other primary sources, students create collage poems by juxtaposing writing by Native Americans and Europeans. (For junior high to adult.)

Step One: Finding Original Sources

History textbooks often give students the impression that past events are immutable facts to be learned, and fail to get them involved in reinterpreting those facts. One remedy for this is to turn to primary sources. For this exercise, these sources include the winter counts discussed above and tribal speeches that were collected by whites. From the 1750s on, whites spread out across the North American continent and left many kinds of records: trading post accounts of pelts exchanged for goods; journals written, and sometimes published, by naturalists who traveled with fur trappers, traders, and soldiers; letters and diaries by women trekking westward; songs such as the ones the French brought, or songs made up to reflect the new life in America.

How do students find these original sources? Many are readily available in libraries and bookstores: editions of journals by artist-naturalists John James Audubon and George Catlin (from the 1830s) have been published for decades. Many books on the voyageurs—those intrepid Frenchmen who were the first to penetrate the Canadian wilderness—include their songs. Collections of oral histories of Native American tribes contain a variety of speeches by tribal leaders, myths, winter counts, etc. Collections of American folk songs are also valuable resources.

With some initial priming, students can go to the library and find these primary sources. And once they have them, the next phase of the project can begin.

Step Two: Selecting Excerpts from Diverse Sources for a Collage Poem

Collage is a technique usually associated with the visual arts. Before the First World War, the Cubist artists began making collages, gluing newspaper, textured papers, and cardboard onto canvas and board to create abstract still lifes. From there some collages became three-dimensional; that is, they approached bas relief and sculpture, some of them including "found objects," such as a toy house, a boxing glove, or wooden spindles from a stairway.

In writing, there are many different ways to use collage. A class can cut headlines and advertising copy from magazines to fashion a humorous collage out of slogans. This kind of collage has a visual as well as literary impact because the typefaces from headlines and ads, juxtaposed, play off each other, showing us how the look of print subtly influences us.

The kind of collage I have in mind for this exercise is more literary, though students can add visual elements to the final presentation, if they wish. An historical collage selects lines or short excerpts from different sources of roughly the same time period and arranges the excerpts so that they inform each other by contrast. The sources I use in the example below are "Ben Kindle's Winter Count," some tribal speeches, and Audubon's "Missouri River Journal of 1843."

Both the Oglala and Audubon traversed the Dakota territory, following the Missouri river during roughly the same time period. The Oglala followed the buffalo and changed camp to find water and grass for their horses and to maneuvre around enemy tribes—all on familiar ground. Audubon took a steamboat with fur traders and stopped at several trading forts along the Missouri. His son accompanied him, but otherwise Audubon was separated from family and home, in unknown territory. He intended to discover new American mammals for his collection. He hunted small and large game—for food, for sport, and for scientific study. When he found a mammal he hadn't seen before, he drew it, skinned it, and made notes in his journal about what he had observed of its habits and habitat.

Students should survey the sources to get a sense of what topics are covered in them. Then, they can decide on certain themes common to the two or three sources, and look for specific passages dealing with these themes. For example, from "Ben Kindle's Winter Count," we know that contact with Europeans was an important theme, as were war and peace, hunting and housing, illness and death. When I ask students to consult original sources, I suggest that they skim for ideas or events that catch their eye, or read carefully a handful of pages, maybe three or four. I recommend using strips of scratch paper to mark the places in books where similar themes occur. Colored paper (or a colored dot at the top of each strip) helps distinguish one theme from another: red for cultural contact, green for hunting, blue for illness, yellow for animals, etc. Next, students should make a list of such themes, or make a group list on the board.

Students are often surprised by what they find in primary sources. For example, in "Ben Kindle's Winter Count," we learn that the 1862 Sioux uprising in Minnesota began in part because even though the Indians were starving and had been promised supplies, the Bureau of Indian Affairs would not release food rations.

In my own research, I became more and more interested by the status of women in Oglala life. Three early counts describe women in lonely places who foretold the future. This shows that women had status and power, even though some of the women were not real—they were seen in visions. I also noted the increasing difficulties between the tribe and white policemen, soldiers, or agents. I found this key entry for 1878:

Cheyenne / Holy / they kill him.
Cheyenne Holy Man was killed this year. He was a Sioux medicine man and at a gathering at the agency, he claimed to be invulnerable. So they shot at him and killed him.

This occurred in the same year the Bureau of Indian Affairs opened the reservation in Pine Ridge, South Dakota, where many Oglala live now. Here, at the outset, the medicine man pitted his power against that of the government agency. Had he claimed among his own people to be invulnerable, I doubt that anyone would have challenged him. Thus the conflict over who would control the tribe was decided.

Step Three: Drafting the Collage Poem

The technique of collage poetry—lifting phrases out of their contexts and putting them in new ones—helps the reader to see the phrases more vividly, and emphasizes their implications.

In his book *The Little Mariner,* the modern Greek poet Odysseus Elytis created some rich poems using historical and contemporary quotations. He listed favorite phrases from other writers in one section, then in another listed descriptions of his favorite places, paintings, and pieces of music. Here is a short excerpt of quotations:

HOMER

dusky water

brightly burnished interiors

then an ineffable ether was cleft from the sky

ARCHILOCHOS
the souls of waves in their embrace

SAPPHO
many-eyed night

HERACLEITOS
extinguish hubris not fire

Child's is the kingdom[11]

The entire work gives us a composite personal portrait of the poet as he connects fragments of history that continue to move him.

A collage poem can start or end anywhere. One guiding principle is to put passages side by side according to their common themes; sometimes the very words will seem to echo from writer to writer.

In my own collage poem, I thought I was arranging the excerpts around the theme of cultural contact, but at the same time I found myself intrigued by the way the different texts used animals, especially wolves. My collage poem also includes snippets of speeches given by various tribal leaders, some from eastern tribes. Many of these speeches are from *The Portable North American Indian Reader* (the same source that reprints the "Winter Count"). The speeches address with impassioned rhetoric some of the same changes recorded so straightforwardly in the "Winter Count." Other sources would have yielded different results. Accounts from the early 1830s by travelers such as George Catlin and Prussian Prince Maximilian would have added quite different tones because these two men knew a lot more about the Indians than did Audubon.

Here is a selection from my collage:

1800 "Ruminant's heart / He eats not" / does a deed.
A man named "Never-eats-buffalo-heart" made a feast for all the people. This was the first feast among the Sioux.

Sat., May 13, 1843. On a sand-bar afterwards we saw three more Indians, also with a canoe frame . . . they looked as destitute and as hungry as if they had not eaten for a week, and no doubt would have given much for a bottle of whiskey . . . I pity these poor beings from my heart!

Powhatan to John Smith, 1609: Why will you take by force what you may obtain by love? Why will you destroy us who supply you with food? What can you get by war?

1801 They break out with a rash.
The second epidemic of measles.

Sun., May 14. When the wolves hunt a Buffalo and have killed it, they drag it to some distance and dig a hole large enough to receive and conceal it; they then cover it with earth and lie down over it until hungry again, when they uncover and feed upon it.

Canassatego, Iroquois, to a white leader, 1742: We know our Lands are now become more valuable: The white People think we do not know their Value, but we are sensible that the Land is everlasting, and the few Goods we receive for it are soon worn out and gone . . . Besides, we are not well used with respect to the Lands still unsold by us. Your People daily settle on these Lands, and spoil our Hunting. We must insist on your removing them . . .

1802 White man / a / good / he arrives.
The first white preacher came to the Sioux.

Mon., May 15: After dinner we went to the heronry that Harris had seen yesterday afternoon . . . Here we killed four fine individuals all on the wing, and some capital shots they were, besides a Raven.

Dragging Canoe, Cherokee, 1768: Finally, the whole country, which the Cherokees and their fathers have so long occupied, will be demanded, and the remnant of the Ani Yunwiya, "The Real People," once so great and formidable, will be obliged to seek refuge in some distant wilderness . . . until they again behold the advancing banners of the same greedy host.

Tues., May 16: I startled a woodcock and caught one of her young and I am now sorry for this evil deed.

Pachgantschilias, Delaware, to a group of Christian Indians, 1787: I admit that there are good white men, but they bear no proportion to the bad; the bad must be the strongest, for they rule. They do what they please. They enslave those who are not of their color . . . They will say to an Indian, "My friend; my brother!" They will take him by the hand, and, at the same moment, destroy him.

Wed., May 17: When the buffalos have leaped or tumbled down from either side of the stream, they swim with ease across, but on reaching these walls . . . fall back dozens of times, give up the ghost and float down the turbid stream...different tribes of Indians . . . no matter how putrified the Buffalo flesh . . . they swim to them, drag them on shore and cut them to pieces; of which they cook and eat this loathsome and abominable flesh.

Tecumseh, Shawnee, to the Choctaws and Chickasaws, 1811: Where today are the Pequot? Where are the Narragansett, the Mohican, the Pocanet, and other powerful tribes of our people? They have vanished before the avarice and oppression of the white men, as snow before the summer sun . . .
   Sleep not longer, O Choctaws and Chickasaws, in false security and delusive hopes . . . Will not the bones of our dead be plowed up, and their graves turned into plowed fields?

1815 Sans-arcs / big house / they live in.
The No-Bows (Sans-arcs) build the first log house.

Thurs., May 18: Mr. Laidlow told us on the 5th of May the snow fell two feet on the level and destroyed thousands of Buffalo calves.

Sharitarish, Shawnee, to President James Monroe, 1812: The Great Spirit made us all—he made my skin red, and yours white; he placed us on this earth, and intended that we should live differently from each other. He made the whites to cultivate the earth, and feed on domestic animals; but he made us, red skins, to rove through the uncultivated woods and plains; to feed on wild animals, and to dress with their skins.

1817 Dead wood / with (as material) / they build house.
They build houses of dry wood.

Sharitarish: There was a time when we did not know the whites—our wants were then fewer than they are now. They were always within our control—we had then seen nothing which we could not get.

Tues., May 23: . . . by hook or by crook these two managed to kill four Buffalo but one of them was drowned, as it took to the river after being shot. Only a few pieces from a young bull, and its tongue, were brought on board, most of the men being too lazy, or too far off, to cut out even the tongues of the others; and thus it is that thousands times thousands of Buffalo are murdered in senseless play, and their enormous carcasses are suffered to be the prey of the wolf, the Raven and the Buzzard . . . we saw some Buffalo and had hopes of shooting one.

Sharitarish: Before our intercourse with the whites, who have caused such destruction in our game, we could lie down to sleep, and when we awoke we would find the buffalo feeding around our camp—but now we are killing them for their skins, and feeding the wolves with their flesh, to make our children cry over their bones.

Whenever I reread my poem, I discover new reverberations of the clash of European and Native American views. Recently I noticed that Audubon's attitude toward death sometimes seems more casual, less grounded than the Oglalas's. Audubon, quintessentially a man of the New World, had left his parents in France and, once established in America, left his home time after time. This rootlessness goes along with both his fascination with the new and his negligence of the damage he did on the way. He left the consequences behind.

The Oglala, on the contrary, suffered all sorts of consequences from their contact with whites: one epidemic after another, the disruption of hunting and food gathering, and the degradation of their lives by alcohol. I think they suffered consequences partly because of their rootedness. I know that such thinking goes against all our Hollywood images of settlers and "Indians"—but the "Winter Count" suggests that the Oglala had a deeper sense of community than did many whites. The Oglala, after all, had a long history that was retold and brought up to date each year. The "Winter Count" referred new events back to former ones. The fate of individuals and the fate of the group were related. But Audubon looked always forward, as we still do, each day a plunge into the new. Even in his private journal, Audubon rarely referred to the recent past. His sense of community was fluid; he easily left one behind and adopted another.

Another interesting approach to this exercise is to have students do one collaborative collage poem over an extended period of time, during which they could add a bit to the collage every day or so, rereading some of what is already in place. You and your students could establish a regular place for the collage, perhaps across the tops of chalkboards and windows, separating some sections by drawings, some by designs, and leaving the quotations up for students to read and think about.

Variation: A Poem about Hunting and Its Native American Ethic

Hunting plays an important role in the "Winter Count" and in Audubon's journals. Hunting was a necessity for many native tribes; they killed only as much game as they could use. For Europeans, however, hunting was sometimes merely a sport, in which they did not eat the animals they killed. They didn't bother to track down wounded animals to put them out of their misery.

These different ethics of hunting underscores the distinction between the native tribes and the Europeans. In the poem below, Bill Ransom, a contemporary poet who is part Cheyenne and Arapaho, highlights these contrasting attitudes toward hunting:

Statement on Our Higher Education
for Ron Lampard, Nisqually

We learned that you don't shoot
things that are wiser than yourself:
cranes, crippled bear, mountain beaver, toads.
We learned that a hunter who doesn't eat his game
is a traitor and should wander the earth,
starving, forever.
We learned to fish the shadow side of creeks
and to check traps every morning before the dew lifts.
It is a kindness in our savagery
that we learned to owe our prey
a clean death and an honorable end.
We learned from our game
to expect to be eaten when we die,
learned that our fathers
learned all this before us.
Because of this you are brother
to cranes, mountain beaver, toads and me.

And to one old crippled bear
that neither of us will ever see.[12]

The author's attentive eye and plainness of diction make this poem beautiful. The poem contains some practical knowledge, such as fishing the shadow side of creeks, but it also expresses a philosophy in action. Not waiting to kill trapped animals is also "a kindness in our savagery"—they don't suffer so long. The Indians learned more than that, however: they learned to see their connection to the animals they killed. Like their prey, they "expect to be eaten when [they] die." This statement on the circularity of all life leads to an even more radical idea: that human life will become brother to animal life because, one way or another, animals will eat what dead humans have fed. In many ways, this mirrors the philosophy behind the "Winter Count": nothing is lost, and everything is related.

For those who hunt, writing about the ethics of hunting might show how we differ from (or resemble) people such as Bill Ransom. Those who don't hunt could write about hunting from the point of view of an historical person vastly different from the Native American—like those railroad agents who, in the late nineteenth century, leaned from train windows and shot indiscriminately at buffalo grazing beside the tracks.

EXERCISE THREE
Circle Poems in the Native American Spirit

This exercise will introduce younger students to the differing attitudes and customs of Native Americans and Europeans, in what I call "A Circle Poem of Praise in the Native American Spirit."

Step One: Reading Model Poems

For this exercise, I first read a poem by Darrel Daniel St. Clair, of the Tlingit tribe. Born in Alaska, St. Clair was a teenager when he wrote this poem. Like Bill Ransom's poem, St. Clair's also suggests another kind of school, one without walls:

My school the earth.
My teachers,
The sky, the clouds, the sun, the moon,
The trees, the bushes, the grass,
The birds, the bears, the wolves,
The rivers, whom I claim to be
My mad genius.

Once I missed a day
Because they tried to make
Me learn it from the books
In a little room
That was really too stuffy.
I hope my teachers don't
Put me on the absent list.
I enjoy going to that school
Where the air is fresh.
Where nothing is said and I learn
From the sounds.
From the things I touch,
From all that I see.
Joy to the world and
I've fallen in love with my teachers.[13]

Step Two: Using Stickers and Circles

After the students and I discuss how St. Clair's school is different from theirs, I hand out a wildlife sticker to each student. (I collect these stickers showing trees, birds, or other animals from organizations such as the Sierra Club, the National Wildlife Federation, and Greenpeace.) I then hand out big sheets of newsprint and have the students fold them in half and draw a moderate-sized circle on one half, leaving enough room to write on either half. "Stick the sticker somewhere on the circle," I tell them.

Fig. 5: Nature stickers.

It's possible to do this exercise without the stickers, but I find that the activity of licking and sticking appeals to young students, and gives them an illustrated example of some growing, living thing—a spruce tree, arctic fox, leopard, chipmunk, or chickadee. This gets them started thinking about what they know of the outdoors.

Step Three: Two World Views

Next I outline two ways of looking at the world: the Indian way and the way of people of European ancestry. To schematize these differences, I draw a pyramid and a circle on the chalkboard.

I tell them that the Indian way sees the world as a circle: humans occupy a place in the circle, but so does everything else in the natural world—rivers and hail and beaver and cardinals and jackrabbits and canyons and meadows and roses and thistles and creeks and ocean and whales and on and on. As I say these names I write them around the circle, as in:

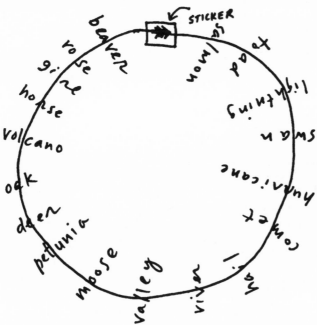

Fig. 6: Example of a nature circle.

Then I tell students that although humans may kill animals and plants for food, humans belong to the circle, too, and must also learn from everything else in it. In other words, we are neither better than, nor separate from, the other life forms in the circle.

The European way tends to see the world as a pyramid, with a supreme divinity at the top. Further down the pyramid are angels and then humans, after which come other living things, ranked according to their smartness or complexity or similarity to us. Students quickly grasp this concept, and can soon say that apes and monkeys should come under humans, then dogs and cats and hoofed animals, then other mammals, then birds and fish, then insects, then trees, then plants, then maybe water, maybe fire, maybe air, maybe dirt. The reasoning goes this way: as we descend lower on the pyramid, the things we add have "less life" and "less importance"—it is all right for humans to use them because these things can't feel anything and don't have a spiritual life.

Step Four: Writing Nature into the Circle

In the next step, the class adds any forms of natural life they want to their circles. I help by listing categories on the board: Animals, Plants, Fish, Birds, Weather, Sky and What's in It, Water, Landscape, Dirt, Fire, Air. I urge students to be as specific as possible in their lists, to put *salmon*, rather than *fish*; to put *eagle* rather than *bird*.

Step Five: Looking at Another Model

Next I read N. Scott Momaday's "The Delight Song of Tsoai-Talee." Momaday, one of the best-known contemporary Native American writers, comes from the Kiowa tribe that originated in Montana but migrated to Oklahoma.

> I am a feather on the bright sky
> I am the blue horse that runs in the plain
> I am the fish that rolls, shining, in the water
> I am the shadow that follows a child
> I am the evening light, the luster of meadows
> I am an eagle playing with the wind
> I am a cluster of bright beads
> I am the farthest star
> I am the cold of the dawn
> I am the roaring of the rain
> I am the glitter on the crust of the snow
> I am the long track of the moon in a lake
> I am a flame of four colors
> I am a deer standing away in the dusk
> I am a field of sumac and the pomme blanche
> I am an angle of geese in the winter sky
> I am the hunger of a young wolf
> I am the whole dream of these things
>
> You see, I am alive, I am alive
> I stand in good relation to the earth
> I stand in good relation to the gods
> I stand in good relation to all that is beautiful
> I stand in good relation to the daughter of *Tsen-tainte*.
> You see, I am alive, I am alive.[14]

The "Delight Song" beautifully expresses the connection of humans to all the wealth and variety of nature. I ask the class to notice how precisely each description brings to life what Momaday has noticed. We also talk about what it means to "stand in good relation." Students often suggest that relation means relatives and good relation means treating relatives kindly and respectfully. I tell them that this poem is a love song, of course, not just to the daughter of Tsen-tainte, but to the whole world.

Step Six: Writing Poems about Nature's Teaching

I tell the class that we are now going to write our own songs of good relation. In our poems, one part of the circle will teach something to another part. Students should begin by connecting with a straight line two names in their circles, such as beaver and moon. To get them started, I take beaver and moon and write the first line of my poem on the board: "The wet brown beaver leaps in the stream and shows the sad sliver of moon how to fill with rain."

Next we brainstorm some other words for *teach*, like *preach, demonstrate, educate, show, display, learn, understand, prove*, etc.

Then on the other half of the paper, beside their circles, I have students start drafting their poems, making each stanza take off from a connection they've drawn between two parts of the circle. Here is such a poem, by Heidi Bakken, a fourth grader:

> The goat teaches
>   the mountain how to sing.
> The moon told
>   the people how to be quiet.
> The old woman made
>   the elm tree come alive
>   and he liked that.
> The hail was in the sky, so
>   he told the star to come too.
> The deer told
>   the old man, I like you.
> The goat got shaped
>   like a cloud because
>   he looked at it.[15]

To cap off this exercise, you can also have students create a collaborative poem using some of the best lines from each student's circle poem. Here is an example from a fifth grade class:

> The parrot can show the moon how to talk.
> The ladybug teaches lava to fly.

The snake shows the hurricane how to eat a mouse.
The Appalachians teach the moon how to make rocks.
The stars demonstrate to the garter snake how to shine brightly.
The rattlesnake teaches the ground to rumble.

Like the collage poems from the previous exercise, the poems from this one circle around and around in an endless chain of influence.

EXERCISE FOUR

Writing at the Frontier

Keeping diaries with women on the Oregon Trail, creating tall tales to match the inflated advertisements and accounts of nature on the American frontier. (Two related exercises for junior high to adult.)

In the nineteenth century, travel was often so arduous and lengthy that, once a family pulled up stakes, they rarely returned. But this didn't seem to deter the 350,000 settlers who, from 1840 to 1870, crossed the Great Plains from the Mississippi to California or the Oregon territory. Most of these people had chosen to migrate. Some of them left not only because of material circumstances, but also to fulfill the dreamer and wanderer in themselves. Many families who took the Oregon Trail had already uprooted themselves once or twice to come to America, then crossed the Adirondacks or the Appalachians on their way west. The impulse to leave had begun in Europe, and the magnet of the New World had drawn them on. The men who immigrated often brought families, but once established, many of them soon developed "itching feet."

Those inclined to emigrate weren't always men; plenty of poor, young women signed on as indentured servants in the colonial period or later came from Europe to work as maids for prosperous families. Once they married, many of them didn't want to leave their newly established homes for the six-to-eight-month wagon ride to the West Coast. In their diaries they often questioned the necessity and sanity of the journey. Author Lillian Schlissel, in researching more than one hundred diaries written by women on the Oregon Trail and selecting an anthology of them (*Women's Diaries of the Westward Journey*), discovered that although they traveled side by side with their husbands, brothers, and fathers, the women "did not always see the venture in the clear light of the expectation of success."[16] The call of open land came at a difficult time for the women, many of whom were in the midst of raising families: "One of every five overland women was seized by some stage of pregnancy, and virtually every married woman traveled with small children." The move often wrenched the women from friends, as well as the churches and schools they had worked hard to establish.

The heroics of hunting and Indian-fighting did not interest the women, who saw their menfolk make fools of themselves or get hurt hunting buffalo. And the women saw another side of the Indians, more often than the men. The Indians portrayed in the Oregon Trail diaries were often quite hospitable to the settlers: they bartered moccasins for bread, helped ferry cattle across rivers, and gave directions to the travelers.

To the women, the trip to Oregon meant illness, discomfort, the death of children, and the loss of familiar amenities (such as a piano left on an upward slope of the Rocky Mountains). Perhaps more than anything else, they were worried by the uncertainty of what they would find. Though the women yoked oxen, drove wagons, picked up buffalo chips for fires, lost and buried children and still kept on, they rarely put their hearts into the trip. Their husbands were spurred westward by visions of a land of milk and honey, such as Oregon, where pigs were said to be "running about under the great acorn trees, round and fat, and already cooked with knives and forks sticking in them so that you can cut off a slice whenever you are hungry."[17] Mixed with the inflated tales of the Golden West were the endless trials of getting there and settling.

Step One: Outlining the Route, Understanding the Dangers, Reading a Song about the Trip

I begin this exercise by tracing with my students the usual route of the Oregon Trail, from its departure points in Missouri and Iowa along the Missouri River (or the Platte) across Nebraska and into Wyoming, then forking across the Rockies and heading either north to Oregon or south to California (see fig. 7 for western portion of the Oregon Trail). Initially the trail was narrow and many travelers had little idea of what to expect— maps and guidebooks were unreliable and only the rivers and setting sun gave direction until the wagon train met a major landmark, such as Independence Rock in Wyoming. But as the years passed, crowds took to the trail, and hundreds of wagons, cattle, and horses pressed on together, the sun shining on the white wagon tops.

Next I discuss the arduous conditions of the trip, trying to give students a vivid picture of it. First, the wagon trains congregated along the Missouri River. Families outfitted the wagons and packed provisions. People bunched together for the trip, usually in extended family groups, with bachelors and an occasional solitary woman joining up with families. On the trail, good water was sometimes hard to find, and the

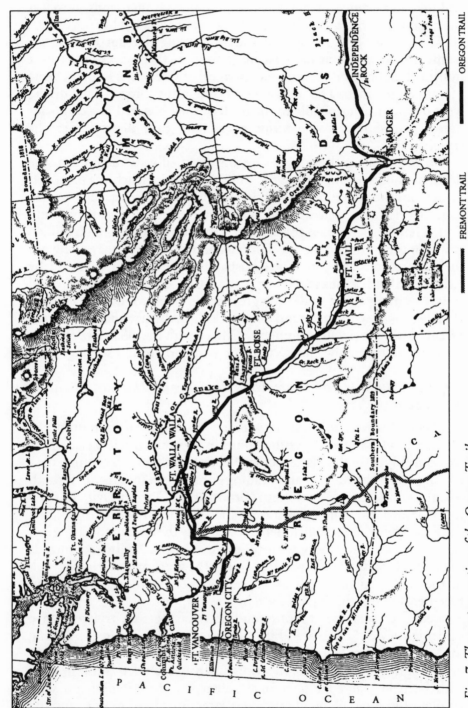

Fig. 7: The western section of the Oregon Trail.

━━━━━━━ OREGON TRAIL

━━━━━━━ FREMONT TRAIL

men often failed at hunting. Hail and freezing rain sometimes fell in torrents, and when rivers swelled too deep to ford, everything had to be unpacked from the wagons and brought across on a raft. Once at the Rockies, the wagons were hoisted up and inched down. Outbreaks of cholera were common; many sick and dead were left or buried along the trail.

Many local libraries and historical societies have collections of letters describing the trip to Oregon. If students have access to such letters, they can bring photocopies to class to read aloud. Especially effective are those addressed to or from the students' geographical region. Another good resource is "Sweet Betsy from Pike," a popular song about the overland trip to California. In it, Betsy and Ike bring three animals along to remind them of home, one spotted hog, an old "yellar" dog, and an old Shanghai rooster. The song describes the trip almost as well as the diaries and letters, and with more levity:

> They swam the wide rivers and crossed the tall peaks,
> And camped on the prairie for weeks upon weeks.
> Starvation and cholera and hard work and slaughter,
> They reached California spite of hell and high water.
>
> Out on the prairie one bright starry night
> They broke out the whiskey and Betsy got tight.
> She sang and she shouted and danced o'er the plain,
> And showed her bare arse to the whole wagon train.
>
> The Injuns came down in a wild yelling horde,
> And Betsy was skeered they would scalp her adored.
> Behind the front wagon wheel Betsy did crawl,
> And there she fought the Injuns with musket and ball.
>
> The alkali desert was burning and bare,
> And Isaac's soul shrank from the death that lurked there:
> "Dear Old Pike County, I'll go back to you."
> Says Betsy, "You'll go by yourself if you do."[18]

Betsy has the nerve to fight Indians and to continue on across the desert; she may be bolder than most of the women diarists, but they too did what had to be done to keep moving. Unlike Betsy, however, they occasionally allowed themselves a regret and a complaint.

Step Two: Reading Excerpts from the Women's Diaries and Listing Their Preoccupations

The Oregon Trail diaries usually begin with the date of each entry. Most women kept diaries for their whole families; thus they weren't particularly private. Most entries were short because the women were busy with children, cooking, walking, or driving the wagons.

If you read excerpts aloud in class, ask your students to listen for repeated subjects. A diary tells as much about a writer by what she repeats as by what she mentions only once. Here is a list of repeated events made by a class of junior high students who listened to the diaries in Lillian Schlissel's anthology:

Sickness in the family
Graves passed, with reason for death marked on a cross
Number of miles traveled
Food, water, wood
Rain, thunder, wind, and their damages
The cattle, oxen, dog, or horse
Children who are lost or left behind
People returning, going the other way
Indians who help or frighten.

The class also noted some things about the Trail that they had not expected to find:

It was crowded, sometimes a thousand head of cattle and fifty wagons traveled together.

It was littered—people dropped off pianos, pickles, etc., left dead animals along the trail.

Indians were more often helpful than not during the early years of the migration; some Indians made money by swimming cattle across rivers or by building toll bridges.

The travelers often took apart the wagons to get them across rivers.

Common diseases were cholera, measles, scarlet fever.

Travelers were shocked to learn that snakes like to sleep next to warm bodies, but found that putting a rough rope around the sleeper would keep the snakes away.

Next I have students consider what makes these diaries particularly distinctive as women's records. To do this, I ask them to consider excerpts from one or two diaries. One good example is Jane Gould Tourtillott's diary, which she called "Touring from Mitchell, Iowa, to California, 1862." At the start of the journey, Tourtillott had two small sons; she and her husband and sons traveled with her father-in-law, her husband's brother, and his wife. Other than her children and husband, Jane mentions her sister-in-law, Lou, most frequently. By 1862, the

Indians along the trail had become hostile. The diary mentions quite a number of warnings or actual attacks. Albert, Jane's husband, was ill for much of the trip, and though he partly recovered once in California, he soon died. She then remarried and raised an additional five children. Here is a selection from her entries:

Tues., April 29: Having no stove it is rather unpleasant cooking. Our road is very good today.

Fri., May 16: Most of the women of our company are washing. I am baking. I made some yeast bread for the first time for three weeks, which tasted very good after eating hot biscuits for so long.

Sat., May 31: . . . Gus was fiddling in the evening . . . They wished us to come up to the house and have a little dance but Albert, feeling rather indisposed, we declined the invitation.

Tues., June 3: . . . In the afternoon we passed a lonely nameless grave on the prairie. It had a headboard. It called up a sad train of thoughts, to my mind, it seems so sad to think of being buried and left alone in so wild a country with no one to plant a flower or shed a tear o'er one's grave . . .

Fri., June 13 . . . A lady on our train was thrown from her horse and injured quite severely. They sent on ahead a mile for Doctor, who was in the next train.

Mon., June 23: . . . Stopped for noon near the Platte. It is filled with small islands. The boys have gone bathing. There is a grave of a woman near here. The tire of a wagon is bent up and put for a head and foot stone, her name and age is filed upon it . . .

Fri., July 4: Today is the Fourth of July and here we are away off in the wilderness and can't even stay over a day to do any extra cooking. The men fired their guns. We wonder what the folks at home are doing and oh, how we wish we were there. Albert is not well today, so I drive.

Sat., Aug. 3: . . . They had buried the babe of the woman who died days ago, and were just digging a grave for another woman that was run over by the cattle and wagons when they stampeded yesterday. She lived twenty-four hours, she gave birth to a child a short time before she died. The child was buried with her. She leaves a little two-year-old girl and a husband. They say he is nearly crazy with sorrow . . .

Fri., Aug 15: We were aroused this morning at one o'clock by the firing of guns and yelling of Indians, answered by our men . . . .It did not take us long to dress, for once. I hurried for the children and had them dress and get into our wagon, put up a mattress and some beds and quilts on the exposed side of the wagon to protect us . . . The firing did not continue long nor do any harm.

Thurs., Aug 21: . . . Albert, Lucy, and I went a short way from the road and got our arms full of currant bushes laden with fruit, both red and white. We ate what we wished and had nearly two quarts to eat with sugar for supper. They were real refreshing.

Sat., Aug 23: . . . Oh dear, I do so want to get there. It is now almost four months since we have slept in a house.

Wed., Aug 27: The first thing I heard this morning was that Mr. McMillen was dead. Died at ten last night . . . .I do feel so sorry for the poor wife and daughter, strangers in a strange land. All of her relatives are in Ohio.

Fri., Aug 29: . . . We came to where there have been Indian depredations committed. There were feathers strewn around, a broken wagon, and a large grave with stones over it, a bloody piece of a shirt on it. It had probably two or more persons in it. There was a hat and a nightcap found near, also some small pieces of money.

Sun., Sept 7: We hear such discouraging account of our road to Carson River that the female portion of our little train are almost discouraged.

Tues., Sept 9: [Mrs. McMillen and Annie, whose husband and father had just died, decided to discontinue the journey and stay in Humboldt City.] I am sorry to leave Mrs. McMillen, it does not seem like a good place for a woman to stay, there are only four families here, the rest are single men. We came on six or eight miles and stopped without much grass for noon (I am as homesick as I can be). I chanced to make this remark and Albert has written it down.

Mon., Sept 15: The road is the worst I ever saw.

Sun., Sept 21: . . . This town [Empire City] is not as large as Dayton, but the streets are full of freight wagons. We see a great many fruit wagons here from Cal[ifornia].

Wed., Oct 1: . . . I walked on before the teams two miles or more, called at a farm for a drink and to rest. Had the pleasure of sitting in a large rocking chair, the first time in five months.

Wed., Oct 8: . . . A lady called by the fence and told us of a house to rent, also gave us some green corn, the first we have had this year . . . The house is one block east of the Lunatic Asylum . . . We pay ten dollars per month rent . . . [19]

Tourtillott's diary focuses on food, washing, and the sorrow of parted families. Hardier than her husband, she could take the reins when he was feeling poorly, survive Indian attacks without an attack of the "vapors," worry about the fate of cattle and female friends, and, after a long day on the road, dance a *shottische* in the California redwood Big Tree Hotel— not unlike Sweet Betsy from Pike.

The women's constant concerns for the physical and emotional welfare of their families and other women and children make their diaries different from the men's. To get a male perspective on the trip, students could read excerpts from Francis Parkman's *The Oregon Trail* and from a diary called *The Narrative of Samuel Hancock, 1845–1860*.[20]

Students can compare Tourtillot's situation to their own by asking questions such as: When we travel, where do we stop and how do we eat? When we travel, is there much danger of any family member dying or getting lost? Are we likely to be attacked by hostile peoples? Would we enjoy spending five months in a bumpy wagon or on foot? Would pregnant women we know balk at traveling in such conditions? If we had to walk half way across the United States without signs or good maps, what would we notice more closely than we do these days, when we whiz by at sixty miles per hour? Such questions help students realize how radically life has changed since the last century.

Step Three: Creating a Character

A good way to start is to give the character a name. Think of women's names typical of the mid-nineteenth century: Lydia, Amelia, Catherine, Jane, Ellen, Myra, Mary, Martha, Roxana, Cora, Lucy, Rebecca, Sarah, Margaret, Louisa, Nancy, Agnes, Beth—these names and others appear in Lillian Schlissel's book. From names, students can move on to invent ages, traveling companions, number of children, dogs, cattle, favorite mementos from home, and temperament.

To help this process, the class can make word maps before writing the diary entries. Have them put the name of the diarist in the middle of the paper—first, middle, and last names. Encourage them to have fun creating the names and adding personal touches: maybe the character has a craving for cake frosting and a rocking chair, neither of which she'll find on the Trail. Maybe the diarist is pregnant and sick to her stomach a lot. Maybe she has three-year-old twins named Clay and Christina who bring mud pies into the wagon and wander off after a garter snake.

Around the name, each student fleshes out the character: age, ethnic and racial background, hometown, temperament, hobbies, and others in the family.

Step Four: Reading a Student Model

Here is an Oregon Trail diary written by junior high student Corri Gilbertson:

The Diary of Beatrice Adams

April 23. Today we crossed a shallow creek. My baby calf almost drowned. Daddy got terribly sick but is feeling better.

May 8. Albert was left behind this morning. Four black people brought him to us. Daddy is much better today.

June 19. We left mama's piano behind at the foot of the mountain. She cried. Boe died late last night. He was caught in a stampede by cattle. Jenna got cholera but we didn't.

June 23. Jenna was buried early today. We all cried a lot. I miss having Boe "scare" the wild animals by barking. The blacks turned back this afternoon.

June 30. We traveled 8 miles today. It was at least 95 degrees. We ate our last loaf of bread. Samantha is getting married tomorrow. I'm in the wedding.

July 1. Sam's wedding was hot. We saw four graves after it. The people died of cholera and the measles.

August 18. Samantha is (possibly) dying of cholera. We hope she will make it. Made only 3 miles today. Passed 9 graves. All had cholera.

August 28. We were attacked by Indians today. Nobody killed. Sam is better.

Step Five: Writing the Diary

Here are a few tips and reminders I give my students before they begin to write:

1. Begin each entry with day of the week and date.
2. Keep the entries short. No need for full sentences.

3. Note both group concerns—family life, work, scenes the travelers pass through, Indian attention, disasters—and something of her inner life, how she reacts to the events occurring to her and her family and the wagon train.
4. Include factual details, embroidered with the personal and imagined.
5. Write a series of entries that cover five to six months, beginning no earlier than April.
6. Make the terrain change as the journey progresses.
7. Remember that you are writing from the perspective of a woman; let her experience as a woman show through in the writing.
8. Remember that this is the nineteenth century, when things like pregnancy were not mentioned, though the woman might refer to being ill, having trouble walking, having to lie down. The birth of a baby was recorded, however.
9. Create repetition of certain kinds of events to emphasize what your character cared about and took time to notice.

EXERCISE FIVE
Writing a Tall Tale

A variation on the diary exercise revolves around creating a tall tale. (For junior high to adult.)

From the very beginning of European settlement, travelers and settlers fell into the habit of exaggeration. Since the size of game, crops, rivers, forests, storms, and distances in Europe were dwarfed by those of America, exaggeration was a natural device for conveying the newcomers' astonishment. Loneliness and solitude no doubt contributed to the tale-telling. Settlers yearned for someone to tell about their adventures. When the occasional traveler—particularly one fresh from Europe—knocked at their doors, they were more than ready to let out long pent-up tales. The wilderness settler could embroider as much as he liked. Who would correct him? He could make out his difficulties three times worse than they'd been, or even go as far as to create an entirely new persona for himself. His fancy could range free, and the long trips by stagecoach or on horseback gave him plenty of time to refine his exaggerations.[21]

Think of Paul Bunyan, with his blue ox Babe, the hero of lumber camps. With his superhuman strength Paul could uproot huge trees with a twist of his wrist, reroute a raging torrent, or stop a tornado, and then sit down in the lumberjack dining hall and consume mountains of pancakes and cascades of syrup. Paul Bunyan was more than a match for the immense new land, and the tales about him heartened lesser mortals who quailed before the endless forests and flash floods.

Step One: Reading an Excerpt from a Tall Tale

True-life accounts of American fecundity suggest some possible origins of these hyperboles: Francis Higginson's 1630 account, *New England's Plantation,* had this to say about corn: "Thirty, forty, fifty, sixty [fold increases] are abundant here." The numbers of animals almost made him stutter with amazement: he knew of fishermen who filled two boats at one time with nets so heavy they could scarcely draw them in. New England, Higginson told his English readers, is more healthful than anywhere else in the world.

Two centuries later (1845) an advertisement for Arkansas talked up the place with even more enthusiasm and exaggeration:

> Strangers, if you'd asked me how we got our meat in Arkansas . . . I never did shoot at but one, and I'd never forgive myself for that, had it weighed less than forty pounds . . . You see, the thing was so fat that it couldn't fly far; and when he fell out of the tree, after I shot him, on striking the ground he bust opened behind, and the way the pound gobs of tallow rolled out of the opening was perfectly beautiful. [22]

Not all the reports of America boasted of its vast benefits; some bemoaned the immensity of American catastrophe. In the 1840s, traveling by stagecoach in West Virginia, J. S. Buckingham recounted hearing men talk about the unhealthy condition of the Illinois river: "One asserted he had known a man to be so dreadfully affected with ague from sleeping in the fall on its banks, that he shook . . . all the teeth out of his head." [23] The next two storytellers topped that tale by describing a man so sick with ague he shook off all his clothes and the fourth had the poor man shake a house down around his ears.

It took men and women larger than life to control and combat the immensity of America. Davy Crockett (1786–1836) was a shrewd politician, hunter, fighter, drinker, and raconteur, and eventually was elected to Congress (in 1828). An English captain traveling through Kentucky heard about Davy Crockett everywhere:

> He took hailstones for "Life Pills" when he was unwell—he picked his teeth with a pitchfork . . . fanned himself with a hurricane. He could . . . drink the Mississippi dry—shoot six cord of bear in one day. [24]

The anonymous tale, "Mike Fink Beats Davy Crockett at a Shooting Match," demonstrates how such exaggeration built on itself. At one point in the exchange of boasts, Crockett bends back Mike's ear with the following tirade:

> "Mike, I don't exactly like to tell you you lie about what you say about your rifle, but I'm d—d if you speak the truth, and I'll prove it. Do you see that 'are cat sitting on the top rail of your potato patch, about a hundred and fifty yards off? If she ever hears agin, I'll be shot if it shan't be without ears." So I blazed away, and I'll bet you a horse, the ball cut off both the old tom cat's ears close to his head, and shaved the hair off clean across the skull, as slick as if I'd done it with a razor, and the critter never stirred, nor knew he'd lost his ears till he tried to scratch 'em.[25]

Step Two: Creating a Character from the American Frontier

Here are some standard frontier types from which students can choose: farmer, blacksmith, tanner, teacher, politician, boatman, trapper, hunter, peddler, housewife, merchant (both male and female), cook (women cooked in logging camps), lumberjack, fisherman, etc. Unlike their urban counterparts, women on the frontier often worked alongside the men.

Part of the fun of developing these types into distinctive characters comes in creating humorous names for them, such as combining a familiar first name with a compound last one (joining an item from the person's life with a common suffix): a boatman might be named Jim Sternfoot; a teacher might be named Nancy Rulerman; a farmer's daughter might be named Karen Shootfast.

Using the word mapping technique, students place the name of the character in the center of a piece of paper. Then they brainstorm the tools the character would use at work, making sure that these are accurate to the frontier: hoe, harrow, plow, oxen and horse, churn, iron kettle, anvil. Next I have students add features of the landscape: a waterfall, meadow, canyon, high bluff, road, or path. Finally, I have them add weather (tornado, hailstorm, drought) and clothing (buckskin breeches, gingham apron, sunbonnet, clogs, sheepskin coat, coonskin cap).

Step Three: Creating Drama through Exaggeration

Many of the tall tales begin with small boasts and end with earth-wrenching occurrences. So, rule number one for writing a tall tale is to start small and gradually build larger and larger. This gradual approach makes the tale more credible.

Next I have students imagine a situation that plays with the standard elements of the American tall tale: fecundity, extreme weather, loneliness, isolation, competition, and reversals of expectations. I ask students to recall the advertisement for Arkansas where the bird falls out of the tree and disgorges gobs of tallow, and to imagine pumpkins the size of wagon wheels, partridges so plump that . . ., corn so tall that . . ., rivers so unhealthy that . . ., hail so big that . . ., snow so deep that . . ., trees so tall that . . .

A variation on this is a tall tale about school. Older students can write such tales, using the strategies suggested in this exercise, but transferring them to such topics as lunch, teachers, lockers and the amount of stuff in them, grades, books, the library or media center, water fountains, stairways clogged with students rushing from class to class, gym, teams, the principal, and so on. Then they can read the tales to younger students from the same school, who will probably make a very appreciative audience.

Back to pioneers. Another thing I remind students is that just as the pioneers competed with the wilderness, they also competed with each other. When the frontiersman who has bested the biggest bear in the mountains meets up with another hunter, he's going to want to boast and outdo with the same stamina that brought down the bear.

Surprise is the staple of good stories; in tall tales it often means that what first seems a blessing turns out to be a curse in disguise: the ten pumpkins the size of wheels rot and spread their stench over the barnyard, the chickens flee, the pigs stampede the children, and the horses break through the barn walls in their eagerness to get away.

Step Four: Reading Some Models

Here are four tall tales by students. Listen for the distinctive voice of the narrator in each example. This is not the normal speaking manner of the author; instead, the narrator is a fictitious persona, a garrulous talker who won't let the listener get a word in edgewise. In a sense, the narrator is a fast-talking con artist, aiming not so much to capture the listener's belief as to keep the listener so interested and so quiet that the question of whether the incidents really happened will never come up.

Karen Shootfast, Farmer's Daughter

Karen Shootfast was a weird child, she did not grow like a regular farmer's daughter. "No way," she must have said at birth, because this child grew strong and beautiful, she had the looks of an angel princess and the shape of a picture that would never be drawn more perfectly. Well, let me tell you about this Karen Shootfast. Her daddy was sickly and her mother died at her birth. She was such a different child. They were so poor they did not even live in a barn. They lived in a cave near town. Karen Shootfast thought from the age of five months that she had better start talkin', walkin' and shootin', and believe it or not, she did. Ol' Karen Shootfast learned to talk an alligator into giving her his skin; she learned to walk better than Lady Isabel herself and shoot, this girl could shoot an ant a mile away. That's where she got her name, Karen Shootfast.

At the age of thirty-two, she came to town with her sickly father and there was a bank robbery. She grabbed her daddy's fifty-year-old pocket pistol and before the sheriff could move to shoot, she shot the socks off both of the robbers as they ran out of the bank, without touching a hair on their legs. Then she showed the town just how good a shot she was. She had a showdown with both robbers and these were the fastest gunmen in the west. She shot them both with one shot. Three women and the sheriff fainted and the preacher dropped dead with such a shock in their bones. Old Karen grew up to be the best and the prettiest gal in the west.

—Markeela Thomas, tenth grade

* * *

Fisherman

How do you do! I'm Mike Salmon, fisherman. I'm gonna tell you 'bout a day that I went fishing. Boy that day I needed more than one man to catch the fish as I brought them in with my pole. I could actually walk on the water there were so many fish. I had to walk (on the water of course) to the shore to get another boat because the one I had was starting to sink from all the fish. I tried to pull up the anchor, but the fish were so thick that it was like trying to pull through ice. By the end of the day, I caught so many fish they filled five boats. I caught all of the fish in the sea with a bare hook. It is now called the Dead Sea.

—David Bixler, tenth grade

* * *

Henry Joes, the Trapperkeeper

Once there was a trapper named the trapperkeeper, alias Henry Joes. His arms were the size of redwood trees. He could lift a log cabin at the blink of an eye. When he walked around, he made trenches wherever he walked. His skills at trapping were excellent. He didn't even use traps. With his monstrous voice, he screamed at the top of his lungs and scared all the animals in the forest to death. To shave his face he had to use a saw blade, and he took baths in the Pacific Ocean and showered at Niagara Falls, and then dried off in a tornado. His knife Charlie is so sharp that he could cut the earth in half. For dinner he ate nails and drank lava from a volcano. Him and Paul Bunyan had a fight and made huge crevices in the ground, which is now called the Grand Canyon.

—Vinny Corbo, tenth grade

* * *

Lena Lutefisk

One day Lena Lutefisk decided to go fishing with her husband Ole Lutefisk and some Germans. They left at 6 A.M. and were to arrive home at 5 P.M. When noon came they still hadn't caught anything and wanted Lena to make a dinner for them. Lena wanted to stay fishing unlike the others who were playing cards. Lena decided to go fishing and serve dinner at the same time. She put the pole between her long toes and mixed up some soapy water. She then waited for a fish to bite. She felt a tug and pulled up the fish with her feet. Then while she cleaned off the scales with a knife, she baited the hook with her feet. She cast the bait into the water with her long toes and threw the fish in the soapy water which produced lutefisk! She repeated the process over and over again and soon the others noticed what she was doing and thought it would be a good idea only they were still playing cards. Each of them tried it, but Ole was the only one to succeed, for the Germans' toes were too short and the pole kept slipping. Soon the news was all over Delaware about the Norwegian's great feet.

—*Joya Bromeland, eighth grade*

Step Five: Shaping the Tale

A good way to start the story is to set the scene and introduce the main character. It's a good idea to emphasize one or two characteristics of the person, using lots of details.

Then the exaggeration can start. It's important to begin with something fairly commonplace—pumpkins, a bear, some logs, pancakes, horseshoes, etc.—then gradually increase the exaggeration until the whole world in the tale seems out of control. The tale should end with a surprise.

* * *

Some of the most recent immigrants to the New World are the Hmong from Laos. After decades of civil war, many Hmong families began the trek out of their mountain country in northern Laos toward refugee camps in Thailand. From there, if they were lucky, they emigrated to the United States. The stories of fifteen Hmong boys who made this journey are collected in David L. Moore's *Dark Sky, Dark Land: Stories of the Hmong Boy Scouts of Troop 100.* Early in the story of Xe Vang (as told to David Moore), the boy describes the civil war in Laos and its effects on many Hmong families:

Hmong farmers lived in Buom Long [the boy's town] for protection while cultivating fields in nearby villages. Small boys learned how to use guns and became soldiers at an early age. Rice, supplies, and ammunition were dropped from airplanes so people trapped in Buom Long could eat, defend themselves, and survive.[26]

Though the stories read sometimes like high adventure serials—complete with daily threats, excitement, sudden ambushes, and hair's-breadth escapes—they also chronicle family ties that are strained and sometimes severed by the wrenching journey. Though the jungle landscape seems exotic and foreign, the trials and endurance of these families sound something like the stories of families on the Oregon Trail. Such journeys are quintessentially American, with huge stresses on individuals and families, testing the identity of each race and ethnic group in a new environment.

As students write older versions of the immigrant story, they might think about the Hmong and other recent immigrants from Haiti, Africa, El Salvador, or the former Soviet Union. We should encourage these new immigrants to tell us about themselves and how they see us, not only to help us understand their cultures as other ways of being human, but also to give us new ways to measure our own culture. What they see with their new eyes will show us ourselves more vividly. They may have new ways of responding to the size of things on this continent, and their own versions of tall tales. For them, as for any other new immigrants, this is, for better or worse, one more time, a new world.

Chapter 5
WAR, VIOLENCE, AND PROTEST

EXERCISE ONE
Civil War Scenes: Writing Civil War Ballads from Photographs and Whitman's Words

In this exercise, students write modern ballads based on photographs of Civil War scenes and Walt Whitman's writing about the war. The combination of visual and literary sources brings us close to the Civil War's particular combination of casual grime and impassioned rhetoric, and helps students consider how the war's photographic record differs from Whitman's literary portrait of it. (For high school and older.)

Photographs brought the Civil War—the first American war to receive an extensive photographic record—home to the civilian population. Stereographic ("3-D") portraits of soldiers and battle scenes sold by the millions. Through engravings based on photographs, the contemporary newspapers and magazines carried the war into people's parlors in much the same way that TV brought the Vietnam War into our living rooms.

The first photographs documenting a war (the Crimean War) were taken in the mid-nineteenth century. Gradually such pictures come to seem universal: we cannot separate them from our images of other wars. Written records age differently. Over time, they seem to accumulate more and more of the spirit, technology, and "look" of a particular war. Walt Whitman's poems and reports from Civil War battlefields and hospitals are filled with the roar of cannons, the flap of flags, the clank of marching, the groans of the wounded and the amputees. Whitman describes the war in ways that seem to me at once archaic and accurate: he writes about dying with an unflinching, almost contemporary show of pain and gore, and about death with a sweetness that seems faded, yet true to his time. His words bring the particulars of the Civil War to mind, real, historical, and distant. In some of Whitman's passages, where the historical predominates over the eternal, we may even forget the universal horrors of war, and be tempted to romanticize the conflict, imagining it like a pageant replete with historically accurate replicas of neat uniforms, mess kits, and hospital tents—and none of the disease and death that so characterized it.

That's when we need to bring in the photographs, the careful studies of camp soldiers, ruined cities, and ditches of Rebel and Union dead. Matthew Brady, Alexander Gardner, and others documented the Civil War with painstaking precision. Their photographs are static, but they also look as if they could have been taken yesterday. Their often casual intimacy is partly due to the camera's insistent realism, but also due to the fact that the photographers documented the common soldiers, not just the generals in heroic studio poses. Combined with Whitman's words, they help students to enter the experience of the Civil War.

Advance Preparation: Selecting Passages from Whitman and Finding Civil War Photographs

Before beginning the exercise, I read poems and prose reports that Whitman wrote about the Civil War and then selected passages to read aloud later to the students. It's better, of course, if students themselves can also read Whitman, especially the "Drum Taps" section of *Leaves of Grass,* and the war passages in his prose collection, *Specimen Days.* (Much of Whitman's Civil War work appears in *The Portable Walt Whitman,* edited by Mark Van Doren.)[1]

The stereograph photographs that I use with this exercise are photocopies of the rectangular, cardboard-backed ones that people in the nineteenth century often bought in sets. Inserted into the holder of the stereopticon, the double images of the slides merged into one and gave the illusion of depth, like 3-D movies. Buying a set was probably comparable to renting a video today—any middle-class family of the time could do it. Stereograph slides are available these days from historical societies, museums, antique stores, and flea markets.

But stereograph photos formed only part of the photographic record of the war. Many photographs were made for newspapers and magazines or for the soldiers to give as mementos before they went to battle. Perhaps the most easily available modern publications of the whole range of Civil War photographs are the two series from Time-Life Books, *The Civil War* and *The Image of War.* Many photographs have also been duplicated in the lengthy but informative PBS video series, *The Civil War,* produced by Ken Burns. In the Time-Life books, the photographs' captions provide helpful information. For example, in the volume called *Tenting Tonight,* one caption reads:

Men of the 1st Texas Brigade engage in a variety of chores—scrubbing clothes, frying corn pone, and chopping firewood—outside their winter quarters at Camp Quantico, Virginia, in 1861. The log hut was opulent by Army standards, featuring a roof of sturdy shingles and a glass window with nearly every pane intact.[2]

If you are short on time or information, the Time-Life volumes will prove especially useful.

State or county historical societies usually have collections of photos taken in their particular regions. These local collections add an immediacy to the writing experience—after all, the Civil War touched nearly every part of the nation. With individual photos, it is also possible to make photocopies for students without too much trouble or expense.

In preparing for my classes, I leafed through the collection of stereopticon slides and other photographs at the Minnesota Historical Society, from which I selected a variety of shots, fifteen in all. Here are the labels and notes on some:

• "Professor Lowe in His Balloon, from the 1862 Peninsular Campaign." From the back of it I took the following notes: Army balloon aided signal service. The Fair Oaks Battle: the balloon followed the enemy's movements and gave warning to the generals on how to head them off. Men holding the ropes permitted the balloon to rise, then anchored it to a tree.

• "The Sunken Road at Antietam." Notes indicate that the Rebels used this ditch as a rifle pit. The Union battery got excellent range of the road and slaughtered the enemy like sheep. The dead were photographed where they fell. (Research has revealed that occasionally the Civil War photographers repositioned dead soldiers in beatific poses and even put crosses in their hands, but this slide is labeled specifically, "The dead were photographed where they fell.")

• "Where One of Grant's Messengers Called." A stereopticon slide. From the notes on the back I learned that the city of Petersburg, Virginia, was under constant fire from July 1864 to April 1865. The Union batteries shelled almost continuously, yet many women and children stayed in Petersburg during the siege. The photo shows the Dunlop house from inside a dim, plaster-littered parlor, looking out a shattered window. "Grant's Messenger" was obviously a cannon ball.

• "Savage Station, 1862." From the back I noted: A crowd of sick and wounded from the First Minnesota Regiment spread out beside a railroad station under a tree and a ladder. June 29, 1862. The Richmond and York River Railroad tracks ran nearby.

The first time I tried this exercise, I worked with a group of eleventh grade humanities students who had just read Stephen Crane's novel about the Civil War, *The Red Badge of Courage*. I have also used it with twelfth grade English students, who had not studied the war. Of course, it's best if the students have done some reading about the war before they try writing from the photographs. Dipping into the Time-Life *Civil War* books or seeing some of the PBS *Civil War* series is good for focusing students on the minutiae that distinguish this war from others—the cornmeal, hardtack, minnie balls, cannons, horse-drawn covered wagons, songs, and slang.

Step One: Choosing a Partner and a Photograph

After initial discussion, students choose partners and select a photograph from the photocopies I've made available to them.

Step Two: Introducing the Ballad Form to Students

To help students envision the exercise as a whole, I describe the ballad form, with its choruses alternating with descriptive verses. (For more discussion of the ballad form, see exercise 2 in chapter 2.) I tell students that for the choruses they may adapt material from Whitman's poetry and prose, or come up with their own. The material for the verses will come from the photographs. Each pair of writers needs to decide whether they're going to create chorus and verses together, or whether one writer will write the verses and the other the chorus.

Step Three: Questioning the Image, Defining the Scene

Here are some of poet Ron Padgett's recommendations for "getting inside" a photograph. Look closely at each object in the photo, identifying each one, if possible. Then look at each quadrant (upper left, upper right, lower left, and lower right) of the photo, one at a time. Try to guess the season, the time of day, the location of the sun, and the weather conditions. Think about what might be just beyond the edge of the photo. Now pick a particular spot in the photo, a place where there is room for another person. Look at that spot for a moment, then close your eyes and imagine that your body has been transported through the surface of the picture and actually inserted into the scene. With your eyes still closed, visualize the details of the scene around you (what was formerly on the left is now on the right, for instance). Let yourself believe that you're really there. You can even see the photographer aiming his camera at you! You can feel the air around you. And now that you're inside the scene, you can hear its sounds, which were silent before. You can even turn your head and see what's happening beyond the edge of the photo. Stay there for a while, relax, and look around. If something "happens," let it happen; otherwise it's fine just to look around. When you've seen enough, open your eyes.

After this individual experience of entering the photo, the teams can work together to interpret the realistic details in the photographs imaginatively, incorporating information that they have gleaned about the war. Having students work in pairs is helpful partly because deciphering the visual details in faded photographs can be difficult. The questions and answers about the image of "Savage Station—1862" (fig. 8) might go something like this:

Question: "Why is there a ladder slanting across the picture to the upstairs of Savage Station?"

Answer: "Maybe because there are wounded men upstairs and the inside stairway has been burned out."

Question: "What do you think is happening inside the tent on the outskirts of the crowd of wounded?"

Answer: "Maybe it's a cook tent or maybe the doctor performs surgery there."

Of course, I also tell students to include simple statements of what they see in the photograph. I urge everyone to look for details that characterize a place or a person: "Notice the man with the wide-brimmed straw hat hunched in the foreground. He doesn't look very sick, just exhausted and discouraged." Or, "The white picket fence around the mass of wounded men looks incongruous—this is hardly a pretty garden with flowers in it anymore."

I encourage the students to write down anything they know that they might bring to bear on the photograph; for instance:

With only ether and chloroform and no antibiotics, the pain of surgery and the danger of infection must have been great.

A partner might respond:

I can imagine the air heavy with the smell of sweat and blood. The scene looks almost idyllic in black and white, but screams are probably coming from the surgeon's tent. When gangrene set in, the doctor could only amputate. The bodies are so close together, there is no privacy, but that probably doesn't matter. With so much pain, you stop caring where you are or who hears you cry out.

Fig. 8: Sick and wounded soldiers at Savage Station, Va., June 29, 1862.

It also helps to ask "What is about to happen next?" We know that the scenes captured in photos are present only for a moment. Trying to imagine what might happen next may help students bring in their knowledge of the war. Of Savage Station, a student might guess, "As soon as the camera clicks, a train will pull in and then start loading the wounded into flatcars for transportation to the hospitals in Washington."

In other words, a close and imaginative examination of the photos helps the students *get inside* them. (See appendix 3 for more about this process.)

Step Four: Taking Notes from Whitman

The "Drum-Taps" section of *Leaves of Grass* forms the core of Whitman's poetry about the war. His prose reports, later collected in his *Specimen Days,* are more heavily grained, casual, and hurried. Many of them were published in New York newspapers. Whitman spent more than three years, from late 1862 through 1865, tracking the Army of the Potomac. Much of the time he stayed in Washington visiting and nursing sick and wounded soldiers, but he also

> went down to the fields in Virginia (end of '62); lived thenceforward in camp; saw great battles and the days and nights afterward; partook of all the fluctuations, gloom, despair, hopes again aroused, courage evoked, death readily risked.[3]

Much of the prose from these years and many of the poems from "Drum-Taps" are in *The Portable Walt Whitman,* from which I select passages to read aloud. I prefer reading aloud in class, rather than letting each student read silently, because it's a better way for students to take in the rich language and long cadences of Whitman's writing. I have the students select and write down Whitman's vivid and telling phrases to use later in their ballads, especially the phrases that seem to relate to the photo they've chosen. The idea isn't just to mimic Whitman, but rather to absorb the precise terms of this one war and enrich our own description of the photographs with Whitman's range and sensitivity.

To give students a sense of how the war initially felt to a civilian, I often begin with a section of the first poem in "Drum-Taps," "First O Songs for a Prelude":

> To the drum-taps prompt,
> The young men falling in and arming,
> The mechanics arming (the trowel, the jack-plane, the blacksmith's
>   hammer, tost aside with precipitation,)

The lawyer leaving his office and arming, the judge leaving the court,
The driver deserting his wagon in the street, jumping down, throwing
    the reins abruptly down on the horses's backs,
The salesman leaving the store, the boss, book-keeper, porter, all
    leaving;
Squads gather everywhere by common consent and arm,
The new recruits, even boys, the old men show them how to wear their
    accoutrements, they buckle the straps carefully,
Outdoors arming, indoors arming, the flash of musket-barrels,
The white tents cluster in camps, the arm'd sentries around, the sunrise
    cannon and again at sunset,
Arm'd regiments arrive every day, pass through the city, and embark
    from the wharves,
    [. . .]
The tearful parting, the mother kisses her son, the son kisses his
    mother
    [. . .]
The artillery, the silent cannons bright as gold, drawn along, rumble
    lightly over the stones . . .
The hospital service, the lint, bandages and medicines,
The women volunteering for nurses, the work begun for in earnest, no
    mere parade now [. . .][4]

I then read the stirring ballad, "Beat! Beat! Drums!":

Beat! beat! drums!—blow! bugles! blow!
Through the window—through doors—burst like a ruthless force,
Into the solemn church, and scatter the congregation,
Into the school where the scholar is studying;
Leave not the bridegroom quiet—no happiness must he have now with
    his bride,
Nor the peaceful farmer any peace, ploughing his field or gathering his
    grain,
So fierce you whirr and pound you drums—so shrill you bugles blow.

Beat! beat! drums!—blow! bugles! blow!
Over the traffic of cities—over the rumble of wheels in the streets;
Are beds prepared for sleepers at night in the houses? no sleepers must
    sleep in those beds,
No bargainers' bargains by day—no brokers or speculators—would
    they continue?
Would the talkers be talking? would the singer attempt to sing?
Would the lawyer rise in the court to state his case before the judge?
Then rattle quicker, heavier drums—you bugles wilder blow.

Beat! beat! drums!—blow! bugles! blow!
Make no parley—stop for no expostulation,
Mind not the timid—mind not the weeper or prayer,
Mind not the old man beseeching the young man,
Let not the child's voice be heard, nor the mother's entreaties,
Make even the trestles to shake the dead where they lie awaiting the
    hearses,
So strong you thump O terrible drums—so loud you bugles blow.

Before moving on, I point out how the changes in the chorus emphasize the growing effect of the war, and that the students' choruses can also change slightly to indicate a deepening of the poem's meaning.

After being aroused by Whitman's battle calls, we next follow him to the Virginia battlefields in a prose selection from *Specimen Days*. Notice how details here echo the subject of the photo of "Savage Station":

Down at the Front

Falmouth, Va., opposite Fredericksburg, December 21, 1862.

    —Began my visits among the camp hospitals in the army of the Potomac. Spend a good part of the day in a large brick mansion on the banks of the Rappahannock, used as a hospital since the battle—seems to have receiv'd only the worst cases. Out doors, at the foot of a tree, within ten yards of the front of the house, I notice a heap of amputated feet, legs, arms, hands, &c., a full load for a one-horse cart. Several dead bodies lie near, each cover'd with its brown woolen blanket. In the door-yard, towards the river, are fresh graves, mostly of officers, their names on pieces of barrel-staves or broken boards, stuck in the dirt [. . .] The large mansion is quite crowded upstairs and down, everything im-promptu, no system, all bad enough, but I have no doubt the best that can be done; all the wounds pretty bad, some frightful, the men in their old clothes, unclean and bloody. [. . .] I went through the rooms, down-stairs and up. Some of the men were dying. I had nothing to give at that visit, but wrote a few letters to folks home, mothers, &c. Also talk'd to three or four, who seemed most susceptible to it, and needing it.[5]

The contrast between the mood of the two poems and the prose of *Specimen Days* is striking. Whitman's heroic poems heighten individual resolve into an immense, democratic contribution. They do not focus much on the grimy, mean, and accidental elements of war that his prose steadily records. Expressing Whitman's noble vision of the Union, the poems frame the war's brutality with images from soothing nature, such as the haunting motifs of lilacs, evening star, and the hermit thrush's "song of the bleeding throat" in his famous poem, "When Lilacs Last in the Dooryard Bloom'd." But in the prose, though he tries to make a new moon "prove an omen and a good prophecy," such hope and comfort don't always carry over into his descriptions of the dirt and pain of battle.

In a paragraph on the battle of Fredericksburg (Sunday, December 14, 1862), Whitman describes an exhausting attack:

> During the whole of that time [twenty-seven hours of attack], everyone, from the Colonel on down, was compelled to lie at full length on his back or belly in the mud, which was deep and tenacious. The surface of the ground, slightly elevated just south of them, served as a natural bulwark and protection against the Rebel batteries and sharpshooters, as long as the men lay in this manner. But the moment the men raised their heads or a limb, even if only a few inches—snap and s-s-st went the weapons of Secesh! In this manner, the 51st remained spread out in the mud all Sunday night, all Monday and Monday night till after midnight. Although the troops could plainly hear the Rebels whistling, etc., the latter did not dare advance upon them.[6]

Even when the scene is a quiet day in camp, Whitman does not ennoble the soldiers; instead he describes them with the precision of an attentive draftsman:

> Nearby was the camp of the 26th Pennsylvania, who have been out since the commencement of the war. I talked with a couple of the men, part of a squad around a fire, in the usual enclosure of green branches fencing three sides of a space perhaps twenty feet square—breaking the wind from north and east. Where there are boughs to be had, these sylvan corrals are to be met with in all the camps, some of them built very finely and making a picturesque appearance for a camp. They serve as the company kitchens and the same purpose of rendezvous of an evening that the public house, the reading room, or the engine house did at home . . .
>
> The tents of this camp were quite comfortable, such moderate weather as we are having now [December 1862]. One of the men came out of a tent close by, with a couple of slices of beef and some crackers, and commenced cooking the mess in a frying pan for his breakfast. It looked very good. Another man was waiting with similar articles to have the use of the frying pan . . .
>
> I thought, rough as it was, that men in health might endure it and get along with more comfort than most outsiders would suppose—as indeed the condition of the men around me was tolerable proof.
>
> The mass of our men in our army are young; it is an impressive sight to me to see the countless number of youths and boys. There is only a sprinkling of elderly men. On a parade at evening there you see them, poor lads, many of them already with the experience of the oldest veterans.[7]

Finally I read students another 1865 poem from "Drum-Taps." Whitman's sympathy for the young soldiers wounded and dying in battle fills the rhythmic, compelling lines of this poem (titled from its first line):

A march in the ranks hard-prest, and the road unknown,
A route through a heavy wood with muffled steps in the darkness,
Our army foil'd with loss severe, and the sullen remnant retreating,
Till after midnight glimmer upon us the lights of a dim-lighted
      building,
We come to an open space in the woods, and halt by the dim-lighted
      building,
'Tis a large old church at the crossingroads, now an impromptu
      hospital,
Entering but for a minute I see a sight beyond all the pictures and
      poems ever made,
Shadows of deepest, deepest black, just lit by moving candles and
      lamps,
And by one great pitchy torch stationary with wild red flame and
      clouds of smoke,
By these, crowds, groups of forms vaguely I see on the floor, some in
      the pews laid down,
At my feet more distinctly a soldier, a mere lad, in danger of bleeding
      to death, (he is shot in the abdomen,)
I stanch the blood temporarily, (the youngster's face is white as a lily,)
Then before I depart I sweep my eyes o'er the scene fain to absorb it all
      [. . .]
Then hear outside the orders given, *Fall in, my men, fall in*;
But first I bend to the dying lad, his eyes open, a half-smile gives he
      me,
Then the eyes close, calmly close, and I speed forth to the darkness,
Resuming, marching, ever in darkness marching, on in the ranks,
The unknown road still marching.[8]

Students often note the following phrases: "the road unknown," "shadows of deepest, deepest black," "wild red flame," "a mere lad in danger of bleeding to death," and "face is white as a lily." Whitman's contrast of light and dark reflects his own extreme emotion, suddenly brought to bear on the dying youth. And the lily he sees in the young face sanctifies this death in the midst of the "smell of ether, the odor of blood." The face "white as a lily" suggests a hope for resurrection. Whitman finds the war modern in its slaughter and size, but because he is living in the nineteenth century, he is not inured to such senseless destruction: he requires some meaning for the sacrifice.

Step Five: Fashioning the Poem

The next step is to write the choruses for the ballads. Depending on the students, I sometimes do a demonstration on the board, using Whitman's phrases suggested by members of the class. Because it's often hard to decide how much of Whitman's language to use in a line—or when to alter it to fit our purposes—I find that a demonstration can be very helpful. First I ask students to swap yesterday's notes and then to read aloud the phrases they like. Let's imagine that from this we have collected the following phrases and paraphrases on the board:

> by common consent and arm
> musketry so general
> on in the ranks
> a ruthless force
> flash of musket barrels
> sunrise cannon and one at sunset
> one great pitchy torch
> in pews laid down
> full length in mud
> dare advance
> youths with the experience of oldest veterans
> face white as a lily
> several dead bodies lay near
> men in old clothes and are dirty
> leave not the bridegroom quiet
> at my feet a soldier, a mere lad
> at the foot of the tree, amputated feet, arms, hands
> no happiness must he have for the bride
> the mass of the men in the army are young
> men dying upstairs and down
> no sleepers must sleep in those beds
> heap of amputated limbs
> our army foiled with severe loss
> orders given to fall in
> 27 hours of attack . . . everyone lying on their backs
> so shrill you bugles blow
> fresh graves of mostly officers
> shadows of deepest, deepest black
> names on barrel boards
> stuffed in the dust
> the eyes calmly closed in death

Playing around with the phrases—condensing and rearranging them, for instance—leads us to some unusual combinations:

Flash of sunrise cannon.
Youths dare advance.
White as a lily
in pews laid down.

Or:

Youths the highest veterans
consent and arm.
One great pitchy torch
full length in the mud.

The lines of the choruses in most ballads use lengths of between four and seven syllables. But reading the expansive Whitman can make everyone feel like using much longer, sweeping lines. "Make a shape that suits you," I tell the students. "If you want to try long lines, add your own words to the phrases you've taken from Whitman." I also tell them that they may use their own words and ideas, or look to Whitman for historical details, and then recast them in their own words. In any case, students should try to make the chorus suggest the essence of the photograph.

The verses, on the other hand, relate a short narrative of events suggested by the photograph. The narrative can be fairly simple, with the photo recording one moment in the narrative. Each verse can disclose a bit more of the imagined events involving the imaginary characters in the narrative. The chorus then comments on the underlying mood and meaning of the developing narrative.

Even with extensive preparation, students sometimes have trouble getting started. In that case, I read aloud several Civil War ballads by other students to show them how the choruses and verses can work together. Often these examples describe some of the same photographs the present class is using, which also helps them move from brainstorming to drafting.

Once the students start writing, they usually need at least thirty minutes to draft a full poem. As they work, I move around the classroom to answer questions. Sometimes I help students decipher a photograph or refer them to a section of a reference book. I also remind them of a strategy we discussed, that of altering the chorus to indicate a change in the narrative. Students also try out ideas on me as they begin to enter the lives of the people in the photographs. Sometimes it's helpful to encourage them to invent people who are not shown, such as a family for the deserted Dunlop House in Petersburg, or a wife or mother at home to whom a soldier is writing.

As the writing emerges, students often show me what they have so far. I respond by emphasizing what I like, occasionally pointing out modern slang that seems anachronistic or suggesting what could happen next in their ballads. Students sometimes ask to see the student examples again.

The following poems by eleventh grade humanities students are fine examples of the brief evocative narratives and choruses the photographs can inspire. The first poem below, titled "First Minnesota Squad—After Fair Oaks," refers to a picture (fig. 9) of a cannon looming in the foreground. In mid-ground, men stand idly by, with timbers and carts strewn around them. In the distance an old frame house seems to survey the quiet of the field where 400 men were buried after battle:

First Minnesota Squad—After Fair Oaks

Steel cannons lie silent,
Helpless in the aftermath,
No comfort for mourners.

Under cloudless skies
Docile cows wander.
Frame house stands silent,
Looking upon the morbid scene.
Immune from this disease of war.

Lone soldier prays,
"End this hell of pain."
Distant soldier strays:
The frame house speaks of home.

Under cloudless skies
Docile cows wander.
Frame house stands silent,
Looking upon the morbid scene.
Immune from this disease of war.

The cold, hard ground
Houses cold, decaying bodies.
Over four hundred perished.

—*Christina Seagren and Bridget DeFrank*

Another student poem finds the story in the photograph of the Dunlop House from Petersburg, Virginia, 1864:

Fig. 9: Squad of the First Minnesota Volunteer Infantry after the Battle of Fair Oaks, 1862.

What Might Have Been

Through a broken window
Past shattered shards of glass
Lies a blurry image
Of what might have been.

Guns sound. Union army.
The shelling has begun.
First one hits. Buildings shake.
Fear spreads through the town.

Through a broken window
Past shattered shards of glass
Lies a blurry image
Of what might have been.

Broken bricks, fire blazing.
Faint sound heard, child crying.
Loud he cries, no one hears
Til death claims its prey.

Through a broken window
Past shattered shards of glass
Lies a blurry image
Of what might have been.

Cannons stop. Night has come.
Dog whimpers. Master fears.
Woman stands by the glass
Looking out at death.

Through a broken window,
Past shattered shards of glass,
Lies a blurry image
Of what should have been.

> —*Bill Shepherd and Dave Barden*

The choruses in these poems are composed of the students' own words. Bill and Dave divided up the work, with one responsible for the verses and the other for the choruses. I like the way the one-word change in the last line emphasizes the poignancy of the family who have watched their house collapse around them.

In another set of poems written by eleventh and twelfth grade students, the choruses are composed of Whitman's own words. The poem below is based on a group photo of men in front of the standard Union camp tent called the "Sibley tent," which housed around fifteen men:

Twenty-Four Hours to Attack

The mass of men in the army are young.
Men in old clothes that are dirty.
Orders given to fall in, twenty-four hours to attack.
The youngster's face white as a lily.

Like the sick man standing in back
too proud to lie on his back
when his country needs him,
patriotic, though facing death.

The mass of men in the army are young.
Men in old clothes that are dirty.
Orders given to fall in, twenty hours to attack.
The youngster's face white as a lily.

Unlike the bearded man,
a veteran of many battles,
nonchalantly sharpening his knife.
Waiting, preparing for battle.

The mass of men in the army are young.
Men in old clothes that are dirty.
Orders given to fall in, sixteen hours to attack.
The youngster's face white as a lily.

The artist, drawing the men,
silent, not wanting to break
the quiet meditating of the troops.
Wondering if he is sketching already dead men.

The mass of men in the army are young.
Men in old clothes that are dirty.
Orders given to fall in, eight hours to attack.
The youngster's face white as a lily.

The youngster, not yet having seen "the elephant,"
writes out a will, mailing it home.

Scared to die,
But will for his country.

The mass of men in the army are young.
Men in old clothes that are dirty.
Orders given to fall in, zero hours to attack.
The youngster's face white as a lily.

The battle is over.
The Yankees are victorious.
The Rebels in retreat.
The survivors gather around the flag.

The mass of men in the army are young.
Men in old clothes that are dirty.
Orders given to fall in, twenty-four hours to attack.
The youngster's face, grim with determination.

—*Tom Pesta, Joe Lounsbery, and Pat Nesburg*

These students created choruses to indicate the countdown to battle, and then in the last line of the chorus they changed the fearful youth with face "white as a lily" to a youth "grim with determination" after he has fought a battle.

In the following poem, students describe the destruction of a Virginia landmark and suggest the failure of secessionist rhetoric. Again, the chorus is drawn from Whitman's phrases, with additions and changes by the students:

Chambersburg Court House

So shrill you bugles blow,
your tone riddles my bare bones.
Several dead bodies lie near,
their eyes closed, calmly closed.
Twenty-seven hours of attack
stripped years upon years away.
Blow you bugles blow.

Men, brave, arrogant men
once filled these walls—
cries of war
boast of victory
bounced from stone to stone,
memories of their forefathers
etched deep in my bones.

So shrill you bugles blow,
your tone riddles my bare bones.
Several dead bodies lie near,
their eyes closed, calmly closed.
Twenty-seven hours of attack
stripped years upon years away.
Blow you bugles blow.

A crack of thunder,
cannons roared.
I stood in pain
weeping.
Feelings, memories drift like smoke
from under my crumpled skin.
The voices heard no more,
the wind is chilling.
Death predominant.

So shrill you bugles blow,
your tone riddles my bare bones.
Several dead bodies lay near,
their eyes closed, calmly closed.
Twenty-seven hours of attack
stripped years upon years away.
Blow you bugles blow.

Years gone by.
A child stumbles through my remains.
He gazes in wonder at my exposed flesh.
He would never know me
or understand my past—
the boasts of men
turned to ghosts
lost.

So shrill you bugles blow,
your tone riddles my bare bones.
The dead bodies are gone,
their eyes closed calmly forever.
Twenty-seven hours of attack
stripped my existence away.
Blow you bugles blow.

       —Brian Young and Kate Terwey

This description of the attack is rather general until the last stanza. But by the end, the authors themselves have gone through the harrowing experience of identifying with the fighting men. The attack has "stripped my existence away," they write, testifying to the power of imagination to recreate war's bloodshed and death.

Writing poetry about the Civil War requires the writer to bridge the distance between now and then. After the exercise, students have commented that they now think more closely about the possibility of war in their own time. When we study history at arm's length, with more emphasis on facts than on individual human responses, such connections are not as likely to happen. The past remains distant, not quite real, safe. But when we invite imagination to enter our study of history, we open the door to character, emotion, irony, and the magic of metaphorical language. We identify individuals, as do the three authors of "Twenty-Four Hours to Attack": the proud, wounded patriot; the veteran who "nonchalantly sharpens his knife"; the artist already sensing death on the faces of his subjects; and the youth who writes his will before his first battle. Historical figures are no longer a faceless group. We become aware of diversity, and of our responsibility to judge carefully any generalization about past or present peoples.

Students also come to recognize that the Civil War, like all wars, affected people whose stories have remained unrecorded. Imagination then does the work that facts cannot. Through metaphor and irony, the students' poems convey the terrible price of the war, the shallowness of its boasts, the extent of its destruction. "Immune from this disease of war," write Christina Seagren and Bridget DeFrank. By comparing war to a disease, they suggest how hard it is for any individual to escape infection. The "cries of war/boast of victory" etch deep in dead bones an inheritance of egotism and slavery far from the orators' intentions.

Whitman's rich and evocative language helps the students to realize in their own writing the power of irony and metaphor. Notice how Brian Young and Kate Terwey link Whitman's "So shrill you bugles blow" to another metaphor: "Your tone riddles my dead bones," suggesting both the riddle of an unanswerable question and bullets striking a body. Whitman's flourishes of patriotic imagery, mixed with his sensitive descriptions of destruction, provide a valuable model for the students and help them bring facts together with their own creative use of language. They are more ironic than Whitman, reflecting the difficulty many of us now have of imagining a just cause for war. Under the surface of our poems about the past lie our own attitudes. As we write about history, we discover ourselves.

EXERCISE TWO
Writing from the Point of View of an Animal at an Historic Moment

(For junior high to adult. Note: the subject matter I focus on later in this exercise—lynching—might be too strong for some students, not because it's any more violent than what they regularly see on TV, but because it is real. The writing ideas, however, could easily be applied to any event.)

Like the boy in the fable who saw that the emperor wore no clothes, and instantly said so, young children who haven't learned the rules of adult decorum will point out things that adults never would. At a certain stage, children are very good at unobstructed observation. The idea of this exercise is to imagine an animal, observing the world without human preconceptions, an animal capable of describing in words what it sees.

Step One: Deciding on an Event, Fictional or Real

Harper Lee's *To Kill a Mockingbird* is widely read in junior high and high school classes. In it are good examples of two "innocent" children faced with an historical moment. Jem and Scout Finch attend the trial of Tom Robinson, a black man accused of raping Mayella, a white woman. Their father, Atticus Finch, is the defense attorney. Scout and Jem are in an unusual position because, although their father has taught them to uphold the southern white tradition of good manners and benevolent paternalism toward people of lesser status, he has also made them quite aware of the South's code of racial segregation. Thus, the children are positioned by their youth and inexperience and by what they have learned from their father to see around the edges of the southern code to its meanness and inconsistency, as they might see around any other complicated and rigid social code.

For students who have read *To Kill a Mockingbird*, imagining an animal in the courtroom (or any of the other scenes surrounding the trial) would allow them to explore more fully and creatively the ramifications of the southern code. An animal would be even more in the dark about the social and political rationale for the way Tom Robinson is treated than are the children. The animal might even see some inconsistency in the way the children behave: they understand Tom's innocence, for example, but they do nothing directly to proclaim it. Maybe the dog could inadvertently help prove that Robinson, with his withered arm, could not possibly have given Mayella a black eye.

For classes who continue working with either *To Kill a Mockingbird* or with the more general subjects of race trials or lynching in American history, the following information might prove helpful.

The word *lynching* comes from Charles Lynch, a Virginia farmer and patriot who during the American Revolution led vigilante bands to hunt down and hang thieves, outlaws, and loyalists. Though not unique to this country, lynching is most often associated with the states of the Old South and the border states of the Civil War, where it was most often perpetrated on black men by mobs of white men.

In his book *The Mind of the South*, W. J. Cash describes the geographical statistics this way:

> Of the grand total of 3,397 Negroes lynched in the nation from the beginning of 1882 until the close of 1938, only 366 were lynched outside the former Confederate States, and of these 185 were lynched in the border states.[9]

What happened in the South during Reconstruction to foster this onslaught of violence? After the Civil War, northerners and freed slaves assumed the political power held by southern whites before the war. Amidst the economic and social upheaval following the war, these southern whites took the opportunity to vent their animosity against black men. As slaves, black men had been considered valuable property and, though they had no legal rights, had often been protected by their commercial worth. But with the end of slavery, southern blacks lost their monetary value. In addition, many white southerners blamed them for the war and the South's defeat.

Scholars have also suggested that white southerners may have had a guilty conscience toward blacks, and may have feared that the sexual aggression that some white owners had practiced on black women during the slave era would rebound on them once the blacks were free. This helps explain why many whites reacted violently to how freed black men related to white women.[10]

In the anarchic conditions of the Reconstruction period, there was no tradition of civil rights or legal constraints to deter lynch mobs. In fact, government in the states of the former Confederacy took years to recover power. Gradually, southern whites regained control of the state governments, southern blacks emigrated en masse to northern jobs during World War I, and the South made something of an economic recovery. Saner, more humane ideas came to the fore. Lynching declined.

Yet it still occurred, and not only in the South. On June 15, 1920, in Duluth, Minnesota, a state with a black population of 0.4%, three black men were lynched by a white mob that had blasted a hole in the police station wall and dragged them through it. The cause: a white girl's accusation that six black men had raped her. Evidently, even in northern states the presumed sexual threat of black men—and the confidence that illegal action would not be prosecuted—could stoke a lynching.

As in other cases, the National Association for the Advancement of Colored People protested the 1920 lynching in Duluth and sponsored a thorough investigation of the charges against the murdered men. The NAACP found that the girl had concocted the rape story, and that the three hanged men had no connection to her, but were swept up in the mob's frenzy; the sheriff and extra police officers had made determined attempts to prevent the mob from removing the black prisoners.[11] Perhaps the resistance displayed by legal officers helped at least to contain the riot, unlike many other lynchings in which mob rage led to violent attacks on entire black neighborhoods, as an attempted lynching did in Tulsa, Oklahoma, as late as 1921.[12]

During the 1920s, 1930s and 1940s, the NAACP lobbied for national legislation to prosecute police and local officials who condoned lynching and the mob leaders who instigated it, but it was not until the Civil Rights Act of 1968 that the acts of lynch mobs were finally outlawed by federal law.

Step Two: Seeing an Event from the Point of View of an Animal

Some of the finest wit in our literature comes from writers who have blended an animal and a human point of view. Aesop's fables, based on the behavior and instincts of animals, develop morals that apply to human affairs. Chaucer's Chanticleer and Pertolet in *The Canterbury Tales* strut and peck across their farmyard with the panache of refined courtiers. Contemporary poet Lawrence Ferlinghetti's witty poem, "Dog," is another example. Ferlinghetti describes a free-thinking animal roaming the streets of San Francisco in the 1950s. As the dog takes note of things human and canine, Ferlinghetti slyly criticizes human pretensions and politics:

> The dog trots freely in the street
> and sees reality
> and the things he sees
> are bigger than himself
> and the things he sees
> are his reality
> Drunks in doorways
> Moons on trees

The dog trots freely thru the street
and the things he sees
are smaller than himself
Fish on newsprint
Ants in holes
Chickens in Chinatown windows
their heads a block away
The dog trots freely in the street
and the things he smells
smell something like himself
The dog trots freely in the street
past puddles and babies
cats and cigars
poolrooms and policemen
He doesn't hate cops
He merely has no use for them
and he goes past them
and past the dead cows hung up whole
in front of the San Francisco Meat Market
He would rather eat a tender cow
than a tough policeman
though either might do
And he goes past the Romeo Ravioli Factory
and past Coit's Tower
and past Congressman Doyle
He's afraid of Coit's Tower
but he's not afraid of Congressman Doyle
although what he hears is very discouraging
very depressing
very absurd
to a sad young dog like himself
to a serious dog like himself
But he has his own free world to live in
His own fleas to eat
He will not be muzzled
Congressman Doyle is just another
fire hydrant
to him
The dog trots freely in the street
and has his own dog's life to live
and to think about
and to reflect upon
touching and tasting and testing everything
investigating everything
without benefit of perjury
a real realist

with a real tale to tell
and a real tail to tell it with
a real live
        barking
               democratic dog
engaged in real
            free enterprise
with something to say
                about ontology
something to say
          about reality
              and how to see it
                       and how to hear it
with his head cocked sideways
              at streetcorners
as if he is just about to have
             his picture taken
                  for Victor Records
          listening for
              His Master's Voice
      and looking
            like a living questionmark
                into the
                great gramaphone
             of puzzling existence
with its wondrous hollow horn
      which always seems
just about to spout forth
               some Victorious answer
            to everything[13]

I read this poem aloud in class, and then discuss it with students. I tell them how much I like the jaunty recurring line, "The dog trots freely in the street," which mimics the dog's motion. We also discuss the dog's-eye view of some things most humans wouldn't see—fish on newsprint, ants in holes. The dog responds differently to things than would most humans—"He's afraid of Coit's Tower / but he's not afraid of Congressman Doyle."

As soon as the students have a good grasp of how Ferlinghetti uses the dog's point of view, I have them start thinking about how they might apply a similar strategy to writing about an historic event such as a trial, a lynching, a demonstration, a protest, or a sit-down strike. There are many public events that express social, economic, or political conditions and that would provide rich material for the animal to witness and comment upon. I encourage students to pick an animal they like or are particularly interested in, but to remember that certain choices might be too restrictive; for example, a whale probably wouldn't have much to say about the Dust Bowl drought.

Step Three: Gathering Information about an Historic Event

The first time I did this exercise (with a ninth grade civics class), I brought in pictures of five racist hangings in Minnesota. I was amazed to discover so many. My students were also shocked that such things had happened in towns where they lived or visited. "There aren't many blacks here," they said. They were right, but they had forgotten about Minnesota's Native Americans.

The earliest hanging I found in my research was what newspapers called the "Execution of the Thirty-Eight Sioux Indians at Mankato, Minnesota, December 26, 1862." The most recent was the Duluth lynching of three black men, mentioned above. In another hanging, two more Sioux leaders of the 1862 uprising were put to death, and in the two other lynchings, single black men—one described as a "rape fiend" and the other a reputed killer of a sheriff—were murdered by mobs of whites. All five pictures showed the bodies strung up and, in all but one, the hanged men were surrounded by spectators. I made enough photocopies of the photographs to give one to each pair of students in the class.

Using pictures of public events helps students identify details they can then use in their poems. They can begin to imagine what a dog or pigeon would do in a particular scene; details of a past era—vehicles, clothing styles, architecture—become immediately recognizable, and with the teacher's help in labeling a "bustle" or a "Model T" or a "warehouse circa 1890" or a "cupola," the students can infuse their writing with the cultural flavor of a particular period.

Some of the photographs of lynchings that I used with this ninth grade class might disturb some students. (The classroom teacher and I agreed that the pictures weren't any worse than what students see in movies.) The subject of lynching might be too grisly for certain students or classes to handle. Of course there are many other kinds of historic events that would easily lend themselves to this exercise.

Take, for example, the baseball games played by women in the All-American Girls Professional Baseball League from 1942 to 1954. In many ways, these games were historically significant: they marked a shift in behavior, dress, roles, and attitudes that reflected the effect of World War II on the entire American population. The "girl" ball players wore short skirts over shorts, with knee socks. After they slid into base, their thighs often were bruised, scraped, and bloody with what players call "strawberries." Yet their original owner, Philip K. Wrigley, chewing-gum magnate and owner of the Chicago Cubs, insisted that they retain their feminine allure with their short skirts, charm-school make-up and manners, and chaperones. Fans who were used to cheering men's teams often didn't know what to make of these muscular, spitting, swearing girls. Just as women entered factories to make airplanes during the war, so the girls of the League challenged stereotypes about women's abilities, roles, and behavior.[14] How would an animal accustomed to such stereotypes respond to the girl ball players? With some background reading about the League and pictures from articles, a class could be ready after one class period to bring that animal into the ball park and find out. It's a pretty wild idea.

Whatever the historic event, I hand out a list that identifies the photographs. Each picture is numbered and keyed to a few sentences about the image. The students pair up to choose a picture and to interview each other about what they see (as in the Whitman exercise earlier in this chapter).

Step Four: Mapping an Animal's Experience (Optional)

Some students may need a little help getting started. If they can't decide what their animal might do in a given situation, I have them make a word map, with the name of an animal in the center of a piece of paper. Around this I have them add some adjectives that describe the animal. For example, here is a word map I made about a tomcat:

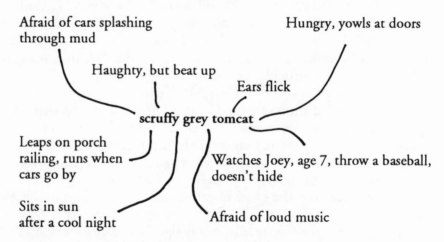

The next procedure—and it can be a bit tricky—is to transpose these modern details back into the era of the event, adding a political slant ("political" in the widest sense of the word). To do this, I have students make a second word map for the event. As an example, here is my second word map for the cat, imagining him at the execution of thirty-eight Sioux in 1862:

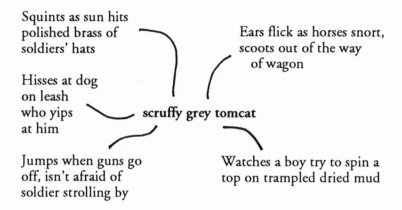

Squints as sun hits
polished brass of
soldiers' hats

Ears flick as horses snort,
scoots out of the way
of wagon

Hisses at dog
on leash
who yips
at him

scruffy grey tomcat

Jumps when guns go
off, isn't afraid of
soldier strolling by

Watches a boy try to spin a
top on trampled dried mud

Step Five: Reading Student Examples

Before students begin writing, they often find it helpful to hear work by other student writers who have tried this exercise in one form or another. The following piece by ninth grade civics student Shelly Rapacz describes the execution of two Sioux chiefs, Shakopee and Medicine Bottle. She adopts the point of view of a dog at Fort Snelling, where the execution took place. Chief Shakopee's actual words conclude her poem.

The Fall of Shakopee and Medicine Bottle

Cold dismal day,
clouds hang overhead and the cold
bites my nose.
Sitting under the field bin
guarding my master's livestock.
On that 11th day of November in 1865,
two Indian chiefs were executed
across the large court. I cross
trying to get a better look at
what a mob is forming and
plotting. I duck under a wagon
hoping not to get trampled.
Two men grab the chains that
bound the Indians to the wagon
and scarred their bodies.
Then slipped nooses over
their heads and the men

heaved. The lifeless bodies
hung swaying in the wind.
I recall, trotting back
to the corral, Chief Shakopee
said, pointing to the train,
"As the white man comes in,
the Indian goes out."

Shelly wrote this poem using only details from a photograph—a buggy with huge wheels, delicately outlined with light; the crowd in one dark mass; in the center, the two bodies swinging—and her imagination.

The following poem by eleventh grade English student Roger Lowe is more in the style of Ferlinghetti's "Dog." His poem gives a definite personality to the dog, and interprets the dog's situation in terms of human divisiveness:

The world is tough.
The food that the shop owner,
Mister George, left is gone. Where has
it gone, who drank it? It's cold
out and snow is falling.
    The world is tough.

There's another. He is in my
alley. Maybe, just maybe he is
trying to take the food away. Or maybe
just passing through. I stop, we
fight until the death to protect what
is ours.
    The world is tough.

There goes Puff, the rich cat, with
a family to take care of her. I
must take care of myself or die.
Just like the funny nice man Disco,
he dances with himself when he walks
down the street. He lives all by himself.
    The world is tough.

There goes my dinner. The garbage
truck took it away. Now I will
have to find a rat or a mouse to
eat. I wish that I had someone
to take care of me.
    The world is tough.

In the next poem, by eighth grade teacher Pat Riley, lynchings become anonymous events told from the point of view of the tree where the bodies have hung:

The Lynchings

My old oak tree's limbs are strong and sturdy.
I am a fine example of my species.
I have a history, my roots run deep.
My story is not pretty
nor told loud or often.
What a burden I bear.
No one asks
No one wonders if I care.
As I stand among those like me
I wonder—Will it be me?
The noise, the feet invade my grove.
I hear them coming, but I cannot escape.
There is nothing I can do to stop the swinging.
I'm always available, an unwilling
participant. I am forced
to listen to the crowd,
their laughter, their profanity, their insults.
I cannot respond.
No women do I see, I feel their presence.
No one notices my beauty.
No one notices my contribution.
I am left with the scrapes and the rope scars.
I am left to wallow in the mess
and misery that remain
limiting what can grow in the world around me.
The awful burden I bear,
The guilt of society, a society who fears
revenge, a society who maintains control.
Will no one come and take
this burden from me,
the sturdy oak tree.

Sometimes students don't want to write about a heavy historical event. The following poem by fifth grade student Dane Anderson sets a good tone for writing about an up-beat experience:

The sleazy teal trots down the street.
He runs into a vet walking home from work.
The sleazy teal trots down the street.

The cat notices it is going to rain so
he starts home for the day.
The sleazy teal trots down the street.
On the way home the teal runs
into a worm trying to crawl up the curb.
The sleazy teal trots down the street.
The teal finds a car full of doughnuts
so he jumps in the open window and eats
as many as he can.
The sleazy teal trots down the street.

Step Six: Drafting the Account from the Animal's Point of View

With the details of the animal's behavior and the details of the event in hand, students are ready to write either poems or prose accounts of the events from the animal's point of view. I urge them to use Ferlinghetti's poem as a model, alternating things only the animal would do with its reactions to the presence of humans. Unlike "Dog," their writing will have more of a narrative line because it will report some of the sequence of events that make up the larger situation the animal is witnessing. So the students' writing should move toward a culmination, as when a "girl" ball player slides home or a lynched body rises into the tree. Students who choose to write poems may also want to use a recurring line, such as Ferlinghetti's "The dog trots freely in the street." This line can vary to indicate a change in locale or attitude.

Perhaps the most important strategy to bring off in the writing is the combination of the animal's innocence with its unwitting commentary on the human situation. This combination will probably have the flavor of irony or, in more light-hearted situations, of humor. "Try to react as your particular animal would," I explain to the students, "but at the same time remember what point you want to make about the event, what attitude of yours you want the animal to express." Students probably understand this strategy better simply by hearing Ferlinghetti's poem than they do by hearing my exhortations, but I give them both.

As students do this exercise, they automatically raise a question they cannot answer except in imagination: what would *they* have thought or done on the occasion described in their poems? The animal persona can be a surprisingly good way for students to see the past from an angle that is both their own and someone (or something) else's, and that is a primary goal not only of the historian, but also of the imaginative writer.

EXERCISE THREE
From Bystander to Sympathizer to Activist

In this exercise, students write pieces that help them learn more about the transition between looking at history and taking part in it. For purposes of discussion, I'd like to focus here on women, racism, and the civil rights movement, though any subject involving the history of a social cause would work well. (For high school to adult.)

The mobs involved in racist attacks in this country rarely included women. But did women condone mob action? Of course some of them did. Others must have objected, but until they began to speak out and organize, the degree of their objection was hard to measure. In the nineteenth century, women's anti-slavery campaigns were often linked to campaigns for women's suffrage. For some white women, working to abolish slavery made them aware of their own servitude. In the 1930s and '40s, many of the anti-lynching groups formed in the South were composed of white women.[15] How did women growing up in the racist South achieve the awareness necessary for reform? Or, to put the question more broadly, how does an individual cross the threshold of mere sympathy and move into activism on behalf of a cause?

To find examples of this process, it's good to look for writers who write in the first person, who not only show us what they believe and how they behave, but who also invest their public politics with autobiography.

Alice Walker's essay "The Civil Rights Movement: What Good Was It?" contains a four-page account of her awakening. As a teenager in Georgia, she recalls, "I walked . . . young and well hidden among the slums, among [black] people who did not exist—either in books or in films or in the government of their own lives."[16] She felt invisible in a world dominated by whites; she "gazed longingly through the window of the corner drugstore where white youngsters sat on stools in air-conditioned comfort and drank Cokes and nibbled ice-cream cones."

At the time, her mother bought a TV to watch the soap operas. "In every scene she saw," Alice Walker's mother imagined herself "with her braided hair turned blond, her two hundred pounds compressed into a sleek size-seven dress, her rough dark skin smooth and *white*." When this fantasy evaporated, "there was always a tragic look of surprise on her face. Then she would sigh and go out to the kitchen looking lost and unsure of herself." Writing her memoir, Walker was angered by the system that completely ignored her mother, an honest woman who raised eight children, who was faithful to her husband, and who never tasted liquor. But her mother never blamed the white system "for making her believe what they wanted her to believe: that if she did not look like them, think like them, be sophisticated and corrupt-for-comfort's sake like them she was a nobody. Black was not a color on my mother; it was a shield that made her invisible." It was a paralyzing stereotype.

Latent at the time, Walker's anger burst forth when, for the first time, she saw a black on TV who was not a menial: it was Martin Luther King, Jr., under arrest and being escorted into a police van while singing "We Shall Overcome." This incident suddenly transformed Walker's life. It gave her an image of black Americans fighting to "become whatever we wanted to become" and made her aware of her power both to choose among many identities for herself and to replace this choice if it no longer suited her.

Step One: Defining a Stereotypical Character

To help students write a first-person account about awakening from seeing people as stereotypes, I've read them the fourth chapter of John Steinbeck's *Cannery Row*. This brief chapter begins with a regular occurrence in the neighborhood: every evening, an "old Chinaman" walks down the hill, crosses the street to the beach, and "disappear[s] among the piles and steel posts which support the piers." At dawn, the old Chinaman retraces his steps. "People, sleeping, heard his flapping shoe go by and they awakened for a moment. It had been happening for years, but no one ever got used to him." The narrator explains that some neighborhood residents think that the old man is God and others think he is Death. The children do not taunt him, "for he carrie[s] a little cloud of fear about with him."

Although sympathetic with the children who were tempted to tease the old man, the narrator recounts that one boy, Andy, braced himself one evening and "marched behind the old man singing in a shrill falsetto, 'Ching-Chong Chinaman sitting on a rail—'Long came a white man an' chopped off his tail.'" This taunt brought the old man to a halt. Andy stopped too:

> What happened then Andy was never able to explain or to forget. For the eyes spread out until there was no Chinaman. And then it was one eye—one huge brown eye as big as a church door. Andy looked through the shiny transparent brown door and through it he saw a lonely countryside, flat for miles but ending against a row of fantastic mountains shaped like cows' and dogs' heads and tents and mushrooms. There was low coarse grass on the plain and here and there a little mound. And a small animal like a woodchuck sat on each mound. And the loneliness—the desolate cold aloneness of the landscape made Andy whimper because there wasn't anybody at all in the world and he was left.[17]

The people of Cannery Row don't see the old Chinaman as an individual; they see him only as an other-worldly symbol; the climactic moment teaches Andy never to taunt the old Chinaman again.

Step Two: Describing a Particular Stereotypical Character

The children in *Cannery Row* know the old Chinaman only by his outward appearance and by his routine behavior. To help the students choose someone comparable in their lives, I ask them to think of places where they go after school or on weekends. "Think of a face you've seen often, someone you would identify as 'the girl at the store' or 'the guy who's always shooting baskets at the gym' or 'the old lady who walks her dog.' If you know the person's name, write it in the middle of your paper for brainstorming. Then make a word map around the name. On the map include small details of the person's dress, gestures, and repeated actions. Make sure you include lots of details of how the person looks."

For students, seeing others as stereotypes is one thing; it is harder for them to see *themselves* as stereotypes. But all children have, at one time or another, been told that they're "this" or "that." Perhaps they're currently trapped in a heavy stereotype—such as "teenager." For this step of the exercise, students could place themselves at the center of the word map, or assume a stereotypical character and use it instead. Either way, it's best if the word map be from a first-person point of view.

In doing this exercise, I chose to write about a woman working for civil rights in the 1960s. Two good sources about civil rights activists turned out to be Anne Moody's *Coming of Age in Mississippi, An Autobiography*,[18] which portrays an embattled black civil rights worker, and Alice Walker's novel *Meridian*,[19] about a young black woman who is assigned a typing job by a male black colleague, who later preys on her sexual compliance. Sara Evans's *Personal Politics*,[20] which describes how feminism grew partly out of the civil rights movement, is also an inspiring resource.

After reading these books, I made a word map for the character of the civil rights worker/secretary, to help imagine myself inside the civil rights movement:

Not used to office
work, but spent
Saturdays at a
settlement house
in the city where her college is located

College student from
the North, majors in history

civil rights Girl Friday

Doesn't like the typical
subordinate secretary
yet fantasizes herself
in three-inch heels
and filmy blouse,

wants the excitement of marching
believes she can help end segregation

taking dictation sitting on her
boss's knee. Hates herself for
imagining this, gets angry.

Step Three: Finding a Setting, Drafting a Beginning

Actually, it's often not necessary to "find" a setting: one usually comes along with the imagined character. Likewise, other characters automatically deepen the setting. Crucial to writing about oneself in a stereotyped role is imagining other characters, particularly those who are perpetrating the stereotype. The following example (a first-person narrative I wrote) presents college students from the North who have gone down South during the summer to help with the civil rights movement:

We are the only ones typing in a room full of organizers. We are the only women working in the civil rights headquarters in this small Mississippi town, summer, 1964. Men jabber, plan, demand, "Girl, when will you finish typing that petition?"

My friend Joyce and I came South from our northern college with a busload of other students to register black people to vote. My grandfather organized for the garment workers' union fifty years ago. I hoped to follow his lead, to go out canvassing, to bring justice to the South. But we two "girls" are stuck in the office while the "men" risk their lives on lonesome dusty roads. "It's too dangerous for you," they tell us.

It's hot in this small office above the hardware store. I wish I could get out of here, but I feel chained to the typewriter, imprisoned by the need to make a difference in the lives of the poor black people we saw on the bus coming into town. This summer job is nothing like Marilyn Monroe's in the movie *The Seven-Year Itch*. Marilyn came to New York to be a typist, but you never saw her work. Instead, she was flirting with the "summer bachelor" whose wife and kid had gone to the country. Marilyn, with the sexy voice, the skirt that swirls up over the grate, and the sly, sleepy eyes, didn't look like she'd ever worked.

Joyce winks at me, yanks a third piece of white paper out of the roller, and balls it up. Neither of us can type. Is this what I went to college for? Fingers stick to the keys and shoulders hurt. The Peter Pan collar of my college blouse scratches against my throat. I don't have enough bosom to make unbuttoning worth it. Who would I flirt with anyway: bossy Negro guys from here, bossy white boys from New York just like the ones from Hebrew class in fifth grade. If I didn't care so much for the movement, I'd take the first bus home.

Step Four: Countering the Stereotype

One way to have characters break out of the stereotype is to have a forceful personality explode onto the scene. A leader may appear suddenly, as Dr. King did to Alice Walker. The leader can be modeled on a famous person, or even on another person the narrator has been casting as a stereotype. For example, if a student is writing about a character he sees occasionally on a playground, and developing this stereotyped character as a black jock who cares only for showing off and one-upping other players, the character may surprise the narrator by showing a side of himself not typical of the jock stereotype.

Sara Evans writes that for many young female civil rights workers, the inspiring figures were black women from the local communities. She quotes civil rights organizer Charles Sherrod, who knew a woman called Mama Dolly:

> "Mama Dolly" . . . was a seventy-year-old gray-haired lady who could pick more cotton, slop more pigs, plow more ground, chop more wood and do a hundred more things better than the best farmer in the area.[21]

When it came to political activism, women like Mama Dolly refused to kowtow to either segregation or second-class womanhood.

Using the example of Mama Dolly, I imagined the following scene for my piece about the civil rights typist:

> Into the office bustles Mrs. Jencks, a small black woman in veiled hat and blue raincoat. She carries an umbrella with a long, pointed tip. The end jabs into the knot of chattering men, and selects Sylvester, one of the young black organizers.
>
> Joyce and I have seen Mrs. Jencks in church, where she plays the organ and directs the choir. We also know her from canvassing meetings where she argues with the pastor, his face glistening with sweat as her sharp voice challenges his fear of what the local Klan will do.
>
> With the end of her umbrella hiking up Sylvester's white collar, Mrs. Jencks marches him over to the desk where Joyce and I are typing. He's half laughing, half angry. She tells us to get right up, saying that Sylvester

can type better than anyone. She knows because before there were any pretty girls from up North, Sylvester typed the church bulletin and did a dandy job.

"You're coming with me," she orders, and pulls Joyce and me outside. "You're gonna drive me to visit three ladies down the road. You'll like their spunk, honey," she says.

Sprung from the hot office, out on the glaring sidewalk with Mrs. Jencks, we can't quite keep up with her quick pace. She sweeps past a parked patrol car with a highway patrol officer in tall boots and wide-brimmed hat leaning against it. "How do, Mr. John," she nods. We sink into her shadow, feeling his eyes follow us from behind mirrored dark glasses.

Later, in the Chevy, she leans across to admit that she's scared of him. Mr. John is mean to dogs and Negroes; his work makes her sick. But she's not going to stop until someone catches her.

I take my eyes off the wide fields and the sun glare, and I study Mrs. Jencks close up. Her jaw is set, lower lip stuck out, dewlaps hang down to her neck. Her skin looks grey and tired, but her eyes are full of humor. "Don't you let those boys do you like that," she works her mouth into a sly smile. "Don't you go hiding yourselves."

My eyes flick to the rearview mirror where I see Joyce's round blue eyes surprised. She sees me watching her and smiles.

Step Five: Achieving the Transformation

As students write themselves into the historical moment of this exercise, they need to imagine their characters being transformed. To express this inner shift, students need to describe moments that correspond to small, psychological shifts. We break out of stereotypes in stages, moving from one level of recognition to another, sometimes slowly, sometimes very quickly. Here are two strategies of dramatic and descriptive writing that will help:

1) As discussed before, *imagine a disruption* of the usual stereotype. In *Cannery Row*, Andy dares to disrupt the routine of the old Chinaman, dares the stereotype of death or God that people have created for him to come alive and show some human emotion. Alice Walker was startled to find a black (Martin Luther King, Jr.) on TV in a role that was not subordinate. I have imagined that an old woman bosses around the young men in the office, and instructs one of them to do a "girl's" job.

2) *Create symptoms* of emotion or thoughts that contradict the stereotype. Ordinarily a white patrolman would not have frightened me, the narrator of my small drama. But as my allegiance to the black movement moves out of the office onto the street, I assume the status of a black and cringe from the threat he represents.

Mrs. Jencks's courage is my shield. Once in the car, safe from the disapproving eyes of the white world, I am freer to investigate her courage. I see fear and determination expressed in her face. Her fear matches my own. The determination and humor she then offers me counter the fear and show me another way to define "woman" and "activist." My awakening has begun.

Before moving on to the next step, I'd like to offer a word of caution about writing about politically or morally charged subjects. Sometimes it's possible to be on the "right" side of an issue and still write stereotypically. Most of us don't approve of taking drugs or of lynching, but writing about them should be more than a knee-jerk expression of our dislike. We should try to see the situation in all its complexity; for example, the people who get swept into drug taking or lynching are not wrong in *everything* they do. The man who rapes and murders a little girl might have kissed his mother goodnight the night before.

Imagining politically "correct" people who stray from the "good" allows us to probe their characters more deeply. Such complex characters lead us to see more clearly, both as readers and writers, the mixture that is involved in everything humans do. In my sketch above, the old black woman who rescues the white girls from their secretarial pigeonholes may, in fact, also be bossy, obstinate, and narrow-minded—just like their middle-class mothers up North! Such a realization helps break what might be called positive stereotypes, and lead to richer, more complex writing.

Step Six: Reading Student Examples

Here are two short sketches from the ninth grade English class who heard the *Cannery Row* selection:

> After school on that cold winter day, me, Nicole, Rosaline, Alexis, and Shareta met in the parking lot of their apartments because their mom didn't want them to go too far away. It would be dark soon.
>
> The old woman sat in her window and stared at us. Her face was wrinkled and dried like a prune. She wore ugly multi-colored moo-moos, with faded flowers from too many washes.
>
> The old woman came out into the parking lot. She shouted and waved her fist about us being too loud. When she turned to go back into the building, you could see her underwear through her moo-moo. We started to laugh, and, in embarrassment, she ran up the stairs and slammed her windows shut. Then the blinds dropped.
>
> —*Lyndzee*

* * *

It was about four o'clock and the air was hot and full of humidity. I walked inside to see if my friends were playing basketball. Shouts from little kids echoed through the building.

Kevin, a black, built, tall man walked into the gym. He was wearing black shorts and a white t-shirt. His sneakers squeaked against the shiny gym floor. His face looked rugged from not shaving for a few days. His big brown eyes were full of excitement. He had crumbs on his face from eating a cookie and in one hand he held some orange juice.

Kevin and I were pretty good friends even though we had just met a few weeks ago. No one yet had beaten him in basketball that I knew. Most of his shots were good, and he had perfect form when shooting. In games, he played around all the time and still ended up beating everybody.

Then a seven-foot thin white man walked into the gym carrying a gym bag and a basketball. I had seen him play on TV once.

Kevin and this man started playing a game. Kevin made the first six points, before the other man won it all.

I could see that Kevin was disappointed, but I knew he wasn't playing his best. It seemed like his only surviving tree in the hot, dry desert had just died.

　　—*Rob*

In both of these sketches, the authors gain sympathy for characters who are different from them. Each piece ends with an image: the old woman's blinds blocking the window suggests that the author realizes that the old woman has to protect herself from the girls' cruelty. Rob's piece ends with a striking image of his new friend. Neither character remains distant and invulnerable: the authors have gotten closer to them as people.

Step Seven: Moving from Bystander to Participant

Using the techniques of journalism, students can imagine themselves dropping the detached stance of a reporter and taking a side in the event they are describing.

Alice Walker's essay and my two scenes above describe the moments when a new political consciousness begins to emerge. What happens next? Meridel LeSueur's essay "I Was Marching" describes her change from neutral disengagement to active involvement.

At first, she set out as a reporter to cover the 1934 Teamsters' Strike in Minneapolis, one of the most violent clashes between labor and management in our history. As a middle-class girl who valued words more than events, she had been brought up to prefer individualistic, competitive actions rather than collaborative, anonymous ones. The blue-collar strike attracted her:

> For two days I heard of the strike. I went by their headquarters. I walked by on the opposite side of the street and saw the dark old building that had been a garage and lean, dark young faces leaning from the upstairs windows . . . I saw cars leaving filled with grimy men, pickets going to the line, engines roaring out . . . I didn't go in. I was afraid they would put me out. After all, I could remain a spectator.[22]

Other people like LeSueur watched from across the street. "I saw in their faces the same longings, the same fears," she wrote. She too was afraid, not of physical harm,

> but . . . of mixing, of losing myself, of being unknown and lost . . . I felt I excelled in competing with others and I knew instantly that these people were not competing at all, that they were acting in a strange, powerful trance of movement *together*.[23]

As her sympathy and curiosity drew her closer and closer to the strike, she entered the building and climbed the stairs. For an hour she leaned against a wall and watched sweaty, dirty, tired men and women sit down to rest. Finally one woman spoke briefly about the kitchen brigade in the adjoining rooms. LeSueur wrote:

> She didn't pay any special attention to me as an individual. I watched her go. I felt rebuffed, hurt. Then I saw instantly she didn't see me because she saw only what she was doing. I ran after her.[24]

LeSueur joined the assembly line to feed the strikers at noon:

> At first I look at the men's faces and then I don't look any more, the same body, the same blue shirt and overalls. Hours go by, the heat is terrific. I am not tired. I am not hot. I am pouring coffee. I am swung into the most intense and natural organization I have ever felt. I know everything that is going on. These things become of great matter to me.[25]

Note the way her shift in verb tense from past to present shows her shift from fearful detachment to active contribution.

With the other workers, she moves out onto the street to listen to the fearsome news of negotiation deadlock and two strikers dead. She realizes that the striking men have formed a human ring to protect her and the other women, and that in some sense she belongs in this circle. Yet the next day at the funeral march, she stands apart, not sure that she, who hates parades, will march. At the last moment, she says, "I don't belong to the auxiliary—could I march?" Three women encourage her gently, and she becomes part of the "giant mass uncoiled like a serpent," and it becomes part of her:

> We passed through six blocks of tenements, through a sea of grim faces, and there was not a sound. There was the curious shuffle of thousands of feet, without drum or bugle, in ominous silence, a march not heavy as the military, but very light, exactly with the heartbeat . . .
>
> I felt my legs straighten. I felt my feet join in that strange shuffle of thousands of bodies moving with direction, of thousands of feet, and my own breath with the gigantic breath. As if an electric charge had passed through me, my hair stood on end. I was marching.[26]

The same initial pattern of holding back, and possibly even looking down on the people in distress, might occur even today if a middle-class student visited, say, a shelter for the homeless. Middle-class people tend to pride themselves on their individualism. They don't want to take part in mass movements if they can help it, and they haven't experienced the bonding together for political change or for survival that happens among poorer people who recognize that their individual fates rely on collective effort.

It might be instructive for a class to do some research on the Great Depression, to collect articles, facts, photographs, and oral history narratives of life during those hard times. John Steinbeck's novel *The Grapes of Wrath* provides rich portraits of a depression family, and how one of its members finds himself compelled to take part in collective action. In *Hard Times*, Studs Terkel has compiled interviews with scores of people about their experience in the depression. Any school library should have sources about this well-documented period in American history.

Below is an outline of the research and writing steps a class could take to enter a historical moment of mass demonstration—or individual experience—to understand it not as an observer, but as a participant:

1. Students might begin by choosing a period of labor or civil or economic unrest and reading historical source material. Later, photographs, maps, songs, and primary materials such as newspaper accounts, letters, and radio broadcasts can help students imagine themselves in the event. Remember to try to have them create a composite picture, recreating the setting, the weather, the sounds, the technology, the personalities, the moment-to-moment details that made up the situation.

2. Next, students can create a persona for themselves—either a heightened version of themselves or an outsider who gradually comes to

share the political beliefs of the demonstrators or strikers. The character of a reporter is an excellent persona because the role requires an account of the background issues and events—and because observing is an important part of a reporter's role.

3. Finally, students can reconstruct a series of historical events and insert themselves in them, reporting them more and more personally as they become more involved, gradually abandoning their outsider's role.

This arc of experience—from outside to inside, and then outside again with a new identity—expresses artistically the psychological change that enables people to act differently in the political world. Students who imaginatively write themselves into this process gain a better understanding of the transformations of people they've read or heard about, those mute, passive, and solitary people who have found the power and voice to join in protest.

Chapter 6
MIGRATION, TECHNOLOGY, AND SOCIAL CHANGE

Change is one of the salient features of the American experience. The migration of European peoples into the American hemisphere dramatically changed the face of the land, the mixture of peoples, the languages, technology, and folkways. Since the beginning of European settlement, the rate of this change has continuously accelerated, giving each generation experiences that the previous ones did not have, and making past ways of life seem peculiar and mysterious to each current generation. This chapter focuses on subjects that reflect dramatic changes in the last one hundred years—transportation and communication; migration due to war, drought, and the economy; and social behavior.

In the first part of this chapter, students learn about the technology of the automobile and radio, and some social effects of World War II.

When an oldtimer describes growing up before World War I, the way people did everyday things such as washing, ironing, cooking, growing food, and getting from place to place seem as odd to us as sleigh bells amid the roar of diesel engines. At that time, families washed dishes, clothes, and themselves in zinc tubs in the kitchen and threw the water out on the roses. There were no toaster ovens or microwaves, either: the wood cookstove required skill and experience to bring it to the right temperature. But if the kerosene lamp overturned and a fire broke out, water from the stove's reservoir was close at hand. People took their Saturday drive to town not in a car but in a wagon pulled by the same horses that pulled the plow on weekdays. Farmers didn't use commercial fertilizers: they used livestock manure. If by around 1910 some city people had installed indoor plumbing, it was for a bathtub only; the toilet was still in an outhouse in the backyard. Many rural homes had to wait until the 1950s for indoor plumbing and electricity.

When the U. S. entered World War II, many regions of the country still contained pockets of people for whom technology had hardly changed since the Civil War. The farm kitchen in, say, Idaho might be covered with linoleum and the family might own a 1941 Chevy, but otherwise they lived with no more technology than tenant farmers in rural Alabama. Yet with the war, American life changed dramatically.

With its huge mobilization of men and women, World War II did more than perhaps any other single national event to alter the speed and spread of technological and social change.

During the war, many families—like the one from Idaho—sold off their farm goods, packed themselves and their furniture into the Chevy and a makeshift trailer, and went to California, where the fathers got jobs in defense plants and shipyards. For the first time in her life, the Idaho daughter went to school with girls from Oklahoma or Texas who wore "black crepe dresses, high heels, silk stockings, their hair piled high, and lots of makeup like the movie stars they had seen."[1] With no shoe-ration coupons, the Idaho farm girl had to be content to wear her brother's black high-top basketball shoes. Her dresses of chickenfeed sacks (her family would have had to spend every extra cent on the purchase of a new car), her braids, and her lack of makeup completed a style that set her apart as a hick.

Even though she wasn't a social success, the Idaho farm girl wanted very much to stay in Southern California, where the new ideas that she encountered in school excited her. But her parents felt hemmed in by the neighborhood of small houses on tiny lots. Her mother missed life on the farm in Idaho, the women's groups, and trips to town on Saturday. She was afraid of city buses and worried that someone would kidnap the baby from his stroller. When the family moved back to Idaho four months later, the daughter vowed to come back to California.

EXERCISE ONE
Radio Dramas about Social Change

In this extended exercise, students write radio sketches modeled after those from the late 1940s, showing how the history of the automobile (or another piece of technology or cultural practice) reflected the economic and social conditions of World War II and its aftermath. (For high school students and older.)

Step One: Presenting a Short Social History of the American Automobile

Henry Ford's Model T—the rugged, affordable American car ($825)—first came on the market in 1908. Six years later, it became the first car to be mass produced on an assembly line, and the nation was presented with an automotive sweetheart most men could embrace.

Before the invention of the automobile, trains had captured the fancy of nineteenth-century travelers and changed the economics and demographics of the countryside by opening remote areas to commerce and immigration. But riding a train, no matter how first class—with swaying dining car, white linen tablecloth, and clinking stemware—required riders to surrender themselves to a huge superior force. Private only in cramped toilets or sleeping compartments, the train failed to meet two major requirements of the American ethic: self-determination and individualism. Americans couldn't drive the train when and where they wanted, and they had to share the ride with dozens of strangers. As the nation's love affair with the automobile intensified, Americans gradually became its slave, altering everything around it for its sake. It wasn't the first time technology has changed places and driven us.

Until the mid-1920s, however, there were limits to how much Americans could use their cars. Snow in winter and mud in spring kept the driving public off the roads. But by 1925, with nearly half the northern population owning cars, state legislatures began to appropriate money for hard-surfaced roads. By the 1950s, an interstate system of highways and byways, with complicated cloverleaf overpasses, motels, restaurants, truck-stops, and gas stations had transformed the face of the nation. No one could mistake the country's devotion to the car.

This is not to say that America's love affair with the car didn't have its opponents. Early on, before Ford's Model T, when the automobile was still associated with its European origins, politicians recognized that it was political suicide to be seen in a car. As president of Princeton University, Woodrow Wilson advised students not to display the "snobbery" of motoring. "Nothing has spread socialistic feeling in this country more," he said, "than this picture of the arrogance of wealth."[2]

Princeton alumnus F. Scott Fitzgerald was fascinated by just this kind of snobbery and wrote about motoring in his stories of sophisticated Eastern college students and the razzle-dazzle society of the 1920s. In *The Great Gatsby* (1925), Fitzgerald gave the fabulously wealthy Jay Gatsby a motorcar to match the excesses of his gin-flowing parties:

> I'd seen it. Everybody had seen it. It was a rich cream color, bright with nickel, swollen here and there in its monstrous length with triumphant hat-boxes and supper-boxes and tool-boxes, and terraced with a labyrinth of wind-shields that mirrored a dozen suns. Sitting down behind many layers of glass in a sort of green leather conservatory, we started to town.[3]

The Great Gatsby is replete with expensive motorcars, deluxe trains, a yacht, a horse-drawn victoria for a romantic ride in Central Park, a horse-drawn funeral carriage (until the 1930s it was considered undignified to carry a coffin to the cemetery in a car)—and thoroughbreds ridden by more aristocratic types than the nouveau-riche bootlegger Gatsby. Fitzgerald's descriptions of all these modes of transportation serve as a subtle commentary on the changing life-styles of the wealthy.

The Great Depression that followed the 1929 stock market crash destroyed much of the wealth generated in the 1920s and put many middle-class and lower-class families through terrible privation. But even the Joads from Oklahoma, who in John Steinbeck's *The Grapes of Wrath* left their farm in the Oklahoma Dust Bowl and headed for California, did so in a truck, not behind a mule.

Later, during World War II, increased migration speeded the social change that the depression had begun. During the war, many Americans were introduced to different landscapes, customs, and beliefs. White Baptists from Oklahoma encountered Japanese-Americans in Los Angeles; rural people who'd never used indoor plumbing and who had lived miles away from their nearest neighbor suddenly found themselves walking down city streets amidst the clatter of buses and indecipherable accents; and black tenant farmers drafted into the armed services found themselves in the French or Italian countryside where their uniforms made them heroes to children whose language they couldn't speak.

Despite all our differences, we Americans, after all, had to unite behind the war. Advertising and radio began to portray stereotypes of national desire and behavior. After the war, this process of creating a national alliance also helped to spread notions of "keeping up with the Joneses." Individual Americans saw themselves portrayed more and more as go-getters whose reward was material success.

The soldiers who fought (according to a 1943 *Life* magazine ad for Community Silverplate) for the right "to love and marry and rear children in security and peace" found, after the war, an additional right, the right to a car and a house. As soon as the war ended, the auto companies raced to produce new and better cars, built by companies such as Packard, which had manufactured "combat engines to measurements as fine as millionths of an inch" (*Life*, November 19, 1945). An October 25, 1948, *Life* ad for Ford showed its new models in a ticker tape parade, like returning war heroes or victorious politicians. With the war over, cars could return to their winning place in American hearts.

Step Two: Looking at Issues of Life Magazine from the 1940s

I have students begin this exercise by leafing through old issues of *Life*. Dividing the class into groups of three or four students, I give each group an issue of the magazine from the 1940s, making sure to include some from the early years of the war and some from after it. I own four issues from the 1940s, but there are circulating copies in many public libraries. If those in your library don't circulate, you can make photocopies of ads and stories. A local newspaper from the 1940s might work almost as well.

What to look for? With my students, I make a list on the board of kinds of news and feature articles and ads in the magazine and the different ways we might interpret them. Here are some kinds of articles and ads to focus on:

1) *Ads about cars* (and other things, especially new items or slants on old products). Look not only at what is said but at how the ads work visually; for instance, one ad uses a censor's black pencil to emphasize the secret work that the company is doing for defense. Note social class, gender, and family relationships—who is driving the car? How are the figures dressed, and what clues to social status do their clothes or surroundings give? What other clues in the ad reflect changes that occurred during the 1940s?

2) *Evidence of the war.* What are the visual cues of the war (such as uniforms or battle equipment)? What messages about the war's effect on the home front come through clearly? Which are more subtle? Many ads emphasize how the men at war value romance, family, and a home to come home to. What does this message suggest about the women at home, the men in the armed forces, and their hopes and worries about each other? What happens to the subject of war in the latter part of the decade? What subjects replace the war?

3) *Stereotypes of class, race, and gender*—reinforced and challenged. In an ad for Father's Day, 1943, four small scenes of men with different connections to the war include only one black man. He is a porter on a train, handing a soldier his hat and uniform. Clearly, he has a subordinate position. (During World War II, the armed forces were segregated, and blacks were often excluded from officer ranks.) In an ad from 1942, a sailor in uniform faces a woman next to a mimeograph machine. The caption, "When 'Man Power' Goes to War," indicates that the woman will take his place when he ships out, but subtle details—like the fact that she has her back turned to the reader—suggest that the word *power* does not belong to her. Here, the stereotype suggests that women are only understudies to the real heroes, "minding the store" until the menfolk return from the business of war.

4) Finally, note how the ads and articles depict America's relationship to the larger world. "Speaking of Pictures," from June 22, 1942, displays photos of ten women from Hawaii, each of a different racial mixture. The November 19, 1945, issue includes a series of sketches depicting the American occupation of Tokyo, with the Japanese gawking at the tall Americans. Both these articles downplay racial stigma or conflict by showing curiosity, rather than hostility, as the first response to foreigners. But does curiosity about the foreign continue throughout the decade? What replaces it?

Comparing articles and ads, students can discover other messages that hint at the complicated realities of the period. The "war brides," who married quickly when their boyfriends were drafted, are left behind by their soldier husbands. But they do not hide their beauty in housedresses. Instead they are working in offices and factories; at night, they take off demure jackets and work clothes, and go dancing in backless dresses. According to the ads, however, romance doesn't get started on the home front because everybody works long hours in aircraft and munitions factories. The only balcony serenades they hear are sung by machines.

In the issues from the war years, the car manufacturers proudly hail their contribution to the war effort. Buick features a plane in its ad for June 14, 1943, under the headline, "Life, Liberators, and Pursuit of the Axis." This pun on Jefferson's "life, liberty, and the pursuit of happiness" implies that Americans at home may have to give up some immediate happiness to defeat the enemy. A few pages later, Mobilgas service stations advise the driving public that "Three-legged Horsepower Won't Get You Far! . . . Prevent Tire Waste—Protect Your *Whole Car*, Too." This plea that Americans take care of their tires is reinforced with a picture of a horse, reminding drivers that in times of scarcity, they may indeed have to park the car and take to literal horse power.

After the war, two new kinds of ads appear: those for radio-phonograph consoles and those for women's undergarments. The ads for the consoles either emphasize family pleasure—"How this smart family picked a fine radio" announces a two-page ad, with cameo appearances by Dad, Mother, and their pretty teenage daughter—or romance, with women in long glamorous dresses either standing entranced by the console or dancing with a handsome man.

An Oldsmobile ad in the same issue of *Life* (October 27, 1947) shows a woman driving a car, an article tells us about women college presidents, and an ad for girdles and panty-girdles features a drawing of a pert woman in Jantzen underwear. A year later, an ad for Playtex includes an action photograph of a model in a girdle and three endorsements by female celebrities. What is going on? It's interesting to speculate on the roots of post-war American consumerism from the clues in the magazines.

Step Three: Collecting the Most Revealing Discoveries from Life

As the students continue with the exercise, I ask them to tell me the most revealing items or connections they've discovered in *Life*. Then, beginning with the earliest issue, I list them on the board. Here is a sample from four issues:

June 22, 1942
• Pontiac, an ad for its cannon, with words blacked out, as a military censor would do to a letter.

• A General Motors ad shows trucks and coaches, but no private cars. Placed next to story of "Furlough Brides." Implication: people can't have a private life during war.
• "Imagine Little Me . . . Helping the Government." A woman in a supermarket advertises the store's policy of low prices. Message: women are too "small" to help in big ways.
• Mobilgas, with a doctor in a suit answering phone. Implication: wartime cars will need extra attention.

June 14, 1943:
• "Home . . . where I want unchanged, just as I remember them now, all the things that I hold dear . . . " —excerpt from lengthy imaginary prisoner-of-war letter, under a drawing of a bedraggled prisoner behind a barbed-wire fence.
• Chevrolet ad: "Help Us to Help You and the U. S. A." Drawing of repair man in clean white coat, with a worried expression, and lists of owners' "responsibilities" and dealers' "responsibilities." Additional slogan: "Save the Wheels that Serve America." Note that—in contrast to the 1920s and earlier—car owners are not the reckless wealthy, but solid, middle-class citizens.
• "*Life* Goes to a High School Graduation, in Forest, Ohio." With the war, boys are not going to college but into the service. Valedictorian is a girl with glasses, fitting into the stereotypical "brain" category.

November 19, 1945:
• "Step Out with Mercury"—the first picture of a new car since the war. Production of new cars stopped between 1942 and 1946.
• Feature called "Speaking of Pictures": "Can you guess what rank these vets had?" All the men are in suits; it's impossible to tell a sergeant from a general. Implication: the war touched all, had a democratic influence, and they all deserve respect.
• Westinghouse—the Combination Kitchen and Laundry. Dreamy drawing of woman contemplating pink kitchen and laundry.
• Plymouth: "Just Wait Til You Get Your Hands on the Wheel . . ." Drawing of man in bow tie and white shirt, leaning forward in easy chair, newspaper dropped to floor, pipe beside him on table, arms up as he grasps an imaginary wheel. Implication: a return to "normalcy" by putting the private citizen, male, in the driver's seat again.
• Ad for a new synthetic material, Textron. Slogan: "Parachute Precision during the War, Now Tailored into Winter Plumage for You." Drawing shows woman in pretty white and pink bathrobe swinging in a birdhouse, with parent birds hovering around her and with snow-topped pink parachutes mingling with autumn leaves. Implication: private consumption is now the primary goal of the company. American private life will benefit from the technical advances of the war. Women can be comfortable and pretty again.

• "Step Right Up, Amigos . . . Have a Coke." "Filipinos thrilled when Yankees came back to the Philippines . . . freedom again . . ." Note association of the soft drink with American victory and with internationalism.

October 25, 1948:
• "Plymouth, the Car with 'Air Pillow' Comfort." This ad shows four other images of comfort: Cleopatra's barge, a back scratcher, Rip Van Winkle's twenty-year snooze, and a ski lift.
• Two other car ads show big rounded photographs of the cars themselves, with text that emphasizes "sweet handling" and comfort.
• "Sleep Like You Never Slept Before!" Two-page ad for Englander mattress has huge photograph of mattress with four family members, each sprawled in a different sleeping position. Funny names for each: Dad is the "Steam Roller," boy is "Bird Dog," Mom is "Twister," and older boy is "Traveler."

Step Four: Combining Oral History with Material from Life

The people in any ad or magazine story are often stereotypes. To understand their real-life counterparts, students can read oral history interviews, diaries, memoirs, or letters from the 1940s. A good oral history of the war, *The Homefront: Americans during World War II,* organizes pieces of interviews under headings such as "A Nation on the Move," "Why We Fight," and "Rosie the Riveter."[4] (Another good collection of oral history for World War II is Terkel's *The "Good War."*)[5] Local historical societies may also have collections of letters from the war years that the class could sample. Interviewing family or neighbors who lived through the war also gives students valuable first-hand accounts.

If the students are pressed for time, they (or the teacher) can read aloud short excerpts from published letters, diaries, or interviews. Then each student can jot down the bits of drama that bring the facts of the war alive in personal ways. Here are some from *The Homefront* that I often use:

1) A Japanese family, sent to an internment camp, later has an opportunity to work at Father Flanagan's Boys Town in Nebraska. The wife and children take the train from California to Nebraska, but the father drives the family car and is almost attacked in Arizona. (In February, 1942, President Roosevelt ordered the internment of anyone with even one Japanese great-grandparent. This order involved 110,000 Japanese-American citizens who were sent to ten remote camps, solely on the basis of their Japanese heritage.)

2) A Southern white woman moves to Seattle with her children and takes a job at the Boeing plant that pays forty-six and a half cents an hour. She has to work seven days a week, with only Christmas off. The daughter

learns that Negro people (as they were called), whom she had thought of as inferior, are as smart and articulate as she.

3) An Iowa farmer is drafted but, at the last moment, not taken because he's over thirty-five. He returns to Iowa, where he starts up a repair shop to keep the farm machines and cars going throughout the war.

4) A young woman gets a job pumping gas, though she doesn't know a dipstick from lipstick. She learns that the farm women in her town don't have much confidence in her ability at the pump.

5) A small Illinois town's population jumps from 2,000 to 6,000 when a defense plant opens there. Before the war, women used to stand and gossip in the middle of Main Street, but now it is crowded with cars. One family rents out upstairs rooms, finally sells their house and moves to pre-fab apartments. Through the paper-thin walls, they hear about the illegal lives of their neighbors, everything from prostitution to Black Market dealings.

6) A young black man from South Carolina moves to Philadelphia to find work. In 1944, he and forty other black men apply to the transit authority to test its hiring policy. When eight are hired, the white drivers stage a long protest strike. President Roosevelt sends in troops to post signs on the transit buildings, labeling them "Government Property." The white drivers are told to go back to work or they will be drafted.

Step Five: Modifying the Oral Histories for More Drama

In the next step, students begin drafting radio dramas based on their research on the 1940s. Radio dramas are, of course, fictional, but in their heyday in the 1940s and 1950s they captured much of the flavor of the times. By writing them, students experience a cultural form of the period and explore the effect of the war on American life.

First, I have students discuss what they've gleaned from *Life* and their research of oral histories. I ask them to recall the most dramatic details. What do these details reveal about social behavior and the war's effect on everyday life? Comparing social behavior from the 1940s to that of today will help classes to recognize how differently people acted in the past. For example, in the 1940s not many students had cars; they depended on their parents, the bus, or the subway, or they just walked. Rationing during the war also affected the way people lived: the use of the family car was limited to going to and from work or special occasions; and having a birthday party would be problematic when a family didn't have enough ration stamps for sugar or butter to make a cake.

I stress to students that in their radio plays the goal is not only to give essential facts about the wartime era, but also to present interesting conflicts and connections. The best historical fiction leans more toward the contrast and variety of the novel than toward the strict accuracy of nonfiction.

If students try imagining themselves in the place of the people in the oral histories, inserting concrete details, blended with the historical facts, they'll begin to create that mix of the universal and the local that can make a good story both believable and historically accurate. For example, an oral history may tell of a group of Air Force cadets being given rooms in a college dormitory, and the young coed being irked at having to find a room elsewhere on short notice. But in fiction, the coed might encounter a cadet in her former dorm room when she goes back to retrieve her hair brush. They strike up a conversation, and he asks her to get a message to his sick mother in the next county. She borrows a friend's car to drive to his house, and from there unwinds a plot that becomes increasingly dramatic and suspenseful.

When I tried this exercise myself, I combined imagined events with what I'd learned from sources such as *The Homefront.* I decided to expand the experience of the Idaho farm girl going to school in California to include some Japanese students who are suddenly sent away to intern-ment camp. Perhaps the girl from Idaho—let's call her Nancy—receives letters from her Japanese friend, Mitsuoko.

I decided that Nancy's situation might be more interesting if she were sixteen rather than twelve (as she is in the oral history excerpt). Wanting to be more accepted by her new friends, she might beg her father to drive her to a class picnic. He hesitates because the tires on the car are getting worn and the picnic is thirty miles away—the family doesn't have extra gas ration stamps for such a long pleasure trip since they're saving up to return to Idaho. Then I imagined that on the way home from dropping her off he has a blowout. Now what will Nancy have to do to help her family fix their tire? How might I connect this to what is happening to Mitsuoko?

As students begin to shape their own characters and stories, I suggest that they include flashbacks from before the war. Studs Terkel's collec-tion of oral histories of the depression, *Hard Times*, is a good source for the 1930s. The Time-Life series called *This Fabulous Century*, with one book for each decade, provides information, photographs, news stories, headlines, and ads.

Variation: Writing a Letter Poem

At this point in the exercise, you could have your students branch off into poetry. It's easy for them to use the characters they have created to write a poem in letter form. This letter might describe one way the war has uprooted them. Here is an example by Japanese-American poet Dwight Okita. Born in 1958, Okita may have been thinking of a relative's experience or of what he had read about the relocation camps:

In Response to Executive Order 9066: ALL AMERICANS OF JAPANESE
DESCENT MUST REPORT TO RELOCATION CENTERS

Dear Sirs:
Of course I'll come. I've packed my galoshes
and three packets of tomato seeds. Janet calls them
"love apples." My father says where we're going
they won't grow.

I am a fourteen-year-old girl with bad spelling
and a messy room. If it helps any, I will tell you
I have always felt funny using chopsticks
and my favorite food is hot dogs.
My best friend is a white girl named Denise—
we look at boys together. She sat in front of me
all through grade school because of our names:
O'Connor, Ozawa. I know the back of Denise's head very well.
I tell her she's going bald. She tells me I copy on tests.
We're best friends.

I saw Denise today in Geography class.
She was sitting on the other side of the room.
"You're trying to start a war," she said, "giving secrets away
to the Enemy. Why can't you keep your big mouth shut?"
I didn't know what to say.
I gave her a packet of tomato seeds
and asked her to plant them for me, told her
when the first tomato ripened
she'd miss me.[6]

The power of this poem lies in its intimate evocation of a particular student's experience: sitting behind Denise in school, staring at the back of her head, hearing Denise's harsh words, offering her the seeds.

In their letter poems, students can include moments that reveal everyday events in a character's life (such as sitting in school, walking in the door at home, having a conversation over dinner) and then show how these events are influenced by various realities of the war—a sudden expression of prejudice, moving away from home, hearing that your father has been killed in combat. I also urge students to consider various emotions the letter writer might have in response to the war's changes— anger, eagerness, grief, embarrassment—and then let these conflicting emotions show through in the poem.

Step Six: Learning More about the Radio Drama Form

To understand the style of 1940s radio dramas, students should listen to some. Cassette tapes of these shows are available at most public libraries. A good example is "The Life of Riley," which portrays a family of four (husband, wife, daughter, and son) who left Brooklyn for California. "By day I'm Riley the Riveter, by night I'm Riley the Romeo," Riley boasts in one episode.

In this episode, Riley's wife Peg is begging for some evening entertainment. She tells her husband that she deserves time out on the town "after cooking for you and picking up after you." He counters that he's taken her plenty of places: "During the war I took you once a month to the Blood Bank. Wasn't it a thrill to watch the blood leak out of my arm?"

When his wife's former flame from Brooklyn, Stanley Monahan, arrives, Riley's jealousy overwhelms his good sense, and he's convinced that Peg is getting ready to leave him. Two of Riley's sidekicks get involved. The first is Waldo, characterized by a whining peevish voice and a wife with "enough there to make three little women." Waldo is a typical hen-pecked husband, but his advice to Riley is conniving and shrewd: don't throw Monahan out, he tells Riley, that will only make a martyr out of him, "and women love martyrs."

The second sidekick is Digby O'Dell, an undertaker. The humor broadens as Digby recounts how he foiled a romance between his wife and an assistant by telling the fellow: "If you don't leave my wife alone, you'll stop being my employee and become my customer." He urges Riley to fight for his love and offers to "lay [Monahan] out. I'm rather good at that sort of thing."

Finally, Riley threatens Monahan at the train station and runs into his fist. When Riley's mistakes are all explained and Peg promises that she won't leave him, Riley closes with his trademark phrase: "What a revolting development!"

With your students, listen to a few scenes of a radio drama such as "The Life of Riley," and then note some of the conventions they use:

1) Characters are distinguished as much by their voices as by their family roles, work, temperaments, etc.

2) No more than three characters are "on the air" at one time; more would probably confuse the listener.

3) Music creates intervals between scenes.

4) Like today's TV sit-coms, most harsh political, economic, and social realities are muted, though not necessarily overlooked. Gender and family roles play a large part in the humor and the drama. (Remember that during the war these roles were shifting, though the characters may not realize it.)

5) Each major character has a sidekick, who serves as his or her foil. Usually the sidekick is more caricatural than the main character: e.g., Waldo is a conniving weakling, more brains and less brawn than Riley; the character of Digger O'Dell is defined almost completely by his profession.

6) Basic fears fuel the drama, but everything ends humorously. Nothing serious happens to hurt anyone. This is comedy, after all.

7) Hallmarks of the 1940s: If father doesn't know best, at least doctors do: in commercials, "Four out of five doctors recommend . . . " is a standard appeal to authority. Teenagers do not seriously rebel. They pursue harebrained schemes and cause their parents to yell at them in exasperation, but ultimately they follow docilely where their parents lead. At least on the radio shows.

Step Seven: Brainstorming for a Radio Sketch from the 1940s

To help students invent characters for their radio sketches, I have them consider TV sit-coms of the 1950s and 1960s—some of which are still in reruns. The "I Love Lucy" show, for instance, with flighty Lucy married to band-leader Desi, revolved around domestic misunderstandings, much like the "Life of Riley." More recent sit-coms have included themes of feminism, bigotry, and sexism, but the old themes persist: parents vs. maturing children; the control of the purse; jealousy. If students can keep in mind some of these perennial family and social conflicts, and place them in the context of 1940s social behavior, wartime economy, and technology, they'll be well on their way to writing their historical dramas.

Students can write their radio dramas either individually or in groups of three or four. For brainstorming, though, collaboration works best. The brainstorming strategy described below is a form of group writing in which each student begins by describing a dramatic situation and creating one character. Then the papers are passed back successively to let others fill out the cast of characters. Finally, each paper is returned to the student who started it.

1) Give each student a large sheet of newsprint or drawing paper, and have them put their names at the top. Then each student will write *a few sentences or phrases describing a dramatic situation for a radio sketch*. Each situation should include a car (or whatever theme you've chosen). For example, "Husband comes home from war to find wife working as a grease monkey in a gas station. She's been driving his retired father's Buick across town to work at the station. The husband wants her to stop, but she likes the work. He wants a new car, but she doesn't want to quit driving the borrowed one."

2) Next, each student *selects one of the characters* from the initial description and *gives this person a full name, including a nickname*. (At this point the class can discuss the mental impact of names by playing around with some extreme examples, such as Ashley Marie Snickerdoodle.)

After naming the character (remembering that main characters' names are not as extreme as those of secondary ones), each student should *write how the war has changed this person's usual situation*. They can also add age, physical description, sound of voice, job, hobbies, and temperament.

For my initial description, I selected the husband:

> William Harding West (Bill), age twenty-four, enlisted at twenty-one right out of college, married quickly before being sent overseas to the Pacific. Fought in Guadalcanal and visited Bali. Returned home to work in the insurance business that his father started. Was a star athlete in college and won decorations for bravery in the war. Has a deep voice, mellow and persuasive.

3) Next, students begin the collaboration by *passing their sheets to the person behind them*. Thus, the students at the ends of the rows bring their papers to those in the front seats, and everyone is then ready to write on someone else's paper. Students should read what is already written on the papers so that the next character will fit into the developing story.

The next character they invent (now for someone else's story) is *the second main character*. If this sketch includes a whole family, students can now decide which other family member is going to play the second largest role, opposite the one designated as the main character. The students should give this second character a *name, nickname, age, physical description, voice quality, work, hobbies, temperament*. And they should also indicate *how the war has changed this person's work or values or goals*.

Working alone on my own sketch, I added:

> Janet Irene Mayer West, age twenty-four. Married Bill the day before he was sent to the Pacific, but stayed in their hometown. Lived in a garage apartment behind her in-laws' house, and after working briefly as a typist, which she hated, got a job pumping gas and eventually learned to be a mechanic. Short, wiry, curly brown hair, a tomboy as a kid, Janet (or Jan) has three brothers. She has a high voice and speaks quickly. She used to think—not very happily—that she'd settle down to the life of a housewife, but she's becoming a good mechanic and doesn't want to quit.

4) Next, students pass the papers one seat back again. After reading over the description, they *add the car (or whatever theme you've chosen) and*

other details of wartime life to the story. I remind them to use what they've learned from the oral histories and the ads and stories from *Life* to describe the make, age, and general condition of the car, and to introduce other details about the war.

For my sketch, I wrote:

> Bill's father and mother, Fred and Nancy West, owned a 1935 green Buick during the war. Due to gas and tire rationing, they have not been able to buy new tires or take any long trips. But now that the war is over, they want to buy new tires and drive to Atlantic City for their thirtieth wedding anniversary. (They live in a small town in Maryland.) They kept a close watch on Janet while Bill was gone and didn't let her go to the movies without a chaperone. On the other hand, they didn't expect Bill to remain totally faithful. Janet, of course, was peeved about this. They told her, "No one will ever know what Bill did during the war. But you live here where people will talk."

5) Have the students pass the papers back again. After reading them over, students add *one of the subsidiary characters*. This character can be a stereotype, playing off the ads and articles in *Life*. Sometimes the stereotypes carry over from earlier decades: the students can look at the 1920s and 1930s for some ideas. Here are some suggestions:

- the busy, harried family doctor
- the stay-at-home housewife
- the rich playboy with criminal connections
- the pretty, giggling bride
- the son going into the family business
- the old-maid schoolteacher (often a reality at the time because school boards would not hire married women)
- the uneducated rural black farmer
- the loyal wife working in a factory but yearning for her sailor husband to return so she can return to her role as homemaker
- the draft reject with flat feet and glasses
- the hobo who rides the rails from town to town, but has a regular route of marked houses where friendly housewives hand out sandwiches
- the heartless tycoon.

For my radio play, I created a friend for the wife:

> Katherine Echo Sanders, age twenty-four, with a flighty voice. Kate worked for Doctor Potts during the war. In the doctor's office, she overheard all the town gossip and relayed it to Janet when they went to the movies or walked around town. Married to Eddie Vincent, a boxer who spent his years in the Army giving exhibition matches, Kate can't wait for

Eddie to come home and release her from the prison of her hometown. She wants him to go into professional boxing and make big money, buy her a fur coat, and take her to Las Vegas.

6) One more time, the students pass the papers back and read what has been written. The final character they'll create, unlike the one above, will *contradict stereotypes.* Here are some suggestions:

- a doctor who trades on the Black Market to keep up his standard of living
- an Army deserter
- a washed-up playboy forced to live off friends from his hometown
- Rosie the Riveter—she loves her job and is good at it
- a young southern black man who becomes a union organizer
- a soldier on furlough during the war who dreads going home
- a daughter who sasses her father, runs away, gets a job, and stays in California while her family returns to their old farm in the Midwest.

For my sketch, I created a secondary character, to be the husband's sidekick:

Howard McKinzie, a fast-talking, jovial Army buddy, called Hap for short because he likes to stay happy. He misses the Army, says being a soldier was like being a playboy at the government's expense. He graduated with Bill West from the state university, but was not athletic. In the Army he played the Black Market and supplied the soldiers with exotic liquor and food. He's perfectly happy to let his wife Gladys work and argues with Bill about persuading Janet to leave her job.

Step Eight: Reading a Model to the Class

The format of a radio drama is much like a theater piece: most of the writing consists of speeches for various characters. Stage directions include narrator's text, sound effects, and music. Music can be used as the show's theme and to indicate mood or the passing of time. A scene often begins with a typical sound that establishes the setting—a doorbell, for instance.

If the class has already heard a 1940s radio show, they'll be familiar with many of the elements, and the following example may not be necessary. But for those who need extra guidance, here is my radio dramatization of the "Bill and Janet West Story."

Scene One

(Sprightly music opens the scene. Sound of a car door slamming and the narrator's voice saying: Our happy couple, newly reunited after the war, return home from their jobs in the small town of Grassville. Bill West, much decorated

Pacific hero, now sports a business suit. His lovely wife Janet jumps out of the ten-year-old Buick. But what's this, a frown on Bill's handsome face? What could be disturbing the calm of our happy couple?)

BILL: Janet, when are you going to give up that dirty job? Ugh! You're as filthy as if you spent ten hours wading through a jungle. I came home to forget all that. *(Sound of their entering front door)*

JANET: Don't frown, honey. I'll ditch this grease-monkey suit and put on the new robe you bought me. *(Her voice fades as she goes into the bedroom.)* I'll look as perky as the bird in the ad in my parachute-light Textron robe.

BILL: *(Rustling the newspaper)* Did you read about Knowlan's new store opening? Boy, that's taking a risk, opening a business out in the boonies like that.

JANET: *(Her voice becomes stronger.)* See, you'd never guess I'd spent all day under cars.

BILL: That's more like it. Now how about some grub?

JANET: I know you're hungry, but I forgot to make something last night. It'll take awhile. Here, go put your feet up and read the paper.

BILL *(Grumbling)*: Honestly, Janet, now that I'm back, you don't have to work.

JANET: I know, you've always wanted me to be a chip off your mother's block. You may get your wish—Mr. Griggs's son was just discharged. He'll be home next week. But really, honey, I like the smell of grease and the heft of a wrench in my hand. Maybe I'll call the other gas stations in town. With the new cars coming out, they'll probably want extra help.

BILL: I can't wait to get my hands on the wheel. We should let Dad and Mother have their old car back anyway. Come on, where's your nesting instinct? I'll buy us a car and then we'll fix up this kitchen so pretty you can't resist spending all your time here.

JANET: Not on your life, sonny. I may give up the monkey suit, but I'll never be happy wearing a fulltime apron. *(Music to indicate time passing)*

Scene Two

HAP: Nice new tires on your Dad's car. Did Janet cash in her ration stash?

BILL: Those are new, brand new. *(Sound of foot kicking tire) (Pause)* I'm fed up, Hap. I told Janet last night she should quit that mechanic job at Griggs's gas station, but she said she'd never wear an apron again. How'd I ever manage to fall for a dame like that?

HAP: There's nothing wrong with Janet. She just wants to live up to her tomboy best. You knew what you were getting, old buddy—the cheerleader who'd rather have played tight end. But, cheer up, if you can't change her, why not change yourself? Look at me, I'm happy to let Gladys support me. I always said the soldier's life is the best—all the leisure in the world at the government's expense.

BILL: Except you might get shipped home in a box. No thanks. I'm finished with extra-curricular heroics. What was I fighting for anyway, if not a safe home to come home to? Gee whiz. *(Pause)* And I wonder where she got the money for the new tires. Probably got a deal through the gas station.

HAP: A working woman, ol' buddy. Remember? She's been pulling down a good wage all the years you were gone, plus probably banking the money you sent her.

BILL: But that was all supposed to go for our little cottage.

HAP: Looks like some of it just went to keep the little woman rolling.

BILL: I won't stand for this. She did this without even asking me. And it's my father's car! I'm going to put a stop to this working nonsense. I'll call every station in town.

HAP: So what? Are you going to tell them she has chickenpox?

BILL: No, I'm going to tell them she's in the family way.

HAP: Oh. I wouldn't, if I were you. This may boomerang. Remember the time I stole all the infirmary's alcohol to make bathtub gin, then when a platoon of fleas took over my body, I couldn't find anything liquid to slosh on them and stop the itching.

BILL: This is peacetime, Hap, and we're not in the Pacific. We're home and I call the shots. *(Music to indicate time passing)*

Scene Three

(Sounds of cans being dropped into a supermarket cart)

JANET: Bill doesn't know it yet but his dad put new tires on the Buick. He's taking Nancy to Atlantic City to celebrate their thirtieth anniversary. I guess that puts an end to my working, for sure.

KATE: Ohhh, look at that whole pyramid of five-pound sugars. I'll bake Eddie a gooey birthday cake. Say, Janet, did I tell you he's heard from the Chicago Civic Center? They want him for a boxing match in April.

JANET: Looks like you'll get your wish right out of this burg. And I'll be stuck behind a kitchen curtain.

KATE: You don't have to let a little thing like a car put you behind bars, honey. Call the Mobil station two blocks up. You could walk.

JANET: I'll call right now. Oh, Mr. Jacobson, may I use your phone?

KATE: I've never known a girl so hep to get her hands dirty. You can spare me the grease *and* the flour.

JANET: Oh hello, Mr. Glen, this is Janet West, Mrs. William West. You remember me? I used to bounce my basketball against your garage. Sure. Listen, I've been a mechanic at Griggs's station for three years and I was wondering if you could use me . . . full- or part-time . . . Oh, is that so? No, not to my knowledge . . . but I see your point. Thanks for telling me.

KATE: What'd he say? Still holding a grudge from your kid shenanigans?

JANET: No, but can you beat this? He's heard I'm in the family way. I thought I'd be the first to know.

KATE: Who'd spread a rumor like that?

JANET: With Father and Mother West watching me like hawks, I haven't spread my wings one tiny bit for years. Either you're the culprit or I've caught something at the movies.

KATE: Stranger things have happened . . . remember that Mrs. Wilks from the farm came in to Dr. Potts's office, ready to deliver, and thought all along she was having indigestion?

JANET: This is no gas. Unless you call my husband's big mouth a sewer. I've got an idea. Come on. I'm going to lay in a supply of diapers, booties, and receiving blankets. He hasn't been home long enough to do me any damage. We'll see what he makes of this. *(Music to indicate time passing)*

Scene Four

MRS. CLARK, *a neighbor*: Yoo-hoo, Mr. West, over here. Can you help me with this sanitary dispenser?

BILL: Yes, ma'am, glad to. Where are the towels?

MRS. CLARK: Oh, Bill West, you always were fresh even when you were a youngster. Here, it's this can, filled with, you know, my discards.

BILL: Oh, are you playing bridge?

MRS. CLARK: Now don't you pretend you don't see that monster repository. If you could elevate that and transport it yonder, I'd be most grateful.

BILL: Glad to oblige. Where's Mr. Clark these days?

MRS. CLARK: Oh my, haven't you heard? He was interred nine months ago, passed on to the great conflagration in the sky.

BILL: Was there a fire?

MRS. CLARK: Hardly. "A sudden clotting of the gluteus minimum," according to the loyal Dr. Potts.

BILL: You mean he choked?

MRS. CLARK: We were entertaining, a sumptuous repast was spread before us. I was in my glory with chicken divan. Poor Mr. Clark, a wishbone, as it were, transported him beyond all carnal desires. But, let us not linger. A package for your lovely Janet was left by the delivery boy at my abode. Please come and retrieve it.

BILL: What's in it?

MRS. CLARK: My dear boy, would I stoop to such snoopery?

BILL: *(Sound of tearing paper)* Booties, diapers, blankets?

MRS. CLARK: They look a mite infinitesimal for you. Does your spouse know something you don't? Is she keeping secrets from her soldier boy? Quickly, sit down. You look pale.

BILL: I didn't know the nesting urge came on so quick.

MRS. CLARK: Yes, your return has been of a short duration, scarcely long enough for much conjunctive bliss.

BILL: It's the plurals I'm worried about.

MRS. CLARK: A serpent in the woodpile, perhaps?

BILL: No, no, nothing like that. Thank you, Mrs. Clark, you've been most kind. This is a garden-variety problem, I think, something about the birds and bees.

MRS. CLARK: While the cat's away, the mice bring home the bacon, eh?

BILL: While the cat's away, the tiger comes out of the foliage for a direct hit on Miss Meow. I'll take off that cat's stripes! I'll turn him into butter and spread something with him.

MRS. CLARK: I advise discussion before accusation. Your spouse may have a perfectly good dissertation.

BILL: We'll see who's got some explaining to do. *(Music to indicate time passing)*

Scene Five

JANET: *(Door slamming)* I saw you helping Mrs. Clark. Glad I don't have to cater to the snoot of the west all by myself. How do you like my tire-mounting job?

BILL: Frankly my dear, I couldn't care less. I've got family matters to worry about.

JANET: But these tires are family matters.

BILL: Nothing compared to these booties and gewgaws. All right, Janet, who's the father? You've been unfaithful and unpatriotic. You've been sneaking around while I was off fighting the enemy.

JANET: Why, Bill, I'm surprised you don't know. You told Mr. Glen all about it, right? "In the family way" is the phrase you used, I believe. I thought it was a little strange you'd know before I did, but like a dutiful wife, I didn't want to argue with my hubby. How do you like my contribution to our bundle of joy?

BILL: This is no bundle of joy. How could you?

JANET: How could I what? Go down to the department store and charge something? To a girl like me, toting a purse and pointing a finger for what I want isn't hard at all. Besides, I've always loved baby clothes. Even the sissy ones for girls.

BILL: You have?

JANET: Why sure. Just because I can mount tires doesn't mean I wouldn't be happy to mix formula.

BILL: But you said you weren't? . . .

JANET: Weren't what? Going to keep working? I guess not. You've put a kibosh on that.

BILL: No, I mean, you're not, you know. . .

JANET: Mad as a wet hen? I was when I got off the phone with Mr. Glen. Imagine, you spreading our family business up one side of Main Street and down the other. Your mother will be shocked.

BILL: Then there isn't anything to it?

JANET: Not anything more than what you started, my romantic fool. You'd better straighten this out with your parents before they hear it from the grapevine.

BILL: And I don't want you lifting anything.

JANET: Bill, remember? I'm not.

BILL: You're not.

JANET: Right. But your parents are.

BILL: No. They're too old.

JANET: You got that right. Boy, a few years in the Army certainly does dust up a guy's lessons from the birds and the bees. Too old for that, but just right to drive to Atlantic City for their thirtieth wedding anniversary.

BILL: *They* bought the new tires?

JANET: What a brilliant deduction. My hero!

Step Nine: Drafting the Radio Sketch

After returning the "pass-it-back" papers to their originators, the class can decide whether to work in groups or individually from this point on. If students collaborate, they should pick one scene or one character. Then each person in the group can be responsible for writing the speeches for that one character. They'll also want to include music, sound effects, and a title for the show; this can be a joint or individual effort.

Before this, though, I outline a basic scheme of five scenes, to show the class the way the plot begins, picks up momentum, comes to a climax, and is finally resolved:

• **Scene one:** The first scene introduces the *two main characters and the conflict.* Conflict can include differences in goals, manners, expectations of each other or of other people. I urge the students to make the car (or whatever theme is chosen) a part of the conflict.

• **Scene two:** *One of the characters overhears or finds or sees something that gives him or her a jolt.* This jolt relates to the conflict. It may be a misunderstanding, or it may be some harebrained act that precipitates a series of unexpected events.

• **Scenes three and four:** The two main characters are separated in the next two scenes. These scenes bring each main character together with his or her sidekick for some plot development. One of the main characters may be scheming; the other may be doing something innocent that looks suspicious.

• **Scene five:** The two main characters are back together and after *one of them challenges the other, the truth comes out and harmony is—at least for the moment—restored.* Remember, this is comedy, in which couples and families remain unharmed and united.

Step Ten: Performing the Radio Dramas

Students can perform their plays for each other in class, taking turns reading the parts they've written and adding the sound effects. But it's even better to tape record some of the dramas, with realistic music and sound effects, and then take the tapes to entertain another class. Another option is to play the dramas over the PA system for the whole school. The dramas could be broken up into scenes, with one scene aired a day, to save time. Serials have a long history that dates back at least as far as the nineteenth-century magazine weeklies. A forum can be held for the school at the end of the dramas, to let the audience ask questions about the era and the plays.

EXERCISE TWO
Technology and Intimacy

Poems that explore the way technology in two different decades affects our relationships with each other and with nature. (For upper elementary to adult.)

Step One: Exploring the Sources

Most of us have vague notions about how people in earlier times lived. To make those notions concrete we need to turn to historical sources. Popular songs from the past include many details about everyday life: think of "a bicycle built for two," for example. Leafing through old magazines or looking at outmoded household implements also gives us hints of how people lived in the past. Old photographs are one of my favorite ways to do research because each image presents—all at once— the architecture, fashion, technology, and sometimes the customs of a particular region and time. Old photos are available in "trash and treasure" shops or in family albums. I bought a group of fifteen anonymous snapshots in a flea market in Sioux Falls, South Dakota, and wrote a poem for each photo. One of these poems is particularly helpful for introducing old-fashioned, turn-of-the-century Midwestern ways to classes. Here is the photo and my poem about it:

Fig. 10: Threshers.

Scissors, Snake, Braid, Metal

Threshers came to cut down wheat,
　　pages of rippling sound.
　　Four horses pulled the scissors.

Four men wore hats whose straw brims
　　skittered chaff like mice in the gutter.
　　Scissors sliced through snake.

Winding through heat and chaff the crew
　　smoked across the field. Behind
　　fell a snake like tarnished metal.

At noon out of the cloud the men
　　limped to the boy. Under four caps,
　　blackened faces begged, "Boy, brush our eyes."

In his hand lay pieces of snake,
　　words that fell silent from the page of field
　　except one watery eye that cried to him.
　　He could not meet the threshers' eyes.

In *Cane* (1923), the African-American poet Jean Toomer also wrote a poem about cutting grain, but from the point of view of black men, possibly slaves.[7] In Toomer's poem, a rat is cut by the scythe, much as threshing kills the snake in my poem. The technology is different, but both poems suggest a loss of empathy that comes with bending to the work of cutting and threshing.

Another way to learn about technological change is to consult our elders. Talking to a grandparent or reading oral histories about growing up sixty to eighty years ago will give students a flavor of earlier ways of life. Memoirs about particular locales are often published by historical societies, churches, or fraternal orders, and are available in local libraries.

In a writing class for residents at a senior citizens' home, I've helped women from eighty to one hundred years old record their memories of daily life. Irene Brodie, now 102, describes wash day at her childhood home in South Dakota, at the turn of the century. The work began with gathering water to fill three great tubs in the kitchen. On one tub a hand-turned wringer was attached.

> Hot water from the reservoir attached to the big kitchen range was bailed into one tub. Pails of water from the hand pump over the sink were poured into the other two for rinsing. A big copper boiler was put on the stove and filled with water into which Fels-Naptha soap was shaved.

Every piece of clothing was scrubbed with Fels-Naptha soap in the hot water tub on a washboard. A washboard has a wooden frame with two legs to stand upon in the tub but leans back against the side of the tub. There is a panel of ridged metal and a ledge at the top to hold a bar of soap. To use it, one soaps the soiled spots of the garment and rubs hard on the ridged panel.

The white clothes were put into the copper boiler after scrubbing and boiled until snowy white.

The colored clothes were scrubbed next, then put through the wringer, into two rinsings, and then wrung again before being put into a clothes basket to be carried to the yard, where they were hung up on a clothes-line to dry.

When the white clothes were boiled, they were transferred by two smooth sticks into a rinse and then a second rinse of freshly drawn water.

[. . .]

The tubs were emptied by bucket into the sink where a pipe carried the water to a tank near the garden. This wash water could be used to water the garden and flower beds if rain failed us. The empty tubs went back into the shed. The reservoir next to the stove was refilled so there'd be hot water for daily use and the nice soapy water from the copper boiler was used to scrub the kitchen floor.[8]

Another rich source of information about the daily life of a previous era describes white tenant-farmers in Alabama in 1936. James Agee wrote *Let Us Now Praise Famous Men* on assignment for *Fortune* magazine, but his text and the accompanying photographs by Walker Evans were rejected. Expanded and published in 1941, the book met with little initial success, but is now recognized as a classic. Some sections, such as the following paragraph about the beds where the members of the Gudger family slept, clearly describe the artifacts of daily life:

The children's bed in the rear room has a worn-out and rusted mesh spring; the springs of the other two beds are wire net, likewise rusty and exhausted. Aside from this . . . the beds may be described as one. There are two mattresses on each, both very thin, padded, I would judge, one with raw cotton and one with cornshucks. They smell old, stale, and moist, and are morbid with bedbugs, with fleas, and, I believe, with lice. They are homemade. The sheaths are not ticking, but rather weak unbleached cotton. Though the padding is sewn through, to secure it, it has become uncomfortably lumpy in some places, nothing but cloth in others. The sheeting is of a coarse and beautiful unbleached but nearly white cotton, home-sewn down the length of each center with a seam either ridged or drawn apart. It is cloth of a sort that takes and holds body heat rapidly, and which is humid with whatever moisture may be in the air, and the fabric is sharp against the skin. The pillows are store bought, the cheapest obtainable: thin, hard, crackling under any motion of the head; and seem, like the mattresses, to carry vermin. The pillowcases are homemade, of the sheeting; one is a washed, soft, fifty-pound floursack. The striped ticking shows strongly through the cloth. The beds are insecure enough in their joints that motions of the body must be gentle, balanced, and to some extent thought out beforehand. The mattresses and springs are loud, each in a different way, to any motion. The springs sag so deeply that two or more, sleeping here, fall together to the middle almost as in a hammock. The sheets are drawn tight in making the bed, in part out of housework ritual, in part, I believe, in the wish to make the chronically sagged beds look level. Sometimes this succeeds. At other times the bed, neatly made though it is, looks like an unlucky cake.[9]

The final example is by poet Phoebe Hanson:

Long Underwear

While my sister is still asleep next to me in the bed,
I lie awake staring
at the cracks in the rough plaster walls
of our little stucco bungalow.
Outside another blizzard
whips snow against our window,
and no one will go to school today.
But I get up anyway,
the only one awake in the house,
grab long underwear
saved from the day before.
Back then, underwear
was worn for a week,
from one Saturday night
bath to the next.
I race to the hot air
register in the living room,
let my flannel nightgown
drop to the floor,
stand in forbidden nakedness
while the rush of Satanic heat
blasts forth from the coal furnace below.
When I hear the rest of the family stir,
I pull the grey underwear
over my legs,
carefully wrap it
around and around my ankles,
hold it in place with long brown stockings,
stare at the wrinkles,

at the ugliness I won't discard
until spring melts the stubborn snow
of my father's caution,
and lets me wear my legs naked again.[10]

Step Two: Mapping the Effects of Technology

Making word maps helps students explore how people of different eras washed, dressed, grew or bought food, cooked, slept, heated and lit their homes, traveled, and communicated, and how these daily activities affect the human relationship to natural resources and to each other. Students can write two word maps: one for past practices and another for present ones.

To begin, have students write, in the middle of a piece of paper, a past practice that is different from ours; for example, "washing clothes by hand," "sleeping in homemade cornhusk beds," or "keeping chickens for eggs and meat." For purposes of illustration, let's use "keeping a cow for milk."

Next, have them draw straight or curved "roads" out from the phrase.

Now students are ready to consider the consequences of this way of life. Have them imagine that they are children in a family that has old-fashioned ways, just as in Phoebe Hanson's poem, living in a small town or on a farm, and that there are at least two children in the family. First, on one of the roads of the map, I have them write about the people who are involved with this item or activity. (See number 1 on the diagram below.)

Next, under numbers 2 and 3, I ask students to add a list of the natural resources the cow needs to stay alive and ways the cow depletes or increases natural resources. Notice here that while cows need space, maybe an acre of pasture to produce grass and hay, they save the family from having to travel to get milk or cheese. The cow also replenishes the soil with manure.

Under number 4, I have students add what a family keeping a cow would know about the cow and her needs:

l. Parents buy cow, grow hay, build barn, child milks cow, parent separates cream, stores milk in ice box—three people.

2. Cow needs hay, wood for barn, water to drink, grass to eat. Maybe a half acre will give enough grass, needs pond or spring.

Keeping a cow for milk

3. Cow manure will help replenish soil. Can also burn cow chips. Milk and cheese keep family healthy. The family doesn't have to burn gas or oil to get milk or keep it cold.

4. Children know the warmth and smell of a cow, also how her body looks & sounds. They may name her and know when she's sick. They know when she needs to be milked and to eat. They'll be able to tell whether she's eaten wild onion because her milk will taste that way. If there's a drought, they'll realize that they can't grow food for her and maybe they'll have to kill her. They may play with her bones.

Step Three: Mapping the Present-day Equivalent

A second word map, based on a modern dairy farm, gives students a better perspective on technology and social change. (In rural schools, I ask students to assume that today none of their families keep a milk cow.) For comparative purposes, let's assume that the modern family consists of a parent or two and at least two children who live in a fairly large urban area.

On this word map, students sketch out the same categories as before, but in present-day terms:

1. An adult to earn money to buy milk, supermarket employees to unload, store, and charge for the milk, a trucker to bring milk to the store, farmers to care for and milk the cows and take the milk to the dairy, workers to process it—twelve people.

2. Need electricity to run milkers, boilers and packagers in dairy, lights, coolers in store, refrigerator at home; gas to bring milk to dairy, to store, to home. Hay, grass, water, shelter for cow, manure possibly used on soil as nutrient.

Buying milk at the store

3. Family knows nothing about cows, except maybe a picture on the milk carton. They do know how to walk or drive to the store. If a drought hurts cows in one part of the country, the family's milk may come from another region. The family is not as closely connected to the natural world of cows, weather, hay, or wild onions. A small child may even think that milk "comes from" the store.

Step Four: Drafting a Poem about Technology in a Previous Era

At this point I ask students to review their word maps and to select a moment on the map that has dramatic possibilities—somebody involved in some activity.

Now, each student (or the class as a whole, if you're doing a class collaboration) can create a character and imagine that character in a location. They should be very specific: for instance, not just a girl on a farm, but rather a sixteen-year-old girl in her grandfather's kitchen in a farmhouse in North Dakota drinking a glass of milk that came from the cows grazing around the pond just down the road. To this they can add notes about what they know about the technology of the period. As they do all this, the students should allow themselves to imagine that they *are* their characters and to "go back in time" to the decade when the technology in question was in use. They should feel free to fictionalize the character as they do this.

To begin their poems, I tell students to emphasize the sights, sounds, tastes, and smells of the place they're in. Then, if they wish, they can expand the scene to include other characters.

Step Five: Reading a Model, Adding Comparisons, Forming an Ending

Before students start their drafts, I sometimes read them one last example, a poem of mine about the cows and milk. Note how, toward the end of the poem, I use two comparisons to show how close I've come to the cow and to the boy who delivers the milk. I encourage students to use comparisons in their poems, because I think it helps them to express their intimate experience with the natural world.

Milk Bottles / Cow Pies

Saturday. Pulled awake
by the early sun, I tiptoe
down the creaking stairs.
Milk bottles clink.
Through the window, the farm boy
grins at me. I crumple—
he'll see my nightgown.
A long stare at the linoleum,
then straightening
I pull open the door,
grasp the cool necks
of milk bottles—can't wait
for a swig of clover-sweet.
I step gingerly across
the splintery shed, pour
a gush of white in a glass
with red chickens, red as
the nameless cow's warm red
side I milked last week
at grandfather's farm.
Her innards sloshed like
water in the bottom of a boat.
The squirt of milk as sharp
as spit from the boy's teeth.
He'll tell on me today
out there in the barn
by the lake. Prissy town girl
he'll call me. The glass
tilts up a big gulp,
pool in the throat.
An aftertaste—wild onion.
It's his bouquet, that rascal.
How can I repay him?
A cow pie in his lunch box
come school on Monday.

Variation: Double-Voiced Poems

This variation is akin to a song with two voices, or, as a dramatist might call it, overlapping monologues. Splicing two poems, each written from a word map of different eras, can give students a graphic sense of how the different technologies affect us differently. Here's a double-voiced poem I wrote:

Drinking Milk—Two Generations

Summer. Pulled awake
by the early sun, I tiptoe
down the creaking stairs.
Milk bottles clink.

> Winter morning. Room
> cold until furnace
> cranks up. Fridge door
> sticks, milk carton
> drips from a wound.

The farm boy grins at me.
I crumple. He'll see
my nightgown. Stare
at the linoleum,
then straightening
I pull open the door,
grasp the cool necks
of the bottles.

> Snap, crackle, pop
> of Rice Krispies
> in a bowl. Milk
> drowns three elves,
> I used to believe
> the box, they could
> talk. Milk so cold
> it hurts my teeth.

Can't wait for a swig
of clover-sweet. I step
gingerly across
the splintery shed.
Gush of white in a glass
with red chickens, red
as the cow's red warm side
I milked last week
at grandfather's farm.

I used to believe
cows lived in the back
of the store, milk
squirted into the carton.
Cows in stalls at the fair,
bad smell, no place to move.
Who wants to wait for the bus
in this weather.

Her gut sloshed like
water in the bottom of a boat.
The squirt of milk
as sharp as spit
from the boy's teeth.
He'll tell on me today,
out there in the barn
by the lake. Prissy town girl,

If I dawdle, I'll miss it
then mom will have to
drive me. Traffic, clouds
of exhaust, windshields
frozen. We don't talk.
She turns off my music.
She can stop at the store.
We're almost out of milk.

The glass tilts up
a big gulp, pool in
the throat, aftertaste
of wild onion.
It's his bouquet.
That rascal. How
can I get even?
A cow pie in his
lunchpail come
Monday at school.

Two discoveries I made in writing this poem intrigued me. The first
is how our distance from the natural sources of food and fuel encourages
cartoon fantasies: when I was little, the three Rice Krispie elves played at
the edge of my cereal bowl. I had no cows to scold for eating onions. I
was also struck by how the speed of our transportation makes life less
intimate. The child in the right-hand side of the poem relies on adult-
driven vehicles to get to school, and her experience of her mother and of

the people in other cars relates primarily to driving and to buying: we begin to resemble the mechanisms supposed to serve us.

Variation

This notion of role reversal isn't original with me. Since the beginning of the Industrial Revolution, writers have observed the effect of what William Wordsworth called "getting and spending" in his Sonnet 38 (in *Lyrical Ballads*, 1807):

> The world is too much with us; late and soon,
> Getting and spending, we lay waste our powers:
> Little we see in nature that is ours;
> We have given our hearts away, a sordid boon!
> This Sea that bares her bosom to the moon;
> The Winds that will be howling at all hours
> And are up-gathered now like sleeping flowers;
> For this, for every thing, we are out of tune.[11]

Henry David Thoreau noted wryly (in *Walden*, 1854) how the locomotive had changed things:

> Far through unfrequented woods on the confines of towns, where once only the hunter penetrated by day, in the darkest night dart these bright saloons without the knowledge of their inhabitants; this moment stopping at some brilliant station-house in town or city, where a social crowd is gathered, the next in the Dismal Swamp, scaring the owl and fox. The startings and arrivals of the cars are now the epochs in the village day. They go and come with such regularity and precision, and their whistle can be heard so far that the farmers set their clocks by them, and thus one well-conducted institution regulates a whole country. Have not men improved somewhat in punctuality since the railroad was invented? Do they not talk and think faster in the depot than they did in the stage-office? There is something electrifying in the atmosphere of the former place. I have been astonished at the miracles it has wrought; that some of my neighbors, who, I should have prophesied, once for all, would never get to Boston by so prompt a conveyance, are on hand when the bell rings. To do things "railroad fashion" is now the byword.[12]

While Wordsworth wishes that we could completely shun the demands and pace of commercialism, Thoreau cannot help but be intrigued by how the railroad has speeded up his logy neighbors. It's interesting to compare these two nineteenth-century responses to technology with Tillie Olsen's grisly description of workers in a meat-packing plant in the 1930s:

In Casings it is 110 [degrees]. A steam kettle, thinks Ella, who had a need to put things into words, a steam kettle, and in a litany: *steamed, boiled, broiled, fried, cooked; steamed, boiled, broiled, fried, cooked.* Tony, Smoky's older brother, lugging his hand truck from fire to chill to fire (casings to cooler to casings) fans the cooler door open for the women as long as he dares. Each time (the hands never ceasing their motions) even those too far away from relief turn their heads in unison toward the second's different air, flare their nostrils, gulp with open mouths. The stench is vomit-making as never before. The fat and plucks, the bladders and kidneys and bungs and guts, gone soft and spongy in the heat, perversely resist being trimmed, separated, deslimed; demand closer concentration than ever, extra speed. A hysterical helpless laughter starts up. Indeed they are in hell; indeed they are the damned. *Steamed boiled broiled fried cooked. Geared meshed.*[13]

Students don't have to enter a factory or railroad yard to understand how technology can dehumanize—or energize—us. They need only to examine what they do every day and to describe it carefully, pinpointing how technology has come to control our lives. I ask students to begin this exercise by thinking of an activity they do regularly—watching TV, or cutting the grass with a gasoline or electric lawnmower, or making a telephone call. I ask them to describe it as if they were giving directions to an alien on how to do it. As they write, they can add repeating lines that mimic the repetition, rhythms, sounds, smells, sights of the technology they're using. In this regard, Tillie Olsen's description of the rendering plant is a good model.

Technology's effect may be enriching or numbing: for example, hearing a voice via telephone across hundreds of miles, especially a familiar and beloved voice, is surely one of the pleasures of modern technology. Being stuck in rush-hour traffic and smelling the exhaust fumes of hundreds of cars isn't. In writing about a specific technology, students should keep in mind how it encourages or reduces some of the qualities we prize: alert attention, careful thought, unexpected ideas, compassionate response, generosity, trust, and so on. In most instances, technological "progress" simultaneously has advantages and disadvantages. For example, the telephone brings a distant friend closer to us than a letter does because we hear the actual voice: the immediacy is something like being in a room with the friend. But some may argue that the telephone encourages shallowness because we speak quickly and without much consideration; the telephone has also reduced our ability to write vividly and with feeling. Letters from a century ago are now valuable documents of daily life: in a hundred years, we won't have such a record of how we have lived. This exercise may help students weigh both the positive and negative effects of technology's increased presence.

EXERCISE THREE
Migration, Neighborhoods, and Housing

Many Americans have immigrated from other parts of the world, and, once they are in the U. S., have then moved from one place to another. During the twentieth century, this migration has developed particular patterns, one of the most pronounced being the exodus from city to suburb. In this exercise, students gather first-hand information and survey historical and literary descriptions of changing neighborhoods, then write pieces about real places and "dream" places. (For upper elementary to adult.)

Step One: Documenting Change in the Neighborhood

Sometimes all students have to do is walk through a neighborhood in their own town or city and look for the changes occurring building by building. Recently, certain neighborhoods have been "gentrified": run-down rental properties have been renovated and spiffed up, sometimes driving out the former tenants, who then are forced to relocate to housing projects or other rental housing. Many cities have such projects, where the newest immigrants mix with Latinos, blacks, and whites. If your classroom is ethnically or racially mixed, all the students have to do is interview each other to discover how migration and neighborhood change are related. They can ask: Where did you live when you first came to the city? Where did your parents, grandparents, great-grandparents come from? Where has your family found better housing? Have your family ever had to withhold rent because the landlord wouldn't make repairs?

Of course, neighborhoods decay or become refurbished for many reasons: it was a freeway that destroyed the black neighborhood along Rondo Avenue in St. Paul, Minnesota, for example. Freeway construction has encouraged suburban sprawl in Los Angeles, Atlanta, and every sizeable American city—think of a state and you can probably name one of its cities affected this way. Upward mobility also changes neighborhoods. As the children of first-generation immigrants grew up with the American language and the know-how to get better jobs, their children in turn often abandoned the old ethnic and racial neighborhoods for the shiny new suburbs. Some outlying small towns have been engulfed by these suburbs.

I usually have students begin this exercise by gathering first-hand information through interviews (with shop owners in a neighborhood, for example) and walking tours. This enables them to delve into written sources (nonfiction, fiction, plays, and poems) with a keener sense of the dynamics of urban change.

Interviews with long-time residents can help students gauge the effect of migration on individuals. Shopkeepers make excellent subjects because their livelihoods are tied to changes in the economic and ethnic composition of a neighborhood. For instance, in the course of eight interviews that I have conducted with grocers, pharmacists, paint store owners, and fuel dealers in a St. Paul neighborhood, I heard all of them comment on two major population shifts in the past hundred years: first, a predominantly Swedish immigrant population arrived between 1880 and 1910 and moved north from the early settlement close to the Mississippi River. (The earliest settlement in St. Paul took place along the river because, of course, the river was the first roadway.) Second, with soldiers returning from World War II and getting married, another major migration occurred, again to the north, to land that had previously been truck farms, woods, or sparsely settled townships. This migration created typical 1950s suburbs of ranch-style tract housing, meaning that the houses were built in large numbers all at once, each with minor distinguishing touches, but essentially with the same floor plans.

This second shift, the migration to the suburbs, was due in part to the automobile: more families now had the cars they needed to reach the goods and services that formerly had been within walking distance. Consequently, business in the old neighborhoods declined, as the older, home-owning residents died and were replaced by less affluent people who rented. Some merchants survived by opening stores in the new suburbs or by absorbing the business of their less fortunate competitors. Thus a complicated group of changes in population, in location and type of housing, and in the use of the automobile altered the way people did business.

Another approach is to invite an old-timer to class, one who's seen the neighborhood change. Each student can ask a question or two, prepared beforehand, and, during the interview, jot down important events, descriptions, and attitudes about the neighborhood.

Step Two: Consulting Written Sources

The Chicago of around World War I provides an instructive example of neighborhood change. Allan Spear's study, *Black Chicago: The Making of a Negro Ghetto, 1890–1920*,[14] describes the huge migration from the Deep South to northern cities that was first spurred by the ruin of the southern cotton industry by the boll weevil prior to the war, and then furthered by the wartime demand for industrial workers. Describing itself as the "leading Negro journal in the country," the *Chicago Defender* appealed to poor black people in the South and depicted migration as a move north to freedom and a blow to southern tyranny.[15] Northern railroad and business representatives went south to spread the enthusiasm for change. Black farm families who had never traveled further than the closest town took the train in the spirit of embarking for the Promised Land. Biblical images helped these rural folks ennoble their risky exodus—the flight out of Egypt . . . Going into Canaan . . . Beulah Land. Their idealized vision of the Promised Land has much in common with that of poor Scandinavians, Italians, or Irish at the end of the nineteenth century, when agents for steamship companies exaggerated the riches and excitement of America and the difficulties of the old world in their advertisements.

Many southern blacks, like newly arrived foreign immigrants, had no notion of how a big city like Chicago operated—they asked for directions, expecting the first person to know their friends, even without an address. Wearing, as Allan Spear put it, "worn, outmoded suits, carrying battered luggage . . . clutching ragged, barefooted children," the black migrants soon found their way to the black neighborhood on the South Side, where "two-story frame houses devoid of paint stood close together in drab, dingy rows, surrounded by litters of garbage and ashes. Ordinary conveniences were often non-existent: toilets were broken or leaky; electricity was rare; heating and hot water facilities failed to function,"[16] just as in the neighborhood where St. Paul's first Swedish immigrants lived.

The southern black men often found work in industry for the duration of World War I, but their wives and daughters had more trouble getting predominantly white factory jobs. These southern black women—like those who'd already lived in Chicago for several generations—eventually found work as domestics in white homes or hotels. The southern newcomers began their adjustment to the pace and expectations of the city, often having less free time—no more Saturdays off, no winter slack time. Now they worked six-day weeks, year round, with the compensation of steady money and rising expectations. They also found racial discrimination: the huge Chicago race riot of 1919 jolted many new residents awake to the violence their presence could unleash.

Lorraine Hansberry's play about a black Chicago family, *A Raisin in the Sun*, is set in a typical South Side "rat trap" apartment. Here, three generations of Youngers dream of using the ten thousand dollars coming to Mama (from her dead husband's insurance) to escape into a better life. Here Mama describes her life in the apartment:

> "Rat trap"—yes, that's all it is. (*Smiling*) I remember just as well the day me and Big Walter moved in here. Hadn't been married but two weeks and wasn't planning on living here no more than a year. (*She shakes her head*

at the dissolved dream) We was going to set away, little by little, don't you know, and buy a little place out in Morgan Park. We had even picked out the house. (*Chuckling a little*) Looks right dumpy today. But Lord, child, you should know all the dreams I had 'bout buying that house and fixing it up and making me a little garden in the back—(*She waits and stops smiling*) And didn't none of it happen.[17]

A poem by Chicago poet Gwendolyn Brooks describes life in one of Chicago's wartime "kitchenette" apartments:

Kitchenette Building

We are things of dry hours and the involuntary plan,
Grayed in, and gray. "Dream" makes a giddy sound, not strong
Like "rent," "feeding a wife," "satisfying a man."

But could a dream send up through onion fumes
Its white and violet, fight with fried potatoes
And yesterday's garbage ripening in the hall,
Flutter, or sing an aria down these rooms

Even if we were willing to let it in,
Had time to warm it, keep it very clean,
Anticipate a message, let it begin?

We wonder. But not well! not for a minute!
Since Number Five is out of the bathroom now,
We think of lukewarm water, hope it get in it.[18]

Brooks imagines hope overcome by the rank smell and decrepitude of the building. When getting a bath takes scheming, a hope for the kind of escape Mama describes does not grow any stronger than the wilting flower Ruth Younger nurses on the ledge outside her window.

Step Three: Freewriting about a Neighborhood

Having done some research into a neighborhood's history, students can now begin drafting a poem of place, about their own or someone else's neighborhood.

I usually have students begin with some freewriting about a neighborhood that they know well, the one where they live now or one they have left or heard relatives talk about a lot. I ask them to think about signs of change in the neighborhood, and the hopes and satisfactions or disappointments families may have experienced with the housing and the way they've been treated by their neighbors. Students should also comment on their favorite and least favorite spots in the neighborhood—the sights, sounds, and smells that either repel or attract them. Landmarks in a neighborhood, such as a fountain, a statue, or a particular house, make good subjects.

Step Four: Creating a Character Who Has a Different Perspective than One's Own

I often encourage students to write from a perspective different than their own. This other perspective may be that of a parent, an older neighbor or friend, or a figure from the students' reading. To give substance to this other character, students can make a list of some of the things that connect this person to the place—beliefs, memories, hopes, etc. For example, if I were to incorporate my mother into a poem about where I grew up (the Old Citadel, a block-long, former barracks for the military college where my father taught in Charleston, South Carolina), I'd list:

  • *Things she did in relation to the place.* The night before we left for a visit to her hometown in North Dakota, she painted the kitchen floor brown with paint from the quartermaster, and laid boards over it for us to cross on our way out to the train. She scolded the peeping tom who came to our back bedroom door. She told us, "Don't run in the halls." She brought us big cardboard boxes from the appliance store across the street to make into play houses. She bought us a two-seated swing for the courtyard.

  • *Ways she felt about the place and the people, things she said about them.* She was appalled by the number of children ("One hundred children in one block!") She invited ladies in for tea occasionally—we made decorated sandwiches, blue moons, green stars, and decorated cookies. She didn't stand and gossip in the halls with other mothers. She hated the lack of privacy. She was proud that the southern church ladies asked her to chair their committees when "they wanted something done." She hated the rats from the ships that ran outside around the courtyard, and she hated the heat.

  • *What the place symbolized for her and how she reacted to its significance.* Living in the Old Citadel was a comedown for my mother, like being sent to a ghetto. She prided herself on being northern and sometimes said she had more energy than the southern women around her. She wanted to make the barnlike rooms attractive. The minute her father gave her money for a downpayment on a suburban home, she bought a huge lot across the river from Charleston and had a small Cape Cod bungalow built, with plenty of space and privacy, just like in her small hometown.

Step Five: Shaping the Poem or Dramatic Monologue

The examples quoted in this step are good literary models for writing about neighborhoods and places. Each suggests a different way of molding the material students have gathered about the history and character of their neighborhoods.

The first poem, by Ricardo Vasquez, was published in Spanish and English in *Fiesta in Aztlan*, an anthology of Chicano poetry:

La Peluqueria del Maestro

Al lado de la iglesia Apostólica de Dios,
cruzando la calle de la iglesia Católica,
se encontraba la peluquería del maestro
donde iba el jefe a cortarse la greña.
Todos los conocidos llegaban sobre la mañana
saludándose uno al otro como amigos que eran
the barrio aristocracy, los hombres de
juicio y de sueños, Lucky Lager instead
of Mint Juleps.
El Maestro con su misma cara todos los sábados;
fuerte, redonda, chimuelo, but kept smiling,
el gran oido, con noble manos
valiendo oro enredadas entre el pelo.
Los sueños de mejoramienta eran realidad
en la peluquería del maestro.
Allí sobre el espejo, un retrato del
muchacho García que pichó por los
Cleveland Indians era la confirmación.

* * *

The Maestro's Barber Shop

Next to the Apostolic Church of God,
crossing the street where the Catholic church was located,
was the barber shop of the maestro
where my father went to have his hair cut.
All the old acquaintances arrived during the morning
greeting one another like the friends they were
the barrio aristocracy, men of
wisdom and of dreams, *Lucky Lager instead*
of Mint Juleps.
The Maestro with the same face every Saturday;
strong, round, some teeth missing, but kept smiling,
the great listener, with noble hands
worth gold entangled in their hair.
Dreams of better things to come were a reality
in the maestro's barber shop.
There over the mirror, a photograph of the

García boy who pitched for the
Cleveland Indians was the confirmation.[19]

Vasquez selects a neighborhood hang-out and starts his poem by placing it in relation to other buildings. Then the poem introduces the characters who frequent the barber shop: the maestro, the poet's father, and other old friends. The maestro becomes the focus, because in his smile, his skillful treatment of men and their hair, he creates a haven for their hopes, with the picture of the García boy, probably in his baseball uniform, as the symbol of hoped-for success. (Mike García was, in fact, a well-known pitcher for the Cleveland Indians in the 1950s.) With gentle irony the poet suggests that for most of these men such hopes are illusory: they will never really step out of the barrio into a larger world.

Students can use Vasquez's poem as a model by beginning their own poems with buildings or spots that are the center of their own neighborhoods—church, hardware store, street corner, backyard fence. Next, they can introduce a regular event—a church supper, a Saturday morning conference of home-repair enthusiasts with the hardware store owner, or an across-the-fence discussion of the weather. Then, I ask them to add details about the appearance of the regulars—stocking caps and torn windbreakers, mud-caked work boots, round bellies, balding heads—and say who is at the center of their discussion. Although the neighborhoods the students describe may be quite unlike the one in Vasquez's poem, I tell them that there should be some object in the scene—like the photo of Mike García—that helps express the emotional meaning of the moment. Perhaps in the hardware store it's a huge snowblower waiting for winter, or in a driveway a brand-new car, or a letter from a relative or traveling friend, with photos.

Variation: Monologues of Escape

It's very human to dream of leaving the familiar rut for somewhere else; it's particularly American to dream of returning to a place left behind (like some women on the Oregon Trail) or forging ahead to new territory, to start over again (like most men on the Trail). These desires suggest another way of writing about neighborhoods and their changes: to create a monologue for a character who dreams of a better place to live.

Paule Marshall's novel about Brooklyn, *Brown Girl, Brownstones*, describes Selina's family (immigrants from Barbados) who rent a deteriorating brownstone row house in Brooklyn during World War II. Selina's mother works hard and saves, determined to buy the house, but her father dreams of returning to Barbados and building a dream house on his tiny piece of land there:

"And when I show these Bajan [Barbadians] here, I gon left them to run temself in an early grave in this man New York. I going home and breathe good Bimshire air 'cause a man got a right to take his ease in this life and not always be scuffling."

He raised the trumpet and again lowered it. "Did I tell yuh I gon plant ladies-of-the-night round the house?"

"What're those?" [Selina] whispered, remembering with a wrench the mother's vow.

"A flower that does smell only at night. When you in you bed you can smell it and it's like the night-self is the thing smelling so sweet . . . And in the front yard I gon have a flamboyant tree. You ain never seen anything like that tree, lady-folks. The blossom does be a blood red and the branches wide so. And when the blossom fall all the ground does be covered in red like a rug," he said, standing absorbed in the middle of the red-faded Oriental rug.

"Daddy," she whispered, and he waved the trumpet, silencing her.

"And I got the house clear-clear in my mind now. I gon build it out of good Bajan coral stone and paint it white. Everything gon be white! A gallery with tall white columns at the front like some temple or the other. A parlor with 'nough furnitures and a dining room with glasses of every description and flowers from we own garden. . ."

"Daddy," she strained toward him.

"And upstairs 'ough bedrooms with their own bathroom—and every bathroom with a stained-glass window like in a church. People gon come from all over to see those stain-glass windows. . ."

Suddenly Selina leaped up, and as the trumpet made another wide dazzling arc she grabbed it, screaming, "She's gonna sell it. She's gonna sell it all."

"What, lady-folks? Who selling what?"

"Mother . . . she's gonna sell the land. Your land."[20]

In this passage, the father daydreams himself out of the New York where he is so often humiliated. When Selina challenges him with the news that her grimly determined mother will ruin his hopes, she not only speaks the truth, but hints at his superfluous role in the new neighborhood.

Students can begin shaping a monologue about a dream place for a character by identifying the place that person would like to escape to. Sometimes people's fantasies about ideal homes or neighborhoods date back to their childhoods, as is the case with Selina's father. Sometimes the "dream house" represents a change in scenery—some people want to move off the farm into the city, or vice versa. Or maybe apartment dwellers yearn for a home of their own, with a yard around it, room for children to play, for entertaining friends, or for a garden.

To develop a monologue, students need to have a character in mind—maybe someone they know or have interviewed, or a fictional character based on a local type: some examples are the farm wife; the college girl; or the father with four children, two mortgages, and a busted furnace. As students develop their monologues, they should keep in mind the age, gender, ethnic and racial background, and general personality of their character. A monologue works best when it includes pet phrases and slang to fit the particular speaker. Selina's father speaks in a West Indian dialect that reflects his background.

Variation: Poems of Cities

It's possible to find meaning and beauty right around the block or in your own backyard. The following poems about cities highlight the power of imagination and perception to discover beauty in the mundane.

In "The Sign," Paul Blackburn imagines two Greek deities, Persephone and Hermes, in the middle of New York City:

> End of September. At
> 19th Street and Fifth Avenue
> on the sidewalk in front of
> the U.S. Employment Service
> a colored lady looks at her watch.
> Five of nine.
> She shines in the sun impatiently

In Madison Square Park
young Persephone from the Bronx
emerges from the subway
ducks her head into
the *Daily Mirror*, walks
not hearing the message
in Puerto Rican Spanish
delivered toward her ear
by a passing young man from Third Avenue and 26th St.
Lady!
You're being flirted with—
enter your life!

I wonder,
does this fountain run all night?
The park smells like an autumn hayfield, dried
leaves, dried grass all heaped together to be

burned in hazy afternoons by men
                    with rakes and visor caps.

Sparrow
looks at fountain ambitiously
and settles for puddle next to it, left
from last night's rain.
In another puddle nearby, a big one,
seventeen disreputable-looking pigeons splutter and
splash and duck their heads
                    and drink and gargle away.
                    Among them a single warbler
green and tan wings splayed
digs long beak into underbelly
                    makes his toilet.

It is settled in already
the birds all employed with their hygiene
the unemployed with their newspapers
on street corners or park benches
Persephone with her page 5
young Hermes off on his errand, hopeless
bums preening outside the public facilities,
and center of it all, this
fountain plashes away   .   And finally
                    today   .   there are
more leaves on the surface of the pool than dixie cups
                    Fall is come[21]

The poem's wit lies in the way Paul Blackburn expands the significance of everyday events in this park by suggesting their connection to each other and to ancient myths: the pigeons "gargle" and the bums "preen," acting like each other; employment is not only the business of people (and some fail at it), but of birds (which are all busy). Persephone from the Bronx may not hear the flirting words of the young Puerto Rican because, after all, the summer is over. Throughout the poem, Blackburn's careful and sympathetic eye catches many signs of the times.

Students can take cues from this poem by focusing on a neighborhood landmark they know well. They might go to the spot and take quick notes of what is happening. The season affects the way plants, people, animals, birds, and machines behave. They should also be on the lookout for small daily urban dramas: the way strangers do or do not interact, or the individual behavior amid the group (like the lone warbler with the pigeons). It's good to capture an image that sums up the essence of the place at one particular moment—like the leaves in the fountain that finally outnumber the Dixie cups.

The next poem, by Patricia Hampl, brings the city of St. Paul, Minnesota, to life by imagining that it has a hand:

St. Paul: Walking

The old city of saints opens its hand again this morning,
    its claw of money and glass rosaries.
I never say no.
Together we have broken bread, promises, hearts,
    whatever drags beneath our muddy river.
I put my bare hand on the red stone of the millionaire's house:
    it sizzled like water in a black pan.
Sometimes I think I will hold forever the hand of this city;
    it shakes its fist of beer and greenhouses at me,
    its long death sways on the stem of an orchid even in winter.[22]

The metaphors and similes in this poem give the city—its industry, its landscape, its character—an almost human personality. I ask students to think about their own cities, and the places and experiences they associate most strongly with them, and then to make a short list of these associations. Some students might want to write as if they were at a vantage point high above downtown, or maybe approaching the city from a distance on a highway. Whatever the point of view, the poet's imagination can create an image that expresses his or her own personal vision of the city—a foot, a flower, a gaze, a kaleidoscope, a web.

In the example below, Denise Levertov, like Blackburn and Hampl, places herself at the scene she is describing:

The Garden Wall

Bricks of the wall,
so much older than the house—
taken I think from a farm pulled down
    when the street was built—
narrow bricks of another century.

Modestly, though laid with panels and parapets,
a wall behind the flowers—
roses and hollyhocks, the silver
pods of lupine, sweet-tasting
phlox, gray
lavender—
        unnoticed—

                              but I discovered
the colors in the wall that woke
when spray from the hose
played on its pocks and warts—

a hazy red, a
grain gold, a mauve
of small shadows, sprung
from the quiet dry brown—

                    archetype
of the world always a step
beyond the world, that can't
be looked for, only
as the eye wanders,
found.[23]

By noticing the otherwise unnoticeable bricks and by realizing that they have a history, Levertov suggests that there is a history behind every overlooked neighborhood artifact—a lamp post, a stop sign, a sidewalk, a garbage can, a garage roof.

The following two examples come from students in their eighties and nineties. Both of the writers have been taking part for many years in a writing class I offer at their senior-citizen residence. In both the poem and the short prose piece, old-fashioned ways of life shine like pearls in the authors' memories. Young students might enjoy comparing their own neighborhoods to those described here:

Memories of Albert Lea

245 W. Clark St.
    The ornate iron fence
    with balls on each point,
    sweet peas
    like young mountaineers
    wearing pastel caps
    climbing the screen porch,
    the long border of nasturtiums
    happy because
    they are so colorful
    and people notice them.

Main Street
    Old men sitting on the bench
    near the barber's pole

talking and watching everybody
walking by.

The enticing cinnamon scent
drifting from
the open bakery door.

Looking over
the whole town
the clock
in the court house tower
tolls each hour
solemnly.

The sweet shop with
its little round tables
and oval backed
wire chairs,
a tall bubbly
chocolate soda,
too soon the sad sound
of air coming
through the straw
in the empty glass.

In Nelson's Grocery
Striped watermelons
piled high
on a table
near the window,
from the ceiling hook
many clusters of bananas
hang down like
long thick
yellow fingers.

The department store's
window with
furniture, men's shoes,
bolts of plaid gingham,
a manikin in a
pink dress
and several straw hats
hanging on a
clothes rack.

Park Avenue
  Impressive big houses
  looking down on
  sparkling Fountain Lake
  rowboats slowly circling,
  canoes racing,
  children swimming near shore.

  —*Dorothea von Berg*

  *   *   *

The County Seat

The town or small city was named for an early settler, Kenton. Five farms reached in all directions. This land was once covered with forests. There are still patches of woods here and there, wood later used for heating and cooking. The town's only claim to fame was the fact that it was the county seat of Hardin County. The Court House, as in most county seats in Ohio, was in the center of Court House Square. On the sides of the square were stores and businesses. Nuises Department Store was on a corner. In the middle to the north side was Schisks, another store that sold sewing material, clothes for women and children. A ten-cent store, a real ten-cent store, Woolworth's was on the west side. On the east side was Sassons Drug Store, where as a child I would buy wonderful ice cream sundaes for a nickel. No lady walked along the south side, for there were saloons and, I have heard, gambling. I was born on N. High Street, also two of my sisters. I remember just a few things about the house, for I was five when we moved. The phone, an old-fashioned one, hung on the wall in the dining room. A big pantry was off the kitchen. Mother was afraid of mice. Women wore long skirts then. She stood on a chair while Dad shut himself up in the pantry, hoping to kill the poor mouse. There was a porch across the back, as well as a pump. The town did have a watering system so we had water in the house. Dad had a strawberry patch and a garden. At the end of the lot was a barn, first for our riding horse Brownie, and then for Colonel, a carriage horse. Very few people had cars.

The town had a public library. Children could take out only one book, that was a hard decision for me. Large grey horses were used in the town fire department.

There were three public elementary schools, first to fourth grade in the East, South, and West Buildings, and a Catholic one. After you finished the fourth grade, you went to Grammar School. I never went to school there, for we moved out of town. Of course, there was a high school, my cousins graduated from there, as well as my father.

I almost forgot the Opera House, mostly for movies, and the movie theater on Detroit Street, not far from the Square. Children could go there for five cents, adults for ten. There were two newspapers, the *Republican* and the *Democrat*. I do not know where men voted, but, of course, Mother couldn't.

People seemed to enjoy living in that town. There were several lodges, Masons and Elks. Mother sang in the church choir, and we children went to Sunday School and we had to behave during the church service.

—*Verna Sweeney*

Final Directions

After hearing these pieces of writing, students will be ready to write. It helps if students have kept a journal of little neighborhood epiphanies, sudden glimpses of materials or workmanship or of interactions between people and things—such a list of small recognitions can be endless. Paying close attention is, after all, common to both the good writer and the good historian, who sees how the present has developed out of countless small actions and reactions. From their notebooks, students can select an entry that still catches their interest, and from that develop a poem or short prose work.

Coda

If this book were a symphony, the themes and variations that echoed and were restated in various registers and keys would now culminate in full force. But teaching, though artful, is not an art form. It is too variable to be an art form. No teacher, no matter how crafty, controlled, or respected, can always lead a classroom full of wriggly eight-year-olds or cautious, skeptical high school seniors through a perfect writing experience. The finest lesson can be derailed by a suddenly beautiful spring day. Even an individual writer, alone with a free hour ahead, can move toward the writing desk, only to be side-tracked by the telephone. This book cannot pretend to a conclusion more definite than its unpredictable human material.

But now, at its finale, this book opens up toward some general comments, a few that look back, a few forward. The healthy practice of crossing disciplines and widening viewpoints is in the wind these days: to give historical substance to peoples previously ignored, students have to look with new eyes and use different tools. Sometimes in such experimentation, a happy combination will occur, like the mixture in one of my favorite exercises—the South American Nerudan ode that celebrates the history of a food that also originated on that continent: the peanut. I hope that this book will point the way to many such conjunctions of literary art and historical substance.

Entering history with the literary imagination is not only aesthetically satisfying, it also may stretch the standards of what belongs in the study of history. This happened in the 1940s, when departments of American Studies systematically began incorporating architecture, music, painting, and sociology into the study of history. Perhaps it's now time for historians to learn the value of student writing that takes a fresh, imaginative, playful view of history. Like juggler's balls, historical facts lie relatively inert until skill and sleight of hand send them dazzling overhead. Each time we bring history's material alive in new ways, we give it a chance to speak to us directly; we also may discover that it has properties we hadn't recognized.

Then there are the students. Imaginative writing doesn't appeal to all teachers and students of history, or of literature, for that matter. But it sometimes brings certain students alive. All of us who visit classrooms to teach creative writing know the sudden excitement of an unexpected success: certain students, who no one ever thought would shine, miraculously do. Usually they are not "academic" in the usual way, may even be "slow." But the oblique, creative approach jogs them awake, and they write with great energy and absorption. When they read their work aloud, the room is hushed with astonishment. They themselves can hardly believe what they have done.

Of course there are many other reasons to introduce creative writing into the study of history, reasons that appeal to the idea of diversity, the use of knowledge, and the reexamination of received ideas. But one of the simplest and best reasons is its ability to transform the many students who slide through American history courses catching only random "facts": George Washington was the first president, the Civil War was fought over slavery, etc. Such facts show no evidence of having been filtered through any process other than that of memorization. Writing a term paper on Mount Vernon may bring some students to appreciate the rich variety of Washington's life, his agricultural bent, and the quasi-feudal management of his plantation, but such a project will result in most students' copying and doctoring segments from encyclopedias, with little grasp of any significance other than that of getting through yet another assignment. However, the instant that standard historical language gives way to metaphor, description, drama, or irony, no one can remain the numb conduit for someone else's thinking.

Writing imaginatively into the American experience requires us to make primary decisions about language, language that then carries the play of temperament and judgment into the past. The past exists only as we continue to bring it alive. We should give our students, who otherwise will fall asleep amidst the drone of what others have said, the chance to dress their own interpretations in strutting colors. It's harder work than snoozing, but a lot more encouraging to those of us who hope that a true and vital study of our past will continue. I'm for that. I dedicate this book to what we have been, to what we can make of that for our edification and delight, and to the richer sense of present identity that will result.

Notes

Chapter One

1. Annie Dillard, *An American Childhood*. New York: Harper & Row, 1987.

2. In *A Geography of Poets: An Anthology of the New Poetry*, edited by Edward Field. New York: Bantam, 1979.

3. In *25 Minnesota Poets*, edited by Seymour Yesner. Minneapolis: Nodin Press, 1974.

4. In *The Large Sky Reaches Down*, a writers-in-the-schools yearly anthology. St. Paul: COMPAS, 1986.

5. In *Three Magics*, a writers-in-the-schools yearly anthology, edited by John Caddy. Minneapolis: COMPAS, 1987.

6. Cynthia Stokes Brown, *Like It Was: A Complete Guide to Writing Oral History*. New York: Teachers & Writers Collaborative, 1988.

7. Joe Paddock, *Boars' Dance*. Duluth: Holy Cow! Press, 1991.

8. In *Looking for Home: Women Writing About Exile*, edited by Deborah Keenan and Roseann Lloyd. Minneapolis: Milkweed Editions, 1991.

9. John Minczeski, *The Spiders*. St. Paul, Minn.: New Rivers, 1979.

10. Ted Kooser, *A Local Habitation and a Name*. New York: Soho Press, 1974.

11. In *The Norton Anthology of Literature by Women*, edited by Sandra M. Gilbert and Susan Gubar. New York: Norton, 1985.

12. Jerome Rothenberg, editor. *Shaking the Pumpkin: Traditional Poetry of the Indian North Americas*. New York: Alfred Van Der Marck, 1986, p. 158.

13. Sandra Cisneros, *The House on Mango Street*. New York: Vintage, 1989, pp. 10–11.

14. Lareina Rule, *Name Your Baby*. New York: Bantam, 1980.

Chapter Two

1. Margot Kriel (Margot Fortunato Galt), "Florence Nightingale Receives a Visitor," *The Iowa Review*, Spring 1980.

2. Thomas Fleming, editor, *Affectionately Yours, George Washington: A Self-Portrait in Letters of Friendship*. New York: Norton, 1967.

3. Walt Whitman, "The Sleepers," in *The Portable Walt Whitman*, edited by Mark Van Doren. New York: Penguin Books, 1973.

4. Frank O'Hara, "The Day Lady Died," in *The Collected Poems of Frank O'Hara*, edited by Donald Allen. New York: Vintage, 1974.

5. Roseann Lloyd, "Lesson from Space," *Minnesota Monthly*, January 1987.

Chapter Three

1. The journals of Christopher Columbus' first voyage to the New World are collected in *Across the Ocean Sea: A Journal of Columbus' Voyage*, edited George Sanderlin. New York: Harper & Row, 1966.

2. Two excellent resources for teaching "The Age of Discovery" are "Quincentennial Education, Grades K–6 or 7–12," from the Central American Resource Center, 317 17th Ave. SE, Minneapolis, MN 55414 and "Rethinking Columbus: Teaching about the 500th Anniversary of Columbus' Arrival in America," from Rethinking Schools, 1001 E. Keefe Avenue, Milwaukee, WI 53212. Both publications review books on the Americas and Columbus' arrival.

3. These two maps are collected in *Discoverers of the New World* by the Editors of American Heritage. New York: American Heritage, 1960.

4. Kelly Cherry, *Relativity: A Point of View*. Baton Rouge: Louisiana State University Press, 1977.

5. Langston Hughes, "The Negro Speaks of Rivers," *The Selected Poems of Langston Hughes*. New York: Vintage, 1959, 1990, p. 4.

6. Robert Francis, "Like Ghosts of Eagles," *The Longman's Anthology of Contemporary American Poetry*, 1950–1980, edited by Stuart Friebert and David Young. White Plains, N.Y.: Longmans, 1983.

7. Henry Gannett, *American Names*. Washington, D.C.: Public Affairs Press, 1947. George R. Steward, *American Place-Names*. New York: Oxford University Press, 1970. Myron J. Quimby, *Scratch Ankle, U. S. A.* New Brunswick, N.J.: A. S. Barnes, 1969.

8. Pablo Neruda, "Birdwatching Ode," translated by Nathaniel Tarn, in *Pablo Neruda: Selected Poems*, edited by Nathaniel Tarn. New York: Delta/Dell, 1970–72.

9. Jack Weatherford, *Indian Givers: How the Indians of the Americas Transformed the World*. Fawcett Columbine, 1988.

10. B.W. Jones, *The Peanut Plant: Its Cultivation and Uses*. New York: Orange Judd Co., 1885, p. 57, and W.R. Beattie, *The Peanut*. Farmers' Bulletin No. 431. Washington, D.C.: Government Printing Office, 1915.

Chapter Four

1. Peter C. Newman, *Caesars of the Wilderness*. New York: Viking, 1987, p. 380.

2. Peter C. Newman, *Company of Adventurers*. New York: Viking, 1985. p. 191.

3. John James Audubon, *Audubon and His Journals*, edited by Maria Audubon, Vol. II. New York: Dover, 1960, pp. 45–46.

4. On the effect of alcohol, see Newman, *Caesars of the Wilderness*, pp. 113–114.

5. George Catlin, *North American Indians, Vol. I*. Edinburgh: John Grant, 1926, pp. 139, 112, 95–97.

6. Chief Seattle, spoken to Isaac Stevens, 1854. Reprinted in *The Portable North American Reader*, edited by Frederick W. Turner, III. New York: Viking: 1974, pp. 251–252.

7. "Ben Kindle's Winter Count," reprinted in *The Portable North American Indian Reader*, edited by Frederick W. Turner, III. New York: Viking, 1974. Another interesting published "Winter Count" is the excerpt, in words and pictograms, from "Battiste Good's Winter Count," in Jerome Rothenberg, editor, *Technicians of the Sacred*. Berkeley: University of California Press, 1968, 1985.

8. Frances Densmore, *Dakota and Ojibwe People in Minnesota*. St. Paul: Minnesota Historical Society, 1977, p. 43.

9. From "Battiste Good's Winter Count." See note 7.

10. Susan Marie Swanson, "Winter Counts, Life Counts, Naming Seasons in Your Life," writing exercise in the in-house collection of *Dialogue Program Materials*, edited by Margot Galt. St. Paul: COMPAS, 1987. I am indebted to Susan Marie Swanson for this idea for a writing exercise.

11. Odysseus Elytis, *The Little Mariner*, translated by Olga Broumas. Port Townsend, WA: Copper Canyon Press, 1988.

12. Bill Ransom, "Statement on Our Higher Education," in *Carriers of the Dream Wheel*, edited by Duane Niatum. New York: Harper & Row, 1975, p. 198.

13. Darrel Daniel St. Clair, "My school the earth," quoted in the introduction to *From the Belly of the Shark, A New Anthology of Native Americans*, edited by Walter Lowenfels. New York: Random House, 1973.

14. N. Scott Momaday, "The Delight Song of Tsai-Talee," in *Carriers of the Dream Wheel*, p. 89.

15. Heidi Bakken, "The goat teaches," from *Three Magics*, a yearly writers-in-the-schools anthology, edited by John Caddy. St. Paul: COMPAS, 1987, p. 73.

16. Lillian Schlissel, *Women's Diaries of the Westward Journey*. New York: Schocken, 1982, p. 14.

17. Ibid, p. 21.

18. *Fireside Book of Folk Songs*, selected and edited by Margaret Bradford Boni. New York: Simon and Schuster, 1947.

19. Schlissel, pp. 217–231.

20. Francis Parkman, *The Oregon Trail*. Boston: Little, Brown, 1889. Samuel Hancock, *The Narrative of Samuel Hancock, 1845–1860*. Hancock, N.Y.: R. M. McBride, 1927.

21. Two fine books about American humor describe the way exaggeration worked in various regions of the country. Constance Rourke's *American Humor* (New York: Harcourt, Brace, 1931) gives us the sly Yankee who took the city slicker in with understatement that amounts to a kind of tall tale in reverse. Walter Blair's *Native American Humor* (San Francisco: Chandler, 1960) describes the actual travelers' accounts that spawned the printed tall tale.

22. Blair, pp. 4–5.

23. Blair, p. 6.

24. Blair, p. 71.

25. Spelling and punctuation as reprinted in Blair, p. 283.

26. David L. Moore, *Dark Sky, Dark Land: Stories of the Hmong Boy Scouts of Troop 100*. Eden Prairie, Minn.: Tessera Publishing, 1989, p. 30.

Chapter Five

1. *The Portable Walt Whitman*, edited by Mark Van Doren. New York: Penguin, 1973.

2. James Robertson, Jr., *Tenting Tonight*, in the series *The Civil War*. New York: Time-Life Books, 1984, p. 12.

3. *Walt Whitman's Civil War*, edited by Walter Lowenfels. New York: Knopf, 1960, p. 12. This work includes some war reports that are not reprinted in *The Portable Walt Whitman*.

4. Walt Whitman, *The Penguin Complete Poems*, edited by Francis Murphy. New York: Penguin, 1989, pp. 305–307.

5. Reprinted in *The Portable Walt Whitman*, pp. 411–412.

6. Lowenfels, editor, p. 34. See note 3 above.

7. Ibid., pp. 36–37.

8. In *The Portable Walt Whitman*, p. 223.

9. W. J. Cash, *The Mind of the South*. New York: Doubleday Anchor, 1941, p. 301.

10. See Winthrop Jordan, *White over Black*. Baltimore: Penguin Books, 1968, and Calvin Herndon, *Sex and Racism in America*. New York: Grove Press, 1966.

11. *Annual Report*. New York: NAACP, 1920.

12. Scott Ellsworth, *Death in a Promised Land: The Tulsa Race Riot of 1921*. Baton Rouge: Louisiana State Univ. Press, 1982.

13. Lawrence Ferlinghetti, *A Coney Island of the Mind*. New York: New Directions, 1958, pp. 67–68.

14. See Margot Fortunato Galt, "The Girls of Summer," *Minnesota Monthly*, May 1991; Jack Fincher, "The 'Belles of the Ball Game' Were a Hit with Their Fans," *Smithsonian Magazine*, July 1989; Jay Feldman, "Perspective," *Sports Illustrated*, June 10, 1985; and articles from the 1940s, "Ladies of the Little Diamond," *Time*, April 14, 1943, and "Girls' Baseball," *Life*, June 4, 1945.

15. See Sara Grimke, "Letters on the Equality of Women . . .," 1838, reprinted in Alice Rossi, *The Feminist Papers*. New York: Bantam, 1973.

16. Alice Walker, *In Search of Our Mother's Gardens*. New York: Harcourt Brace Jovanovich, 1983.

17. John Steinbeck, *Of Mice and Men* and *Cannery Row*. New York: Penguin Books, 1945. pp. 133–134.

18. Anne Moody, *Coming of Age in Mississippi*. New York: Dial, 1968.

19. Alice Walker, *Meridian*. New York: Simon & Schuster, 1976.

20. Sara Evans, *Personal Politics*. New York: Knopf, 1979.

21. Ibid., pp. 51–52.

22. Meridel LeSueur, *Ripening, Selected Work, 1927–1980*. Old Westbury, N.Y.: The Feminist Press, 1982.

23. Ibid., pp. 158–159.

24. Ibid., p. 160.

25. Ibid., p. 161.

26. Ibid., p. 164–165.

Chapter Six

1. Laura Briggs, quoted in *The Homefront: America During World War II*, a book of interviews taken by Mark Jonathan Harris, Franklin D. Mitchell, Steven J. Schechter. New York: Putnam, 1984, p. 34.

2. Quoted in Samuel Eliot Morison, *The Oxford History of the American People*. New York: Oxford University Press, 1965, p. 889.

3. F. Scott Fitzgerald, *The Great Gatsby*. New York: Scribners, 1925, p. 64.

4. See note 1 above.

5. Studs Terkel, *The "Good War": An Oral History of World War II*. New York: Pantheon Books, 1984.

6. Dwight Okita, "In Response to Executive Order 9066 . . .," in *Braided Lives: An Anthology of Multicultural American Writing*. Minneapolis: Minnesota Humanities Commission, 1991.

7. Jean Toomer, *Cane*. New York: Liveright, 1923, 1951, p. 3.

8. Irene Brodie, *The Childhood Memories of Irene McEathron Brodie*. St. Cloud, Minn.: Northstar Press, 1989.

9. James Agee, *Let Us Now Praise Famous Men*. New York: Ballantine, 1960.

10. Phoebe Hanson, *Sacred Hearts*. Minneapolis: Milkweed Editions, 1985.

11. William Wordsworth, *Poetical Works*, edited by Thomas Hutchinson, revised edition edited by Ernest de Selincourt. London: Oxford Univ. Press, 1960, p. 206.

12. Henry David Thoreau, *Walden*. New York: Harper & Row, 1965, p. 88.

13. Tillie Olsen, *Yonnondio: From the Thirties*. New York: Delta/Delacorte Press, 1974, p. 125.

14. Alan Spear, *Black Chicago: The Making of a Negro Ghetto, 1890–1920*. Chicago: University of Chicago Press, 1967.

15. Ibid., p. 134.

16. Ibid., pp. 147–148.

17. Lorraine Hansberry, *A Raisin in the Sun*. New York: Signet, 1958.

18. Gwendolyn Brooks, *Selected Poems*. New York: Harper & Row, 1945.

19. In *Fiesta in Aztlan*, edited by Toni Empringham. Santa Barbara: Capra Press, 1981.

20. Paule Marshall, *Brown Girl, Brownstones*. New York: The Feminist Press, 1981.

21. Paul Blackburn, *The Cities*. New York: Grove Press, 1967. pp. 47–48.

22. Patricia Hampl, *Woman Before an Aquarium*. Pittsburgh: University of Pittsburgh Press, 1978. p. 78.

23. Denise Levertov, *O Taste and See*. New York: New Directions, 1964, p. 60.

How to Create a Writing Assignment with an Historical Slant

Many of my writing ideas come from collaborating with classroom teachers. Usually I arrive for a one-week writing residency and find, after discussion, that the teacher and I agree where writing will fit into the curriculum. Maybe the teacher already uses an "American Studies" approach, teaching about a particular historical period not only from the political and military perspective but also from the cultural one, playing records of seventeenth-century English folk songs and showing slides of Williamsburg houses, candle-making molds, cross-stitched samplers, and curtained beds.

Imaginative writing fits almost anyplace in the history or social studies curriculum. Some courses offer this opportunity more readily than others, of course. Learning about the houses of Congress and the doctrine of separation of powers is fairly abstract and hard to respond to personally, but following a tax bill all the way from its proposal to its application can show how families with different incomes are affected by such a bill. In such a case, creative writing can draw out an empathetic response.

But how to structure an exercise? What models to use? Let's start with the last question first. Over the years I've developed a sense for what kind of literature makes teachable models for elementary or high school students. I can't trace how this sense developed, but I can indicate some hallmarks of a good model.

First, it has to be structured clearly. Structural techniques include ones you probably learned in freshman English: comparison and contrast; sequence (in other words, an organized list of some kind); a gradual accretion of detail that reaches a climax; a story (or image) within a story (for instance, an essay might begin with a contemporary experience, recall an historic one, then return to conclude in the present). If by its structure a piece of writing can't help students order and focus their ideas, it won't work well in the classroom.

I've also learned that the historically apt model isn't necessarily the one most likely to elicit interesting writing from students. Writing a ballad about a Williamsburg tailor, in the mode of ballads popular in the 1700s, might give students practice using details of daily life from the period, but chances are it wouldn't spring them across the distance between their own lives and the past. A contemporary model, however, might lead students to see the relationship between "hip" styles of dressing and the tools and fabrics of the 1990s, and so begin to give them an understanding of the history of the dandy. Such an approach links an historical period and a contemporary writing model, and opens the students' writing to empathy, one fundamental reason for introducing creative writing into the study of history in the first place. When students empathize with people from the past, they dig a tunnel through the years and the accumulated ideas about the past, and let voices echo back and forth from past to present.

But a contemporary model has to be rooted in the same cultural background as an historical one. Having a Williamsburg tailor sketch out his life in Japanese haiku might be funny, but the value would end there. Haiku is too divergent from the Western tradition to capture the swagger and panache of the comic-heroic Western dandy, circa 1750 or 1990. A rap song, on the other hand, blends rhythms and oral exaggeration that have come into the U.S. from the complicated cultural mixture of the Caribbean: distinctive but not totally divorced from the mixture that formed the ballads sung in a Williamsburg tavern a few hundred years ago.

The point is to help student writers take a fresh look at the past. If you're dressed in knee pants, with your hair in a queue, and wearing a flared frock coat, you may be almost as well suited to riding a motorcycle as a horse, but fighting a battle in the French and Indian War from a motorcycle would be nearly impossible: no roads through the woods, no gas stations. When students bring contemporary models to bear on historical experience, they begin to appreciate significant differences in the way life was lived, felt, and valued.

Contrasting past and present is not the only hallmark of an evocative literary model or writing exercise. Sometimes introducing an unusual point of view into the past can also activate the imagination. Take the poem "Dog" by Lawrence Ferlinghetti, used in chapter 5. A modern work—free verse, urban details, 1950s politics—this teachable poem is easy to analyze, with its repeating refrain, jaunty rhythm, and humorous take on the urban scene from a dog's perspective. All these elements are easy to adopt, but the crucial one is the dog's attitude toward human affairs: he sees through human pretense, and measures it against his own reality.

When I first brought "Dog" into a classroom, I hadn't begun to plumb the psychological possibilities in the dog as a historical witness. I simply used the poem to help students of all ages become keener observers of their surroundings. The poems that students wrote were all contemporary. Then a social studies teacher asked me to create an exercise on racial prejudice. I wanted to show his ninth grade class that racial prejudice existed even in Minnesota, with its small percentage of people of color and its history of racial tolerance. A trip to the state historical society's audio-visual room netted a surprise: engravings and photographs of lynchings that had taken place in the state between the 1880s and 1920s. Since I had already used photographs to inspire writing (as in the exercise on the Civil War in chapter 5), I sensed that I could devise an exercise around the photos. I made photocopies and wrote down what little information existed about them.

I still needed a point of entry, some slant to help the class address the admittedly horrible scenes. For some reason I can't explain, I thought of "Dog." Using it, I could show the students how to create an animal witness to the lynchings, and the relief of escaping from the heavy human atmosphere would, I hoped, help the writers leaven the horror and see past the rationale for the lynchings to their sad reality.

The results were mixed: the students did a good job of trotting out animal characters, but their take on the lynchings was too pat. The animals either simply reported what happened without interpreting it at all, or they mouthed the standard liberal assessment of racism.

Back to the drawing board. For chapter 5 an eighth grade teacher gave me another hint: using *To Kill a Mockingbird* in conjunction with "Dog" gives students a full-fledged reading experience about the racism that led to lynching in the early decades of the century. You can't read Harper Lee's novel without experiencing from the inside the complicated social and psychological realities of living in a racist town. Students today may experience their own versions of prejudice, but they probably need this novel, or other readings like it, to understand the particular mixture of ignorant suspicion, hair-trigger mob psychology, and the codified division between the races that spawned lynchings. The children in Harper Lee's novel not only grow up learning the racial code, but they are also innocent enough to see around it: similar to the animal character that initially attracted me.

It was, then, an easy step from reading the novel to writing about the trial in it or an historical lynching from an animal's point of view. I had fleshed out the exercise with enough background information to help students understand the complications of historical experience, and in "Dog" I had also given them a fresh, provocative model for framing their insights.

Where can you find wonderful models like "Dog," and how can you bring students through a writing process that will prepare them to draft their work? As a writer myself, I am always on the lookout for poems and stories and essays that inspire me. I happen across lots of writing simply by dipping into anthologies, attending readings of new writing, and taking tips from friends about good books. None of these activities demands any special expertise—anybody with a reasonably open mind and some teaching experience can encounter pieces of writing that bring out an "ah-ha" of certainty: this poem (or essay or story) will work with students.

Mainly, you have to be on the lookout, and not only for the standard fare. Try established writers and newcomers, writers from various ethnic, racial, and geographical backgrounds. Pablo Neruda's odes appeal to many contemporary poets in the United States; yet, few classroom teachers seem to know of them. The odes exist in various editions and anthologies in good bookstores and libraries, but they haven't really made it into standard textbooks. The moral here is: branch out. Go into a bookstore or library occasionally on Saturday mornings, wander around, leaf through books, let yourself read a little here and there. If you find something that you like, pause and ask yourself if you can make it relevant for your students. If the answer is yes, buy the book or borrow it from the library. You're on your way to devising an exercise.

Then, as you create the exercise, remember some of these general steps for leading students into and through their own writing:

• Use conversation to explore students' personal responses to the historical and literary material. Conversation in a classroom can do more than question and answer. Conversation can begin to give students language about their own experiences and reactions to history that can then be set down in writing.

• The next logical step is to create a classroom collection of words and images. I usually do this on the board, with some sort of word mapping to which the whole class contributes; or with older students I make a map of my own on the board, and let the students make their own. Often what students put on their maps is a flushing out of received or hackneyed ideas (sometimes along with fresh, personal observation), but when the time comes to draft, the students will go beyond what they've put on their maps and write with new inspiration.

• Talking about ways to organize a piece of writing with a class can next point students toward selecting, shaping, and intensifying what resources they have gathered. The exercises in this book offer examples of how this has worked with various models and historical resources.

• I try to remain attuned to the mood and understanding of a class as I am presenting an exercise. Each group of students differs—some need a lot more talking to, a lot more breaking up of directions into little steps, than do others. Sometimes I have to improvise on the spot when

I discover that students don't know what to do with a set of instructions that I thought were clear and helpful. Often, first doing some of the work collectively will then allow students to proceed individually.

• Once students are writing, I move from desk to desk to identify strong phrases, answer private questions, read aloud good drafts, and help students who are stuck. As I work with individual students in this public setting, I am beginning to develop the class as an audience for each other's writing and to prepare them for reading it aloud.

• Reading aloud what they have written satisfies students' curiosity about each other's work and helps them learn other strategies for writing. For the readers, the experience helps gauge what is communicated—the class laughs or responds soberly at appropriate places. Reading aloud also lets the writer hear clunky or marvelous phrases and begin to assess the total impact of the piece.

• Revision is an important step but is not necessary for every piece of writing. I often pair students to work on revision and ask them to give each other several questions or comments to identify strengths and weaknesses that the writers can then address.

• As a final step for the kind of writing proposed in this book, a class can consider what their creative responses to the past have helped them understand. This response may be as simple as a second grader's, who created a new name for herself "in the Indian spirit," and said, "I like my new old Dakota name." Or it may be as complex as a high school student's reflecting on his new understanding of war, after writing a Civil War ballad. This analytical coda to the writing exercise is important, I think, because it allows students a wider sense of the various purposes of writing and the many ways we gain new knowledge of an historical period.

So you see, there isn't a simple method that will result in an instant assignment. What matters most is that the historical material really interest you, that you think it can interest your students, and that you be willing to enter into the adventure of trying it with them.

Historical Sources

In this age when so much learning comes prepackaged, you owe it to your students to expose them to primary sources. These sources are often available on microfilm, like the reams of passenger arrival lists kept in the National Archives for ports of entry like Buffalo, Philadelphia, Baltimore, Boston, and New York. If you want to find out what people ate on the Oregon Trail, there are diaries that will tell you. If you want to know who marketed the first roasted peanuts in the United States, you can probably track that down. If you want to know the names of the Civil War soldiers who fought from your state (assuming it was in the nation at the time), your state historical society or the National Archives in Washington can tell you. Libraries, historical societies, museums and historical sites—even family attics and heirlooms—are full of stories and information, more or less old, more or less accessible, more or less formal or personal.

For the exercise I devised about the peanut (in chapter 3), I called the city library and requested everything the government documents' division had on peanuts. The manila envelope that arrived contained an odd assortment of materials from the U. S. Department of Agriculture, the U. S. Food and Drug Administration, and state farmers' organizations. The collection was so odd that it intrigued me and led to an entertaining and informative writing exercise.

But even in that grab-bag of materials, I found some facts repeated. In doing research, I know I've done enough when I keep meeting the same facts or quotations again and again. This suggests that I'm familiar with the subject and have probably exhausted the originality of my sources. This happens more often when you're using secondary sources. Primary sources often seem endlessly varied: no matter how many of the dispatches and letters from Civil War generals you read in the official documents collected from the war, the next letter will surprise you, much like a friend whose responses aren't always predictable. Yet you'll come to recognize a personality on the page. Once this happens, you may be ready to write about this historical person, whoever it is.

The archives of state historical societies or the National Archives contain, among other things, census data, papers from various presidential or gubernatorial administrations, newspapers, and fire-insurance plats. Though digging through such materials is only for advanced secondary students, it can produce some interesting discoveries. One of my favorite finds was the insurance plat books. At intervals of two, five, and ten years, the city published outsized map books. Inside, carefully drawn plans for city blocks with buildings sketched in and labeled showed not only when buildings were constructed on particular sites, but what their functions had been.

It's best to go looking in libraries and archives with some general question to guide you, but once there, be prepared for surprise. Surprise and delight at historical sources have taken many forms for me, but the two best are discovering materials that are not duplicated in the present and unearthing "found stories" in documents that did not intend to be literary. The poet Charles Reznikoff created two volumes of such discovered dramas, titled *Testimony* (Santa Barbara: Black Sparrow Press, 1978). Drawn from court testimony, Reznikoff's poems present the intense experiences of ordinary people, experiences that, in ordinary textbooks, are lost in large generalizations.

My own favorite discovery came in the St. Paul Public Library in *The Unfinished Autobiography of Henry Hastings Sibley* (Minneapolis: Voyageur Press, 1932), edited by Theodore C. Blegen. Sibley was the first territorial governor of Minnesota. One chapter describes a nightmarish shooting of a Dakota woman with a bow and arrow in the groin, Sibley's pell-mell ride for a doctor, and the later marriage between the woman and Sibley's friend, the one who had accidentally shot her! As far as I'm concerned, this story deserves to be reborn as literature.

So far the most startling artifact I've found (in a small-town historical society) that does not have a modern counterpart is a small book for gentlewomen, written in the middle 1800s. The book describes how to use a fan to flirt with a man. The subtlety of gestures astounds me: a fan carried in the left hand meant the woman was "desirous of an acquaintance," but if she twirled it with the same hand, she was saying, "I want to get rid of you." Twirled in the right, the fan meant, "I love another." Drawn through the hand: "I hate you." Drawn across the cheek, "I love you." Fanning slowly, "I am married." And I had thought that Scarlett O'Hara and her friends were improvising!

The National Archives in Washington, D.C., form the mother lode of information about the U. S. Facsimiles of many primary source materials are available for purchase at reasonable prices from the National Archives (Education Branch, Office of Public Programs, National Archives, Washington, DC 20408, tel. 202/724-0456) and from SIRS, Inc. (PO Box 2348, Boca Raton, FL 33427-2348, tel. 800/347-7477). Many state historical societies and public or university libraries have acquired National Archives materials on microfilm for their own collections. These institutions tend to specialize in documents that put their own state or region in the historical context of the whole country. But the whims of librarians and patrons also bring unexpected treasures into any library's holdings. Before you know it, you may be leafing through an 1857 *Harper's Weekly*, or spinning through reels of the National Archives materials on "Civilians during Wartime" to find what butchers and cooks contributed to the War of 1812.

The National Archives also houses the following kinds of materials, should you ever need them:

- Census Records.
- Passenger Arrival Lists for many ports of entry.
- Immigration and naturalization records.
- Military Records for up to 1912; the later ones are housed in St. Louis, at the National Personnel Records Center (Military Records), NARA, 9700 Page Blvd., St. Louis, MO 63132.
- Pension and Bounty Land Warrant Records. These list rewards in pensions or land given to soldiers in various American wars.
- Civilians during Wartime. As mentioned above, this category includes people who aided military endeavors as suppliers, workers, doctors, and nurses, during the Revolutionary War, the War of 1812, and the Civil War.
- Records of American Indians. This huge and vastly informative collection holds papers of the Bureau of Indian Affairs, Indian Agencies, the names of Indians enrolled in various tribes, Indian scouts in the regular U.S. Army through 1940, and much more.
- Black Americans. Another rich collection that includes various kinds of censuses, military service records, Freedman's Bureau records, lists of people enslaved in the U. S., and papers on the slave trade and African colonization.
- Merchant Seamen records of service on ore boats, cargo boats, etc.
- Civilian Government Employees. A huge collection on the postal service, Indian Agencies, the diplomatic corps, etc.
- Land records, claims, court records for the District of Columbia.
- Cartographic records.

Finally, a word about historical societies and associations. Local societies often publish illustrated magazines full of interesting articles that may offer ideas and materials for teaching. Two national organizations also publish work that may help teachers keep abreast of new interpretations and new documents in American history: the Organization of American Historians (112 N. Bryan St., Bloomington, IN 47408, tel. 812/855-7311) produces the *Journal of American History* and the *OAH Newsletter,* as well as classroom materials and curriculum guides. The American Historical Association, whose membership consists mainly of college and graduate-level teachers, publishes the *American Historical Review*, as well as pamphlets such as *Studying History: An Introduction to Methods and Structure* and *Teaching History with Film and Television.*

Tips for Looking at Photographs

Conventions about taking photographs have changed since the mid-1800s, when photography entered the mainstream of Western culture. In the early days, the photographic processes demanded long, still poses. People couldn't hold a sweet smile for five minutes; so they assumed monotone expressions that would not "freeze up." Today when we look at our great-grandparents' wedding photo, the bride and groom look mean enough to spit. We're tempted to think they were repressed and stiff-necked. But more likely, they were simply uncomfortable sitting still for five minutes. Chances are, they joked and flushed when the shutter finally clicked.

The technology that allowed breezy, informal, transient expressions to be captured on film came much later: compare a snapshot of backyard fun from the 1960s with the formal wedding photograph of a hundred years earlier. You can almost see your sister start to pout when you broke the piñata before she did!

The first job in reading photographs is to remember the formal restrictions on the people in them. We need to ask ourselves, what kind of behavior did the actual photographic process require? Then, what were the reasons for taking the photo? Over the years, reasons have changed almost as much as the photographic process itself.

For years, professionals were the only people who took pictures. You couldn't decide to take a photo on the spur of the moment. You had to plan: a family made an appointment at the photographic studio, dressed up, went downtown, and posed. It was a fairly long, involved occasion that was meant to record a notable moment in someone's life, or to give posterity a permanent record of the way a family looked.

In remote areas, traveling photographers arrived unexpectedly and created the occasion for posing. Take, for example, a photograph (circa 1890) that I bought in an antique shop in Minnesota. A photographer had come to visit a remote logging camp: presto, instant fun, while the lumberjacks posed with guns, two rabbits recently shot, and the three women cooks. Almost a hundred years later, I look at this group picture and find that the women in their white summer dresses have blanched out like filmy ghosts among the clowning men in plaid shirts and high boots. Eerie, interesting, provocative: the aberrations of the imperfect photograph actually suggest something about what life was like for the women in their separate roles among the predominantly male group.

Today we live in an era when cameras are inexpensive and easy to operate. The occasions for taking photos have become much less formal, more personal, more subject to interpretation, as in, for instance, family photos: what does the particular scene say about your family, and especially about the person who took the photo? In my family, my mother was likely to record accomplishments: it was she who photographed my sister and me dressed in the wallpaper kimonos she made us for Halloween, saving money and displaying her creativity to boot.

Often when I use family photographs in the classroom, I ask students not to bring them from home, but to sketch them in class from memory. Sketching the photographs helps students to notice and remember details that they might overlook in the overly familiar image. Once the rough sketch is in place, I write a list of questions on the board for students to answer alongside the sketch:

• Who is in the photo? Give nicknames and "pet" names as well as full ones.

• Who took the photo and why? What is the occasion? As I suggested above, the reason for a photo differs according to the person snapping the picture. There are also as many interpretations of a photo as there are people in it: my sense of the photo of me and my sister is quite different from hers: I was pouting because she got more Halloween candy than I did; she was smiling a big goony smile, knowing mother would not make her share the loot.

• What are people wearing, doing? What items show in the photo? Photographs are excellent evidence of changes in fashion, architecture, technology, games, etc. But to tap this evidence, we have to give specific names to the kinds of clothes, cars, and houses that photographs capture. I remind students to be as specific as possible: to say, "My mom is wearing pedalpushers," not "My mom is wearing pants."

• What story or vignette might the photo suggest? For instance, what are the people in it feeling? What are the expressions on their faces? What history do we know to help us to interpret the story beneath the surface? The more familiar we are with a photograph, the more faceted will be the story we can tell. But it is also surprising how much anonymous photos reveal about the friendliness or discomfort among the people posing, the way they position themselves, hold their bodies, grin or shy away from each other.

• Even old photographs that took minutes to shoot are relatively transient, brief glimpses of more fluid life. What will happen once the shutter clicks? Or what has just happened before the photo? In answering these questions, you begin to create a sequence that leads into past and future, you begin to give a story to the moment held still in the photograph. Another question is: what is taking place beyond the frame of the photo? What is just beyond the fluted phonograph horn, in the other corner of the living room? Who has refused to be in the picture?

Once students have labeled their work, they are ready to begin drafting. Even with all the words on the sketch, some may have trouble. I tell them to ask themselves, "Where does my eye go first in the photo?" Maybe to the rose on the bride's hat, maybe to the spray of water from the watering can. I tell the students to begin by describing the detail that first captures their attention, and to alternate bits of information, history, or story with description. The story of the photograph is fundamentally about what we see, and what we make of what we see. The words we choose have to bring across on the page what the eye almost unconsciously registers. But the beauty of the words is that they name the surface and probe beneath it, allowing the imagination to enter the historical record.

Bibliography

Agee, James. *Let Us Now Praise Famous Men.* New York: Ballantine, 1960.

Audubon, John James. *Audubon and His Journals.* Edited by Maria Audubon. New York: Dover, 1960.

Blackburn, Paul. *Collected Poems.* Edited by Edith Jarolim. New York: Persea, 1985.

Blair, Walter. *Native American Humor.* San Francisco: Chandler, 1960.

Boni, Margaret Bradford, ed. *The Fireside Book of Folk Songs.* New York: Simon & Schuster, 1947.

Braided Lives: An Anthology of Multicultural American Writing. Minneapolis: Minnesota Humanities Commission, 1991.

Breckenridge, Jill. *Civil Blood.* Minneapolis: Milkweed, 1986.

Brodie, Irene. *The Childhood Memories of Irene McEathron Brodie.* St. Cloud, Minn.: Northstar Press, 1989.

Broker, Ignatia. *Night-Flying Woman: An Ojibway Narrative.* St. Paul: Minnesota Historical Society, 1983.

Brooks, Gwendolyn. *Selected Poems.* New York: Harper & Row, 1945.

Brown, Cynthia Stokes. *Like It Was: A Complete Guide to Writing Oral History.* New York: Teachers & Writers Collaborative, 1988.

Burnett, Paula. *The Penguin Book of Caribbean Verse in English.* London & New York: Viking Penguin, 1986.

Caddy, John, ed. *Three Magics.* Minneapolis: COMPAS, 1987.

Carter, Forrest. *The Education of Little Tree.* Albuquerque, N.M.: Univ. of New Mexico, 1976.

Cash, W.J. *The Mind of the South.* New York: Doubleday Anchor, 1941.

Catlin, George. *North American Indians.* Edinburgh: John Grant, 1926.

Cherry, Kelly. *Relativity: A Point of View.* Baton Rouge: Louisiana State Univ. Press, 1977.

Chesnut, Mary Boykin. *Diary from Dixie.* Edited by Ben Ames Williams. Boston: Houghton Mifflin, 1905, 1949.

Chin, Frank. *Donald Duck.* Minneapolis: Coffee House, 1991.

Cisneros, Sandra. *The House on Mango Street.* New York: Vintage, 1989.

_____. *Woman Hollering Creek and Other Stories.* New York: Vintage, 1991.

Clark, Septima. *Ready from Within: Septima Clark and the Civil Rights Movement.* Edited by Cynthia Stokes Brown. Trenton, N.J.: Africa World Press, 1990.

Columbus, Christopher. *Across the Ocean Sea: A Journal of Columbus' Voyage.* Edited by George Sanderlin. New York: Harper & Row, 1966.

Davis, Marilyn P. *Mexican Voices/American Dreams: An Oral History of Mexican Immigration to the United States.* New York: Holt, 1990.

Dillard, Annie. *An American Childhood.* New York: Harper & Row, 1987.

Densmore, Frances. *Dakota and Ojibwe People in Minnesota.* St. Paul: Minnesota Historical Society, 1977.

Durnham, Philip, and Jones, Everett L. *The Negro Cowboys.* Lincoln, Neb.: Univ. of Nebraska, 1965.

[Editors of American Heritage]. *Discoverers of the New World.* New York: American Heritage, 1960.

Ellsworth, Scott. *Death in a Promised Land: The Tulsa Race Riot of 1921.* Baton Rouge: Louisiana State Univ. Press, 1982.

Elytis, Odysseus. *The Little Mariner.* Translated by Olga Broumas. Port Townsend, WA: Copper Canyon Press, 1988.

Empringham, Toni, ed. *Fiesta in Aztlan.* Santa Barbara: Capra Press, 1981.

Evans, Sara. *Born for Liberty: A History of Women in America.* New York: The Free Press, 1989.

_____. *Personal Politics.* New York: Knopf, 1979.

Fairbanks, Evelyn. *Days of Rondo.* St. Paul: Minnesota Historical Society, 1990.

Feldman, Jay. "Perspective." *Sports Illustrated,* June 10, 1985.

Ferlinghetti, Lawrence. *A Coney Island of the Mind.* New York: New Directions, 1958.

Field, Edward, ed. *A Geography of Poets: An Anthology of the New Poetry.* New York: Bantam, 1979.

Fincher, Jack. "The 'Belles of the Ball Game' Were a Hit with Their Fans." *Smithsonian Magazine,* July 1989.

Fitzgerald, F. Scott. *The Great Gatsby.* New York: Scribners, 1925.

Fleming, Thomas, ed. *Affectionately Yours, George Washington: A Self-Portrait in Letters of Friendship.* New York: Norton, 1967.

Friebert, Stuart, and Young, David, eds. *The Longman's Anthology of Contemporary American Poetry, 1950–1980.* White Plains, N.Y.: Longmans, 1983.

Galt, Margot Fortunato. *Dialogue Program Materials.* St. Paul: COMPAS, 1987.

_____. "The Girls of Summer." *Minnesota Monthly,* May 1991.

Gannett, Henry. *American Names.* Washington, D.C.: Public Affairs Press, 1947.

Gilbert, Sandra M., and Gubar, Susan, eds. *The Norton Anthology of Literature by Women.* New York: Norton, 1985.

Hampton, Henry, and Fayer, Steve. *Voices of Freedom: An Oral History of the Civil Rights Movement from the 1950s through the 1980s.* New York: Bantam, 1990.

Hancock, Samuel. *The Narrative of Samuel Hancock.* New York: R.M. McBride, 1927.

Hanson, Phoebe. *Sacred Hearts.* Minneapolis: Milkweed Editions, 1985.

Hampl, Patricia. *Woman Before an Aquarium.* Pittsburgh: Univ. of Pittsburgh Press, 1978.

Hansberry, Lorraine. *A Raisin in the Sun.* New York: Signet, 1958.

Harris, Mark Jonathan; Mitchell, Franklin D.; and Schechter, Steven J. *The Homefront: America during World War II.* New York: Putnam, 1984.

Herndon, Calvin. *Sex and Racism in America.* New York: Grove, 1966.

Hughes, Langston. *The Selected Poems of Langston Hughes.* New York: Vintage, 1959, 1990.

Jacobs, Harriet. *Incidents in the Life of a Slave Girl (1813–1897).* New York: Oxford Univ. Press, 1988.

Jones, B.W. *The Peanut Plant: Its Cultivation and Uses.* New York: Orange Judd Co., 1885.

Jordan, Winthrop. *White over Black.* Baltimore: Penguin, 1968.

Josephy, Alvin M., Jr. *The Indian Heritage of America.* Boston: Houghton Mifflin, 1969, 1991.

Keenan, Deborah, and Lloyd, Roseann. *Looking for Home: Women Writing about Exile.* Minneapolis: Milkweed, 1991.

Kooser, Ted. *A Local Habitation and a Name.* New York: Soho, 1974.

LeSueur, Meridel. *Ripening, Selected Work, 1927–1980.* Old Westbury, N.Y.: The Feminist Press, 1982.

Levertov, Denise. *O Taste and See.* New York: New Directions, 1964.

Lowenfels, Walter, ed. *From the Belly of the Shark: A New Anthology of Native Americans.* New York: Random House, 1973.

_____. *Walt Whitman's Civil War.* New York: Knopf, 1960.

Marshall, Paule. *Brown Girl, Brownstones.* New York: The Feminist Press, 1981.

Martin, Jr., Bill, and Archambault, John. *Knots on a Counting Rope.* New York: Holt, 1987.

Minczeski, John. *The Spiders.* St. Paul: New Rivers, 1979.

Monegal, Emir Richard, ed. *The Borzoi Anthology of Latin American Literature from the Time of Columbus to the 20th Century.* 2 vols. New York: Knopf, 1990.

Moody, Anne. *Coming of Age in Mississippi.* New York: Dial, 1968.

Moore, David L. *Dark Sky, Dark Land: Stories of the Hmong Boy Scouts of Troop 100.* Eden Prairie, Minn.: Tessera Publishing, 1989.

Morison, Samuel Eliot. *The Oxford History of the American People.* New York: Oxford Univ. Press, 1965.

Mura, David. *After We Lost Our Way.* New York: Dutton, 1989.

[NAACP]. *Annual Report.* New York: NAACP, 1920.

Neruda, Pablo. *Selected Poems.* Translated and edited by Nathaniel Tarn. New York: Delta/ Dell, 1970–72.

Newman, Peter C. *Caesars of the Wilderness.* New York: Viking, 1987.

_____. *Company of Adventurers.* New York: Viking, 1985.

Niatum, Duane, ed. *Carriers of the Dream Wheel.* New York: Harper & Row, 1975.

O'Hara, Frank. *Collected Poems.* Edited by Donald Allen. New York: Vintage, 1974.

Olsen, Tillie. *Yonnondio: From the Thirties*. New York: Delta/Delacorte Press, 1974.

Paddock, Joe. *Boars' Dance*. Duluth: Holy Cow! Press, 1991.

Parkman, Francis. *The Oregon Trail*. Boston: Little, Brown, 1889. Reprinted, Hancock, N.Y.: R.M. McBride, 1927.

Quincentennial Education. Minneapolis: Central American Resource Center, 1992.

Quimby, Myron J. *Scratch Ankle, U.S.A.* New Brunswick, N.J.: A.S. Barnes, 1969.

Rethinking Columbus: Teaching about the 500th Anniversary of Columbus' Arrival in America. Milwaukee: Rethinking Schools, 1992.

Reznikoff, Charles. *Testimony*. Santa Barbara: Black Sparrow, 1978.

Robertson, Jr., James. *Tenting Tonight*. New York: Time-Life Books, 1984.

Rossi, Alice, ed. *The Feminist Papers*. New York: Bantam, 1973.

Rothenberg, Jerome, ed. *Shaking the Pumpkin: Traditional Poetry of the Indian North Americas*. New York: Alfred Van Der Marck, 1986.

_____. *Technicians of the Sacred*. Berkeley: Univ. of California Press, 1968, 1985.

Rourke, Constance. *American Humor*. New York: Harcourt, Brace, 1931.

Rule, Lareina. *Name Your Baby*. New York: Bantam, 1980.

Schlissel, Lillian, ed. *Women's Diaries of the Westward Journey*. New York: Schocken, 1982.

Spear, Alan. *Black Chicago: The Making of a Negro Ghetto, 1890–1920*. Chicago: Univ. of Chicago Press, 1967.

Steinbeck, John. *Of Mice and Men* and *Cannery Row*. New York: Penguin, 1945.

Steward, George R. *American Place-Names*. New York: Oxford Univ. Press, 1970.

Swanson, Susan Marie. *The Large Sky Reaches Down*. St. Paul: COMPAS, 1986.

Terkel, Studs. *The "Good War": An Oral History of World War II*. New York: Pantheon, 1984.

Thoreau, Henry David. *Walden*. New York: Harper & Row, 1965.

Toomer, Jean. *Cane*. New York: Liveright, 1923, 1951.

Turner, III, Frederick W. *The Portable North American Reader*. New York: Viking, 1974.

Walker, Alice. *In Search of Our Mother's Gardens*. New York: Harcourt Brace Jovanovich, 1983.

_____. *Meridian*. New York: Simon & Schuster, 1976.

Weatherford, Jack. *Indian Givers: How the Indians of the Americas Transformed the World*. New York: Fawcett Columbine, 1988.

Whitman, Walt. *Complete Poems*. Edited by Francis Murphy. New York: Penguin, 1989.

_____. *The Portable Walt Whitman*. Edited by Mark Van Doren. New York: Penguin, 1973.

Whiteman, Roberta Hill. *Star Quilt: Poems.* Minneapolis: Holy Cow! Press, 1984.

Wilson, August. *Fences.* New York: New American Library, 1986.

Wordsworth, William. *Poetical Works.* Edited by Thomas Hutchinson, revised by Ernest de Selincourt. London: Oxford Univ. Press, 1960.

Yarbrough, Camille. *Cornrows.* New York: Coward, McCann & Geohegan, 1979.

Yates, Elizabeth. *Amos Fortune, Free Man.* New York: Aladdin Books, 1950.

Yessner, Seymour. *25 Minnesota Poets.* Minneapolis: Nodin, 1974.

Other T&W Publications of Interest

Like It Was: A Complete Guide to Writing Oral History by Cynthia Stokes Brown. This how-to guide was written by a teacher who won the American Book Award for her work in oral history. For students 12 and up and for English, social studies, and history teachers. "A solid, well-organized introduction, covering everything" —*Booklist.*

The Teachers & Writers Handbook of Poetic Forms, edited by Ron Padgett. A clear, concise guide to 74 different poetic forms, their histories, examples, and how to use them. "A treasure" —*Kliatt.*

Personal Fiction Writing: A Guide for Writing from Real Life for Teachers, Students, & Writers by Meredith Sue Willis. "A terrific resource for the classroom teacher as well as the novice writer" —*Harvard Educational Review.*

Origins by Sandra R. Robinson with Lindsay McAuliffe. A new way to get students excited about language: the fascination of word origins. Includes many writing exercises and a brief history of English. "Refreshing and attractive" —Robert MacNeil, author of *The Story of English.*

The Writing Workshop, Vols. 1 & 2 by Alan Ziegler. A perfect combination of theory, practice, and specific assignments. "Invaluable to the writing teacher" —*Contemporary Education.*

The Whole Word Catalogue, Vols. 1 & 2. T&W's best-selling guides to teaching imaginative writing. "*WWC 1* is probably the best practical guide for teachers who really want to stimulate their students to write" —*Learning.* "*WWC 2* is excellent... Makes available approaches to the teaching of writing not found in other programs" —*Language Arts.*

•

For a complete catalogue of T&W books, magazines, audiotapes, video-tapes, and computer writing games, contact:
Teachers & Writers Collaborative
5 Union Square West
New York, NY 10003-3306
(212) 691-6590